MARK TWAIN'S
WESTERN YEARS

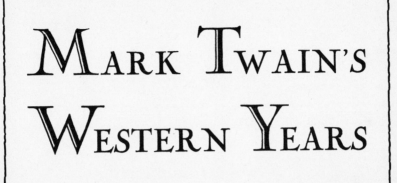

Mark Twain's Western Years

By IVAN BENSON

Together with
hitherto unreprinted
Clemens Western Items

STANFORD UNIVERSITY PRESS
STANFORD UNIVERSITY, CALIFORNIA

LONDON: HUMPHREY MILFORD
OXFORD UNIVERSITY PRESS

STANFORD UNIVERSITY PRESS
STANFORD UNIVERSITY, CALIFORNIA

LONDON: HUMPHREY MILFORD
OXFORD UNIVERSITY PRESS

———

THE BAKER AND TAYLOR COMPANY
55 FIFTH AVENUE, NEW YORK

MARTINUS NIJHOFF
9 LANGE VOORHOUT, THE HAGUE

THE MARUZEN COMPANY
TOKYO, OSAKA, KYOTO, SENDAI

———

COPYRIGHT 1938 BY THE BOARD OF TRUSTEES
OF THE LELAND STANFORD JUNIOR UNIVERSITY

PRINTED AND BOUND IN THE UNITED STATES
OF AMERICA BY STANFORD UNIVERSITY PRESS

PREFACE

THIS study of the development of Mark Twain during his five and one-half years in Nevada and California, from 1861 to 1866, reveals this period as of real significance in his career. The examination here made of material previously unavailable, including a number of unreprinted items, throws light on Twain's literary growth in the West.

Before coming to Nevada, at 25, Twain had made no sustained effort at authorship, and his writings had been of an amateurish, immature type. Certain elements in this earlier writing, however, presaged further development. These include his predilection for humorous writing, his preference for writing travel letters rather than local items, his aptitude for editorial controversy, and his tendency to satirize individuals, often unjustly, for the sake of building a good story or making a point which in itself may have been justified. In the West, Twain continued to write about politics and legislatures, but he abandoned the use of exaggerated dialects, misspellings, and other elements of style found in his earlier writings.

Twain had served two apprenticeships before coming West—as a printer, and as a pilot on the Mississippi. For his first year in Nevada he chose the career of silver miner. Contrary to the views of some critics, there is no evidence that there was anything abnormal in this choice.

After his silver-mining experience, Twain became a reporter on the *Territorial Enterprise*, Virginia City, Nevada, where he came into association with journalists who were to have much to do with his development as a writer. On the *Enterprise*, Twain

first took up writing as a career; here he adopted the pen name by
which he was to become known throughout the world; and here
he first attracted a reading public beyond his own locality, since
his work was widely reprinted in the West and gained the notice
also of Eastern publications. When he left the Comstock Lode for
San Francisco he had served his final apprenticeship; he had made
writing his career.

Mark Twain chose his pen name while he was a reporter on the
Territorial Enterprise. Evidence does not support the view that
he and other Western authors chose pen names because they were
ashamed of their profession and feared the criticism of frontier
society. Moreover, that there was no "original Mark Twain" other
than Samuel Clemens himself is revealed by a study of Captain
Isaiah Sellers' Mississippi River logbook, now made available for
the first time for scholarly examination. Neither the name "Mark
Twain" nor any single reference to Samuel Clemens occurs in the
Sellers journal, which covers the period from 1825 to 1862. The
Sellers material also reveals that Twain had adopted the pen name
before the death of Captain Sellers, rather than after, as Paine
believed.

Discovery of detailed correspondence between Twain and a
rival newspaper man in Virginia City throws additional light on
the duel controversy. These letters, reprinted in the Sacramento
Union, show the progress of the editorial battle and indicate that
no duel was actually fought.

There is little evidence that Artemus Ward influenced Mark
Twain except in an indirect way. Twain found in Ward a congenial companion whose advice he was willing to take. A chain
of linked circumstances stretches from their Virginia City companionship to the publication of the "Jumping Frog" story and
to Twain's beginnings on the lecture platform.

Widespread acceptance of the fiction of Bret Harte's influence
on Mark Twain is shown, through examination of new material,
to have little foundation in fact. True, Harte sought Twain's
sketches for the *Californian;* but that magazine was only one of

several publications to which Twain contributed. Other channels through which his writings reached the public during his Western period were the *Territorial Enterprise,* the San Francisco *Call,* the *Golden Era,* the *Napa County Reporter,* the Sacramento *Union,* the *Hawaiian Herald,* the San Francisco *Bulletin,* and the *Alta California.*

An important factor in Mark Twain's Western development was his growth as a personality. With few exceptions, the Western magazines and newspapers gave him complete freedom, permitting him to develop his eager, vigorous, enthusiastic, dynamic spirit. He lived the Western experience to the full, and his response to it in his writings was personal and emotional.

Had Mark Twain been only a humorist during his stay in the Far West, his Western writings would merit less consideration. But from the beginning he was more than just a humorist. During his Western period he became an accomplished social satirist, and with a gradually broadening scope he wrote artistically, with a variety of effects, from the coarsest burlesque to fine descriptive and informational articles.

Many persons have given generous co-operation in the preparation of this book. Dr. Louis Wann, of the University of Southern California, has been especially helpful. I wish to express my appreciation of those who made available to me material in the Bancroft Library, the University of Nevada Library, the Nevada State Library, the University of California Library, the California State Library, the Clarke Library, and the Willard S. Morse collection. I am also indebted to the following publishers for permission to quote from their books: Bobbs-Merrill Co., E. P. Dutton & Co., Harper & Brothers, Houghton Mifflin Co., Hutchinson & Co., Ltd., Little, Brown & Co., and the University of North Carolina Press.

I. B.

Los Angeles, California
January 17, 1938

CONTENTS

LIST OF ILLUSTRATIONS

CHAPTER 1

BEGINNINGS
OF AUTHORSHIP

At twenty-five Samuel Clemens had written nothing of literary distinction, and, as Paine says, had shown no signs of an ambition to become a writer. The development whereby he was to adopt writing as a life career was to come during his five and one-half years in the frontier West. Although Clemens' pre-Washoe writings are meager, it is important to ascertain what was his author-equipment by the time he penned his first "Josh" letter in the mining camps of Esmeralda.

His literary biographer may appropriately look back to the earlier years which Clemens spent as a boy in Hannibal, Missouri, as an assistant editor, as a tramp printer, as a pilot on the Mississippi, and as a temporary soldier. What background of authorship did he have when he arrived in Nevada in 1861? What previous writing had he done that would show the point which he had reached in his literary development when he departed for the frontier West?

Going back to his print-shop and journeyman printer days, and to the days of piloting on the Mississippi, one discovers an unusually meager output of writings for a young man who obviously had an aptitude for authorship and who certainly had more than ordinary opportunities for publication of his work. The fact is that Samuel Clemens' literary development was remarkably slow for one with his potential abilities. Paine, in discussing the clairvoyant powers of a Madame Caprell whom Clemens had consulted in New Orleans early in 1861 and who predicted that Sam would one day be a great writer, comments on this as follows:

If we may judge by those [letters] that have survived, her prophecy of literary distinction for him was hardly warranted by anything she could have known of his past performance. These letters of his youth have a value to-day only because they were written by the man who was later to become Mark Twain. The squibs and skits which he sometimes contributed to the New Orleans papers were bright, perhaps, and pleasing to his pilot associates, but they were without literary value. He was twenty-five years old. More than one author has achieved reputation at that age. Mark Twain was of slower growth; at that age he had not even developed a definite literary ambition.[1]

Samuel Clemens' first contact with the profession of writing came when he began service as an apprentice printer under Joseph P. Ament, publisher of the *Missouri Courier*. Ament had bought the *Missouri Courier* in Palmyra in 1841. Later the paper was merged with the *Hannibal Gazette,* which Ament purchased in the latter part of May or the first of June, 1848, and publication took place in Hannibal. The merged papers went under the name of the *Hannibal Gazette* until October 12, 1848, when the title *Missouri Courier* was permanently adopted.[2]

Sam's printing apprenticeship began about fifteen months after the death of his father, which occurred on March 24, 1847. The boy's formal education ended then; he was through with school at a little more than eleven years of age.

Circumstances of this early printing apprenticeship have been the subject matter of a variety of interpretations. Mark Twain himself gave three different versions of it in later years. Van Wyck Brooks sees the cub printer beginning his long and tragic frustration, the artist in him receiving its first rude assault.

The first great incident of frustration occurred, according to Brooks, at the scene of the death of Sam's father. Paine's account of these events is the basis of Brooks's theory:

[1] Albert Bigelow Paine, *Mark Twain's Letters* (Harper & Bros., 1917), I, 51. Hereafter referred to as Paine, *Letters.*

[2] Bernard De Voto, *Mark Twain's America* (Little, Brown & Co., 1932), p. 85.

The boy Sam was fairly broken down. Remorse, which always dealt with him unsparingly, laid a heavy hand on him now. Wildness, disobedience, indifference to his father's wishes, all were remembered; a hundred things, in themselves trifling, became ghastly and heart-wringing in the knowledge that they would never be undone. Seeing his grief, his mother took him by the hand and led him into the room where his father lay. "It is all right, Sammy," she said. "What's done is done, and it does not matter to him any more; but here by the side of him now I want you to promise me——." He turned, his eyes streaming with tears, and flung himself into her arms. "I will promise anything," he sobbed, "if you won't make me go to school! Anything!" His mother held him for a moment, thinking, then she said: "No, Sammy, you need not go to school any more. Only promise me to be a better boy. Promise not to break my heart." So he promised her to be a faithful and industrious man, and upright, like his father. His mother was satisfied with that. The sense of honor and justice was already strong within him. To him a promise was a serious matter at any time; made under conditions like these it would be held sacred. That night—it was after the funeral—his tendency to somnambulism manifested itself. His mother and sister, who were sleeping together, saw the door open and a form in white enter. Naturally nervous at such a time, and living in a day of almost universal superstition, they were terrified and covered their heads. Presently a hand was laid on the coverlet, first at the feet, then at the head of the bed. A thought struck Mrs. Clemens: "Sam!" she said. He answered, but he was sound asleep and fell to the floor. He had risen and thrown a sheet around him in his dreams. He walked in his sleep several nights in succession after that. Then he slept more soundly.[3]

This is the version of the story as Paine gives it. That Mark Twain decisively contradicts this story, in at least one other version that he gave,[4] did not deter Paine or Brooks. The scene is loaded with significance for Brooks:

Who is sufficiently the master of signs and portents to read this curious episode aright? One thing, however, we feel with certitude, that Mark Twain's fate was in a sense decided in that moment. That hour by his father's corpse, that solemn oath, that walking in his sleep—we must hazard some interpretation of it, and I think we are justified in hazarding as most likely that which explains the most numerous and the most significant phenomena of his later life. . . . . His "wish" to be an artist, which had been so frowned upon and had encountered such an obstacle in the disapproval of his mother, was now repressed, more or less definitely, and another wish,

[3] Albert Bigelow Paine, Mark Twain: A Biography (Harper & Bros., 1912), I, 74-75. Hereafter referred to as Biography.

[4] Infra, p. 4.

that of winning approval, which inclined him to conform to public opinion, had supplanted it. The individual, in short, had given way to the type. The struggle between these two selves, these two tendencies, these two wishes or groups of wishes, was to continue through Mark Twain's life, and the poet, the artist, the individual, was to make a brave effort to survive. From the death of his father onward, however, his will was definitely enlisted on the side opposed to his essential instinct.[5]

Harnessing such a rigid life pattern on a little boy of eleven who is feeling bad because his father died would seem a bit illogical. And yet, here the little fellow is supposedly doomed to a tragic life of frustration, because a story, which he himself contradicted and which possibly is not true in most of its details, got itself written into a biography. The whole complex analysis is pretty discouraging to little boys. Thus, in the "frustration" version, Sam is permitted to quit school, but he must go to work, be respectable, assume responsibility. An apprenticeship will provide the proper channel: he becomes a cub printer.

In *Mark Twain's Autobiography,* another version of the circumstances leading up to the printing apprenticeship is told. This version concerns an attack of the measles which Sam achieved by deliberately exposing himself. There was an epidemic of the disease in Hannibal, and everybody in the village, Mark Twain wrote in *Harper's Bazaar* in 1910, was "paralyzed with fright, distress, despair," until Sam could not stand the agony of suspense any longer. He crept into bed with a playmate and acquired the disease. "Everybody believed I would die." But the illness was not fatal, for "on the fourteenth day a change came for the worse and they were disappointed." He calls this the turning-point of his life:

> For when I got well my mother closed my school career and apprenticed me to a printer. She was tired of trying to keep me out of mischief and the adventure of the measles decided her to put me in more masterful hands than hers. I became a printer and began to add one link after another to the chain which was to lead me into the literary profession.[6]

[5] Van Wyck Brooks, *The Ordeal of Mark Twain* (E. P. Dutton & Co., 1933), pp. 60–62.

[6] *Harper's Bazaar,* February 1910.

This is a different story, and one hardly knows what to think of it in relation to other versions. It is probably at least true in spirit, since it was written when Mark Twain was trying his very best to be serious, truthful, and sincere in setting down the facts of his life. At any rate, whatever the circumstances of the printing apprenticeship may have been, in becoming a cub printer Samuel Clemens was, in fact, making his first progress toward the literary profession.

Sam's apprenticeship under Ament did not begin immediately after his father's death, as various accounts would lead one to believe, but fifteen months later, since Ament did not establish his paper until late in May or early in June, 1848, and there is no mention from direct and reliable sources that Sam served any previous apprenticeship. De Voto believes that the first employment was unquestionably under Ament.[7] Miss Brashear, although admitting an uncertainty about the date of Sam's first apprenticeship, feels that there is a possibility that he may have worked as a cub printer on the *Journal* or the *Gazette* before Ament came to Hannibal:

It was so fixed a memory of Mark Twain's, however, that he dropped out of school immediately after his father's death and that his mother believed the best place where he could become self-supporting, and at the same time continue his education, to be in a newspaper office, that the assumption seems justified that he worked either on the *Journal* or the *Gazette* from the spring of 1847 until the summer of 1848. The better theory is that he went to work on the *Gazette* and that after Mr. Ament bought it the boy proved to be so intelligent that he was formally taken on as an apprentice when the *Courier* and *Gazette* were consolidated.[8]

Board and clothes were the terms of Sam's apprenticeship— "More board than clothes, and not much of either." There is no reason to believe that he was not as well treated by Mr. Ament as any apprenticed cub was treated in that day, for Mark Twain's account in later years was unquestionably somewhat unreasonable with respect to the man who gave him his first job. Both in

[7] De Voto, *op. cit.*, p. 85.
[8] Minnie M. Brashear, *Mark Twain, Son of Missouri* (University of North Carolina Press, 1934), p. 98.

Paine's biography and in *Mark Twain's Autobiography,* Ament is described as a niggardly character; but Miss Brashear quotes newspaper comments of the early days to show that even Sam and his brother Orion had respect for Ament in those days. In the *Hannibal Journal* of November 25, 1852, the Clemens paper, commenting on Ament's sale of the *Courier,* said that Ament's ability had

made him an efficient supporter of his party principles, while his courtesy, and uniformly manly course, procured him many friends among his opponents. We heartily wish him success wherever he may bend his steps, and in whatever business he may undertake—except making proselytes to his party.[9]

The friendly jibe at the end of the editorial concerns the political affiliations of the two newspapers, which had been political rivals. Ament had been interested in conducting his newspaper as a party organ, and the columns of his paper had shown the party loyalty suitable to the oldest Democratic newspaper in the state.

Sam, in later years, criticized, though not too seriously, the circumstances of his employment with Ament.

"I was supposed to get two suits of clothes a year, like a nigger, but I didn't get them," [he said]. "I got one suit and took the rest out in Ament's old garments, which didn't fit me in any noticeable way. I was only about half as big as he was, and when I had on one of his shirts I felt as if I had on a circus tent. I had to turn the trousers up to my ears, to make them short enough."[10]

Sam seems to have got along very well at Ament's. He was quick to learn, his intelligence was recognized, and the boy was soon entrusted with more than the ordinary duties of a cub printer. Paine says:

When he had been with Ament little more than a year Sam had become office favorite and chief standby. Whatever required intelligence and care and imagination was given to Sam Clemens.[11]

It was not long before the boy was a kind of a "sub-editor" on the weekly paper and the importance of his duties mounted. During the last year of the Mexican War, telegraph communication

[9] Brashear, *op. cit.,* pp. 99–100.   [10] Paine, *Biography,* I, 76.   [11] *Ibid.,* pp. 77–78.

was completed to Hannibal, and news of the war came to the village. Sam was placed in charge of the extras containing the war news; that is, he was permitted to perform the task of circulating them. He gloried in it: "the burning importance of his mission, the bringing of news hot from the field of battle, spurred him to endeavors that won plaudits and success."[12] The young cub printer felt that now he was really becoming a newspaper man.

Sam Clemens' brother Orion established the *Hannibal Western Union,* printing the first number in September or October, 1850.[13] From Ament's paper, Sam went to become a printer on his brother's new weekly Whig newspaper. Now he was definitely established in the printing trade, and he stayed on through a variety of changes in Orion's publishing ventures. The *Western Union* continued under that name until August 28, 1851. On September 4, 1851, the following week, it became the *Hannibal Journal and Western Union.* It became the *Hannibal Journal* on September 9, 1852, and retained this title until the last issue under the ownership of Orion Clemens, dated September 21, 1853. Seven months of an erratic existence were enjoyed by Orion's *Hannibal Daily Journal,* which was started in March 1853, the weekly being continued along with the publication of the daily.[14]

Sam was a printer on each of these newspapers published by his brother. However, three months after the *Daily Journal* began publication he left Hannibal, in June 1853, for St. Louis, to begin his travels as a journeyman printer.

Looking at this period of Sam Clemens' career, when he was printer and sub-editor of his brother's *Hannibal Journal,* we discover the nature of his early writings. These experiments in authorship are placed in four groups by Miss Brashear.[15] The writings in the first group concern an editorial altercation that

[12] *Ibid.,* p. 78.

[13] C. J. Armstrong, Hannibal authority on Mark Twain, has recovered what is believed to be the earliest extant number of Orion's newspaper. The date is October 10, 1850. Miss Brashear places the establishment of the *Western Union* as September 1850.

[14] Cf. C. J. Armstrong, "Mark Twain's Early Writings Discovered," *Missouri Historical Review,* July 1930.   [15] *Mark Twain, Son of Missouri,* p. 107.

Sam had with a rival Hannibal editor. The second group consists
of some experiments in feature writing in which Sam used the
pen name, W. Epaminondas Adrastus Blab. The third group
centers around the poem, "To Miss Katie of H—l."[16] The fourth
consists of three columns of miscellaneous short items under the
heading, "Our Assistant's Column."

In "My First Literary Venture," written about 1870, Mark
Twain mentions the writings of the first, third, and fourth groups
listed above. The events of the "week" mentioned in this auto-
biographical sketch, in the period of Sam Clemens' editorship of
the *Hannibal Journal* during his brother's absence, occurred actually, according to Miss Brashear, during "two separate adventures
in editorship, about eight months apart, and were apparently the
first expressions of the youth's restless energy becoming conscious
of itself and impelled inevitably to break out of the narrow limits
of its small-town routine."[17]

As assistant editor of the *Journal,* Clemens engaged in his first
editorial controversy and made his first venture into authorship.
The local editor of the *Tri-Weekly Messenger,* rival Whig paper
of Hannibal, was the butt of Sam's satirical writing in this instance.
This editor had written an item concerning mad dogs in the
vicinity and had warned citizens against the danger. Mark Twain
later told about the follow-up of this incident in the columns of
the *Journal:*

I was a printer's "devil" and a progressive and aspiring one. My uncle
[*sic*] had me on his paper (the *Weekly Hannibal Journal,* two dollars a
year, in advance—five hundred subscribers, and they paid in cord-wood,
cabbages, and unmarketable turnips), and on a lucky summer's day he left
town to be gone a week, and asked me if I thought I could edit one issue
of the paper judiciously. Ah! didn't I want to try! Higgins was the editor
on the rival paper. He had lately been jilted, and one night a friend found
an open note on the poor fellow's bed, in which he stated that he could
no longer endure life and had drowned himself in Bear Creek. The friend
ran down there and discovered Higgins wading back to shore. He had
concluded he wouldn't. The village was full of it for several days, but
Higgins did not suspect it. I thought this was a fine opportunity. I wrote

---

[16] Paine refers to the poem as "To Mary in H—l."   [17] Brashear, *op. cit.,* p. 108.

an elaborately wretched account of the whole matter, and then illustrated it with villainous cuts engraved on the bottoms of wooden type with a jackknife—one of them a picture of Higgins wading out into the creek in his shirt, with a lantern, sounding the depth of the water with a walking stick. I thought it was desperately funny and was densely unconscious that there was any moral obliquity about such a publication.[18]

Much of this account was apparently correct, but the origin of the editorial controversy had nothing to do with the romance of Higgins, Miss Brashear believes after a study of the files of the newspapers, but arose from the mad-dog items published by the editor of the *Messenger*.[19]

Thus Sam Clemens' first editorial venture is conducted as a writer signing himself "A Dog-be-Deviled Citizen."[20] Several short items were apparently written, but the chief one—the earliest one extant—was published by Sam during the absence of Orion, who had gone to Tennessee on business in connection with a Clemens land tract in that state.

In the issue of the *Journal* of September 16, 1852, the sixteen-year-old editor presented the item that he felt would make spicy material during his brother's absence. Under the heading " 'Local' Resolves to Commit Suicide," and with a cartoon showing the rival editor, with the face of a dog and carrying a lantern and a cane, the following item appeared:

"Local," disconsolate from receiving no further notice from "A Dog-be-Deviled Citizen," contemplates Suicide. His "pocket-pistol" (i.e. the *bottle*) failing in the patriotic work of ridding the country of a nuisance, he resolves to "extinguish his chunk" by feeding his carcass to the fishes of Bear Creek, while friend and foe are wrapt in sleep. Fearing, however, that he may get out of his depth, he *sounds the stream with his walking-stick*.

[18] Mark Twain, "My First Literary Venture," *Sketches New and Old* (Harper & Bros., 1906), pp. 110–11.

[19] Brashear, *op. cit.*, p. 110.

[20] Franklin J. Meine of Chicago has identified an early sketch of Samuel Clemens in the *Carpet-Bag*, a humorous weekly published in Boston from 1852 to 1853. The sketch, which appeared in the issue of May 1, 1852, was entitled "The Dandy Frightening the Squatter." It was about Hannibal, Missouri, and was signed "S. L. C." This is presumably the earliest extant literary work of Samuel Clemens. Mr. Meine believes that this is the contribution Mark Twain was thinking of when he told Mr. Paine of two humorous anecdotes which he contributed to the *Saturday Evening Post* in 1851.

The artist has, you will perceive, Mr. Editor, caught the gentleman's countenance as correctly as the thing could have been done with the real doggerytype apparatus. Ain't he pretty? and don't he step along through the mud with an air? "Peace to his *re*-manes."

                                        A DOG-BE-DEVILED CITIZEN[21]

Following the *Messenger's* sarcastic editorial on the *Journal* item, there is another story, accompanied by two more woodcuts, in the issue of the *Journal* for September 23:

"PICTUR'" DEPARTMENT.

"Local" discovers something interesting in the *Journal,* and becomes excited.

("Local," determined upon the destruction of the great enemy of the canine race, charters an old swivel (a six pounder) and declares war. *Lead* being scarce, he leads his cannon with *Tri-Weekly Messengers.*)

"Local" is somewhat astonished at the effect of the discharge, and is under the impression that there was something the matter with the apparatus—thinks the hole must have been drilled in the wrong end of the artillery. He finds, however, that although he missed the "Dog-be-Deviled Citizen,"* he nevertheless hit the man "who has not the decency of a gentleman nor the honor of a blackguard," and thinks it best to stop the controversy.

MR. EDITOR:
    I have now dropped this farce, and all attempts to again call me forth will be useless.
                                        A DOG-BE-DEVILED CITIZEN

* Who walks quietly away, in the distance, uninjured.[22]

Orion had returned to Hannibal by the time this story appeared, and in the same issue of the *Journal* he had an editorial in which he praised the local editor of the *Messenger;* he added that the jokes of the *Journal* correspondent had "been rather rough; but, originating and perpetrated in a spirit of fun, and without a seri-

[21] *Hannibal Journal,* September 16, 1852. Miss Brashear credits this story to the *Daily Journal,* but it was printed in the weekly; the daily was not established until March 8, 1853.
[22] *Hannibal Journal,* September 23, 1852. Miss Brashear also credits this to the *Daily Journal,* but the daily was not yet established.

ous thought, no attention was expected to be paid to them, beyond a smile at the local editor's expense."

Such, then was the character of Sam Clemens' first newspaper writing. In the second group of his early experiments are four feature stories, three of which appear in the same issue of the *Journal* which contained the first woodcut and story. One of the latter, a long story accompanied by a woodcut, is entitled "A Historical Exhibition." Another is entitled "Editorial Agility." Both of these have introductory notes written by Orion Clemens. The third story of this group, in the September 16 issue, is signed W. Epaminondas Adrastus Perkins, and tells of a drunken brawl on Holliday's Hill. The last of the stories of the second group was published in the September 23 issue of the *Journal*. It is entitled "Blabbing Government Secrets," and concerns the writer's success in having the extra session of the legislature convened for the purpose of changing his surname from Perkins to Blab.

> Well, the request was granted: the Legislature was convened; my title was altered, shortened, and greatly beautified—and all at a cost of *only a few thousands of dollars to the State!*—These Democratic Legislators work cheap, don't they, Editor?[23]

The story is signed by W. E. A. B. In the same issue, the young editor bows his way out of public life in a note over the signature W. Epaminondas Adrastus Blab.

Clemens' first poem is the central theme of the third group of *Hannibal Journal* writings. To liven up circulation, apparently, during a second absence of his brother, Sam composed and published the following verses in the *Journal*:

LOVE CONCEALED.

To Miss Katie of H——l.

Oh, thou wilt never know how fond a love
    This heart could have felt for thee;
Or ever dream how love and friendship strove,
    Through long, long hours for mastery;

[23] *Hannibal Journal*, September 23, 1852.

How passion often urged, but pride restrained,
  Or how thy coldness grieved, but kindness pained.

How hours have soothed the feelings, then that were
  The torture of my lonely life—
But ever yet will often fall a tear,
  O'er wildest hopes and thoughts then rife;
Where'er recalled by passing word or tone,
  Fond memory mirrors all those visions flown.

For much I fear he has won thy heart,
  And thou art but a friend to me;
I feel that in thy love I have no part,
  I know how much he worships thee;
Yet still often will there rise a gleam of hope,
  Wherewith but only time and pride can cope.

                                                RAMBLER[24]
HANNIBAL, May 4th, 1853

This poem, appearing first in the *Daily Journal* of May 6, 1853, was reprinted in the weekly edition of the paper May 12, 1853. In a few succeeding issues of the paper Sam contributed items of comment on the poem, over the signatures of "Grumbler," "Rambler," and "Peter Pencilcase's Son, John Snooks."

The fourth group of Clemens' *Journal* writings is contributed by the young sub-editor in the role of columnist. The three columns written by the "Assistant" appear in the issues of May 23, May 25, and May 26, 1853. Under the heading "Our Assistant's Column," the contributions include such matters as reports of smallpox cases; "man's rights," as illustrated by a man beating his wife and children, tar and feathers being recommended for the man concerned; warm weather, "niggers begin to sweat and look greasy"; "The Burial of Sir Abner Gilstrap," which was a parody of "The Burial of Sir John Moore" and satirized a rival Missouri editor; a note on editorial-pilfering; and notes on emigrant parties bound for California. The three columns are assigned to the authorship of Sam Clemens by Miss Minnie M. Brashear.[25]

[24] *Hannibal Daily Journal*, May 6, 1853.
[25] *Op. cit.*, pp. 128–39.

In the May 27, 1853, issue of the *Hannibal Journal* appeared this notice: *"Wanted!* An Apprentice of the Printing Business. Apply soon." Samuel Clemens left, a few days later, for St. Louis on the first of his travels as a journeyman printer.

When Sam left Hannibal in June 1853 he informed his mother he was going to St. Louis, but his real purpose was to go on to New York.[26] He set type on the *Evening News* of St. Louis long enough to earn expense money to New York. He was working as a job printer in New York by August 31, 1853. He writes a letter from Philadelphia on October 26 of the same year, informing his brother that he is "subbing at the *Inquirer* office"[27] and is being laughed at by the other compositors because he is slow. After a period of visiting in Washington he returned to Philadelphia and set type on the *Ledger* and the *North American* during the spring and summer of 1854.

In the meantime Orion had moved to Muscatine, Iowa, and had established the *Journal* there. In the autumn of 1854 Sam went to Muscatine, set type for a few weeks on his brother's paper, then returned to St. Louis and went back to work on the *Evening News*. During the winter Orion gave up his Muscatine paper and established a job-printing office in Keokuk, Iowa. Soon Sam came to work for Orion, and he stayed in Keokuk almost two years. The Keokuk period of Mark Twain was neither distinguished for its achievements nor was it unimportant. Says Paine:

> At a printers' banquet he delivered his first after-dinner speech; a hilarious speech—its humor of a primitive kind. Whatever its shortcomings, it delighted his audience. . . . . They impressed him into a debating society after that and there was generally a stir of attention when Sam Clemens was about to take the floor.[28]

Clemens spent the winter of 1856–57 in Cincinnati working at his printing trade. In Keokuk he had become fired with a desire to go to the Amazon to make his fortune, and he was now on his

---

[26] Incidents and dates of the *Wanderjähre* period, 1853–1861, are given in Brashear, *op. cit.*, pp. 151–95.

[27] Paine, *Letters*, I, 26.   [28] Paine, *Biography*, I, 107.

way, via Cincinnati and New Orleans. In April 1857 he started down the river, met Horace Bixby, decided to become a Mississippi River pilot, and forgot about South America.

The literary ventures of the journeyman printer days, not counting his personal correspondence, which was now taking on a readable travel-letter tone, consist of two series of "Thomas Jefferson Snodgrass" letters. There is some doubt as to the second series being authentic Mark Twain material. The first series consists of three letters[29] written when Sam was presumably on his way to South America, after having left Keokuk some time in the autumn of 1856. The three letters were published in the *Keokuk Post* and were paid for at the rate of five dollars each. They are the first writings for which Sam Clemens received pay.

No doubt the Snodgrass letters were attempts of Samuel Clemens to write material that would be suitable for a "funnier book," which he had predicted during his printing days in Keokuk. As he was reading in bed one night a young man named Ed Brownell, a chum, came into the room. "What are you reading, Sam?" he asked. "Oh, nothing much—a so-called funny book—one of these days I'll write a funnier book than that, myself." Brownell laughed. "No, you won't, Sam," he said. "You are too lazy ever to write a book."[30]

The first Snodgrass letter, dated St. Louis, October 18, 1856, was published in the *Keokuk Saturday Post* of November 1. It tells of how Snodgrass was sitting in the parlor when one of his friends suggested that they go to the theater to see Mr. Nealy play *Julius Caesar*. They go to the theater, and Snodgrass thinks he will show the orchestra some class by playing on an old coarse comb, in that way taking "them one-hoss fiddlers down a peg and bring down the house, too," if he'd "jest give 'em a tech of 'Auld Lang Syne'" on it.

[29] Paine knew of only two of these Snodgrass letters when he wrote his Mark Twain biography. He had obtained his information from Thomas Rees, of the *Springfield* (Illinois) *Register*. Paine tells of the letters of November 14 and March 14 in the *Biography*, pp. 112–14.

[30] Paine, *Biography*, I, 107.

With the audience laughing at the country hick, Snodgrass gets "riled."

> Darn my skin if I wasn't mad. I jerked off my coat and jumped at the little man and, says I, "You nasty, sneakin degenerate great grandson of a ring-tailed monkey, I kin jest lam—."

Finally the curtain goes up. Snodgrass doesn't think much of the play, but

> at last it come time to remove Mr. Cesar from office . . . . so all the conspirators got around the throne, and directly Cesar come steppin in, putting on as many airs as if he was mayor of Alexandria. Arter he had sot on the throne awhile they all jumped on him at once like a batch of Irish on a sick nigger.

After the final curtain, Snodgrass attempts to orate:

> "Gentlemen and Ladies—I'm a peaceable stranger from Keokuk, and my name is Thomas Jefferson—" . . . . and in a twinklin a couple of police had sot me down in the street, advisin me to go to the devil and not come back there any more. Now, Mister Editors, Saint Louis may fizzle out and be derned.[31]

In his second letter, dated Cincinnati, November 14, 1856, and printed both in the *Daily Post* of November 29 and the *Saturday Post* of December 6, Snodgrass tells of his ride on the railroad during his journey from St. Louis to Cincinnati. He had planned to keep a daily journal of his voyage, a " 'Snodgrass' Dierrea,' or somethin of that kind, like other authors that visits forren parts." Having consulted a map he determines that the best route from St. Louis to Cincinnati was "to go back to Keokuk, and from Keokuk to Quincy, and from Quincy to Chicago, and from Chicago to Indianapolis, and then down to the end of [his] ultimate destination."

On the trip by river packet to Quincy, Snodgrass finds interest in the race between the steamboat and "an old fellar with a carpet bag, who calculated it was good exercise to walk to Quincy." The steamboat was delayed on a sand bar but finally got clear,

---

[31] Samuel Langhorne Clemens, *The Adventures of Thomas Jefferson Snodgrass* (Pascal Covici, Inc., Chicago, 1928), pp. 3–16.

and away she went walkin down the river on four inches of water, and jumpin over three acre patches of dry land, jest as though she had legs. The old man and her had a mighty tight race of it, and she only saved herself by takin a nigh cut across the bottom, comin in fifteen minutes ahead.

When Snodgrass sees his first locomotive he isn't *"skeered,"* but he "had three chills and a stroke of palsy in less than five minutes," and his face a "curus brownish-yaller-green-bluish color in it which was perfictly unaccountable." No conductor was going to get any ticket from Snodgrass.

"Not by a derned sight," says I. "You can't come any o them tricks on me, old feller. You can't get my ticket and then stick me ashore at the first wood yard your old cook stove stops at."

Snodgrass becomes nonchalant, a seasoned traveler:

It didn't take me long to git used to the cars, and then I begun to put on airs like an old traveler—stickin my feet over the back of the next pew, puttin my ticket in my hat band, pretending to go to sleep, and so on, and never lettin on to keer a cent where we was going to.

On the last lap of the journey the train tears along "at the rate of four hundred and thirty-seven miles a minute, leavin the rail track red hot behind us—in some places it melted."[32]

In the third letter Snodgrass tells of the extreme cold in Cincinnati: The Ohio River was "friz to the bottom." The city council had decided to sell coal at a low price to the poor people. But there were complications.

Here's a instance. A indigent Irish woman—a widow with nineteen children and several at the breast, accordin to custom, went to the Mayor to get some of that public coal. The Mayor he gin her an order on the Recorder; Recorder sent her to the Constable; Constable sent her to the Postmaster; Postmaster sent her to the County Clerk, and so on, tell she run herself half to death, and friz the balance, while she had sixteen places to go yet, afore she could git the coal.

A young lady asks Snodgrass to hold her basket for a moment, and the young man is left with a baby on his hands. He "was ketched by a perliceman about midnight down to the river, trying to poke the dang thing through a hole in the ice." There is a

[32] S. L. Clemens, *The Adventures of Thomas Jefferson Snodgrass*, pp. 19–33.

trial. Snodgrass is accused of being an "onnateral father." He finally is released from jail. "It pears to me that baby'll larn to swim yit afore its six weeks older—pervided it don't perish in the attempt."[33]

Crude as they are, the Snodgrass letters are nevertheless significant as showing a stage of literary development that Samuel Clemens was going through during his journeyman-printer days. Later, in his Far Western writings, we find that the exaggerated dialect of the Snodgrass letters has been abandoned. Also abandoned is the humor based on misspelling. These letters are a somewhat sustained attempt at dialect writing; seemingly there was enough of conclusiveness in this experiment to show Clemens that a more limited use of dialect would be preferable in his sketches. The letters have a forced humor that will be hard to find in the Mark Twain sketches of later years. They illustrate "the distance between the comic-strip humor of Twain's boyhood and the bitter satire of his age."[34] "The genius that a little more than ten years later would delight the world flickerered feebly enough at twenty-one."[35]

Searching through the files of the *New Orleans Crescent,* Miss Brashear discovered a series of four Snodgrass letters which she believes can reasonably be assigned to the authorship of Samuel Clemens. She thinks Sam was still at work on his "funnier book" in New Orleans.

The first of the letters appears in the *Crescent* of January 21, 1861. The nom de plume used, as in the other letters of the series, is Quintus Curtius Snodgrass. The title of the first letter is "The Expedition to Baton Rouge," and the narrative concerns Louisiana's joining the Confederacy. Snodgrass tells of how he joined the Louisiana Guard, sailed up the Mississippi on the steamer "National," and planted the flag of the Confederacy in front of the

---

[33] *Ibid.,* pp. 37–48.

[34] Vincent Starrett, in his Foreword to *The Adventures of Thomas Jefferson Snodgrass,* p. viii.

[35] Paine, *Biography,* I, 113.

state house. Miss Brashear feels that since this new Snodgrass
series was written four years later than the first, there would,
naturally, be a difference in style and mood.

> Instead of the vernacular of the traveler from the country, the language
> of Snodgrass, metamorphosed with a classical given name, is ambitiously
> literary. He quotes from Shakespeare, Dickens, and Tom Paine.[36]

Miss Brashear gives some logical points concerning the authen-
ticity of the letter as Clemens' work, but on reading the letter one
finds it difficult to believe that it does belong to Clemens.

The second letter of the series, printed February 25, 1861, is
another satire on military affairs, entitled "Hints to Young Cam-
paigners: with the Manual of Arms." The third, printed March 11,
1861, is an "account of a night's epicurean adventures in which
Snodgrass, his friend Laryndor Kydd, and a few other happy
companions participated."[37] The fourth letter is a report by Snodgrass of his attendance at a dinner at the President's mansion in
Washington. "The letter reflects the common Southern ridicule
of 'Old Abe' and his family at the beginning of the Civil War."[38]

Miss Brashear finds difficulty in justifying the lack of exaggeration, anti-climax, and irony found in the earlier Snodgrass series.
She admits that the *Crescent* letters do not satisfactorily suggest
the later Mark Twain. "And yet, if it can be proved that they are
authentic, they are immensely significant as a link in Mark Twain's
development as a humorist."[39]

Only one other attempt at newspaper writing was made by
Samuel Clemens before he departed for Nevada. During his pilot
days he wrote "squibs and skits" for New Orleans papers.[40] His
interest in writing was evidently not very great while he was enjoying the adventurous life of a Mississippi River pilot, as there is only
one item preserved—not including the second Snodgrass series, of
which the authorship is doubtful. Horace Bixby remembered later
that "Sam was always scribbling when not at the wheel," but

[36] Brashear, *op. cit.*, p. 189.   [37] *Ibid.*, p. 191.   [38] *Loc. cit.*
[39] Brashear, *op. cit.*, p. 192.   [40] Paine, *Letters*, I, 5.

Paine says that if Clemens "published any work in those river-days he did not acknowledge it later—with one exception."[41]

The one exception is the burlesque written about Captain Isaiah Sellers, referred to by Paine as an old pilot

who made the other pilots weary with the scope and antiquity of his reminiscent knowledge . . . . and contributed paragraphs of general information and Nestorian opinions to the New Orleans *Picayune*, and signed them "Mark Twain."[42]

The old pilot, no doubt sincere enough in his intentions, gave a somewhat egotistical tone to his newspaper correspondence by such phrases as "My opinion for the benefit of the citizens of New Orleans." Sam Clemens wrote a burlesque imitation of Captain Sellers' correspondence, signing it "Sergeant Fathom." The letter tells of a supposed trip of the steamer "Jubilee" with a Chinese captain and a Choctaw crew. High-water predictions of Captain Sellers are treated ironically.[43]

Later Mark Twain was sorry for the injury he had done the old pilot, and in the West, a few years later, he adopted the "Mark Twain" pen-name as his own. To his biographer, Mark Twain expressed his regret over the writing of the burlesque. Paine writes of the effect of the satire:

It broke Captain Sellers's literary heart. He never contributed another paragraph. Mark Twain always regretted the whole matter deeply, and his own revival of the name was a sort of tribute to the old man he had thoughtlessly wounded. If Captain Sellers has knowledge of material matters now, he is probably satisfied; for these things brought to him, and to the name he had chosen, what he could never himself have achieved—immortality.[44]

Samuel Clemens' pre-Washoe writings were, then, of an amateurish, premature type. There had been no sustained effort at au-

---

[41] Paine, *Biography*, I, 149. Surely Mark Twain, if he actually had written them, would have remembered and acknowledged the four letters of the second Snodgrass series.

[42] *Ibid.*, p. 149. See below, chapter 5, pp. 79–82.

[43] The satire is reprinted as Appendix B in the fourth volume of Paine's *Biography*, pp. 1593–96. Its original publication was in the *New Orleans True Delta* of May 8 or 9, 1859.

[44] *Ibid.*, p. 150.

thorship, and none of the writings extant has any particular literary merit. There was still nothing important enough that Clemens had done in his writings to point toward authorship as necessarily his future career.

Certain elements, however, in the earlier writings do presage further development in the frontier West. One is Sam Clemens' predilection for humorous writing. A second is his preference for writing travel letters, as a correspondent, rather than writing local items for the newspaper. A third is his weakness for editorial controversy; he enjoyed picking fights with other editors, or with anyone who would carry on a controversy through the columns of newspapers. A fourth is his tendency to satirize individuals, often injuring them unjustly, merely for the sake of a good story or to make some point that in itself may have been justified. In the West we shall find him continuing to write about politics and legislatures. In the West, however, Samuel Clemens abandons the use of exaggerated dialects, misspellings, and other elements of style found in his early Middle Western writings.

CHAPTER 2

IMPACT
OF THE FRONTIER

WITH his twenty-five formative years behind him—his years as a boy in Florida and Hannibal, Missouri, his years as assistant editor to his brother Orion, his years as tramp printer, his four years as pilot on the Mississippi River, and his few weeks as soldier in the Civil War—Samuel Clemens left for the West with his brother Orion. He went as private secretary, without pay, to his brother, who was the newly appointed secretary of Nevada Territory. Sam had saved a considerable sum of money out of his wages as river pilot and was more than willing to finance the Overland Stage trip across the plains to Carson City. So they went up the Missouri River to "St. Jo" and paid the stage fare of three hundred dollars for two passages. On July 26, 1861, the two brothers set out on the adventurous seventeen-hundred-mile journey over the plains and through the passes of the snowclad Rockies, a journey that is described in *Roughing It*.[1]

It would be a mistake to assume that Samuel Clemens went on the trip to the West moved merely by a sudden impulse or whim. On the contrary, he had been hearing for years of the adventure and the romance of the frontier West and had been looking with a restless curiosity at the horizon out there where men were living as in the adventurous days of '49.

Three lures that were beckoning Clemens during his journalis-

---

[1] Mark Twain, *Roughing It* (Harper & Bros., 1906).

tic days with his brother on the *Hannibal Journal* are suggested by Miss Brashear:

There was the Crystal Palace Fair in New York, at which Hannibal was to be represented by a bale of hemp and two barrels of flour, and there was always the river, with its "Die Vernon" and its "Jeannie Deans" making the fast time of thirteen or fourteen hours between St. Louis and Hannibal. Then there were parties passing through Hannibal on their way west.[2]

To all three of these lures Samuel Clemens responded. The first resulted in his travels as a journeyman printer, the second in his four years as a Mississippi River pilot, and the third in his five and a half years as a miner and a journalist in the West.

The third of these lures, and the one in which we are primarily interested in this study, was extensively publicized during Clemens' Missouri days. Newspapers of the time were carrying much information about the emigrant parties on their way to the frontier, whether they consisted of Mormons on their way to Salt Lake or of goldseekers on their way to the California El Dorado. The *Journal* published its share of this kind of news. A typical item, from the columns of the *Hannibal Daily Journal* of May 18, 1853, is the following:

Several California teams passed through here this morning. Messrs. T. W. Bunberry, A. J. Price, and Sam'l Fry started this morning with a good, light wagon and four yoke of fine oxen.

One of Sam's companions, a boy of twelve, left Missouri to play his part in the saga of the golden era of the West. Mark Twain writes, in his *Autobiography,* of this incident of the days of '49:

I remember the departure of the cavalcade when it spurred Westward. We were all there to see and to envy. And I can still see that proud little chap sailing by on a great horse . . . . We were all on hand to gaze and envy when he returned, two years later, in unimaginable glory—for he had traveled.[3]

And Clemens himself gave publicity to the westward trek by publishing such news a few days after he, as a seventeen-year-old

[2] Minnie M. Brashear, *Mark Twain, Son of Missouri* (University of North Carolina Press, 1934), p. 151.   [3] *Mark Twain's Autobiography* (Harper & Bros., 1924), II, 183.

assistant editor, had made his debut as a newspaper columnist. Beginning with the May 23, 1853, issue of the *Hannibal Daily Journal,* there are three issues that contain his contribution entitled "Our Assistant's Column." In the second of these, for May 25, 1853, are reprinted two items from the *St. Joseph Gazette:*

It is estimated that considerably upwards of ten thousand cattle alone have crossed the river at St. Joseph, destined for California. How many have crossed at other points, we have not understood. But it is very certain an immense amount of stock will cross the plains, this spring, cattle, sheep, horses, and mules. The number of cattle it is supposed will exceed *one hundred thousand head.* Persons can now readily account for the high prices of beef and stock.—(*St. Joseph Gaz.*)

The grass on the other side of the river is said to be getting very good now. Many of the emigrants are now on their winding way, having bid adieu for a while to busy scenes of civilization, to try the realities of a life upon the uninhabited plains, save by the red man and the game. They are in search of what a wise man once said is the root of all evil—gold. We wish them a safe journey and prosperous time.—(*St. Joseph Gaz.*)

These two items are the only exchange reprints used by the Assistant in the three issues of his column.

Samuel Clemens had no doubt looked toward the West many times before the great opportunity arrived. Would he not have gone West eventually even if Orion Clemens had not been appointed secretary to the territorial governor of Nevada? Probably not even the possibility of continuing as a pilot on the Mississippi would have kept Clemens from his manifest destiny. It would seem to have been temperamentally impossible for him to continue in any one occupation at any one place for an extended time, particularly as a young man. Among all the phobias, complexes, repressions, frustrations, and innumerable other abnormalities that have been considered in connection with Mark Twain by such analytical scholars as Van Wyck Brooks, possibly but one can be justifiably attributed to this great American humorist—a restless urge for travel, moving, seeing new things, experiencing new adventures.

Civil War or no Civil War, it is unlikely that Clemens would have tied himself permanently to the River. Possibly a year or so more would have been sufficient. In the light of the traits of personality that Mark Twain reveals in the works of his later years, one cannot imagine him staying on indefinitely as a pilot after he knew every town, sandbar, point, snag, landmark, bend, island, dead tree, bank, and reef on the twelve hundred miles of Mississippi River from St. Louis to New Orleans. Pattee feels that "it is very possible that but for the war and the change which it wrought upon the river, Mark Twain might have passed his whole life as a Mississippi pilot."[4] This is not consistent with the temperament of the young Sam Clemens. Of course, many years later he looked back reminiscently on the River days and said: "I loved the profession far better than any I have followed since, and I took measureless pride in it."[5] But is there any evidence there that he would have preferred to make piloting on the Mississippi his life work? Hardly. In fact, the very limitation of only four years of pilot life had much to do with establishing it as a pleasant memory to look back on in future years. His pilot days were over before they palled on him. The opportunity to go West was one for which he had been looking, and was a natural fulfillment of his desire for travel, for adventure, for new experiences in a romantic, colorful land. He had heard about it, and he had read about it. Now he could see for himself.

The thrilling twenty-day journey by Overland Stage from St. Joseph, Missouri, to Carson City, Nevada Territory, is colorfully described by Mark Twain in *Roughing It*. This first contact with the frontier made a profound impression upon the young adventurer. He was really traveling now! Previous excursions about the country, as journeyman printer and otherwise, had made so little impression on him that he writes in *Roughing It:* "I had never been away from home, and that word 'travel' had a seductive charm for me."[6] He wrote:

[4] Fred Lewis Pattee, *A History of American Literature Since 1870* (The Century Company, 1915), p. 49.

[5] Mark Twain, *Life on the Mississippi* (Harper & Bros., 1906), p. 119.

[6] Mark Twain, *Roughing It,* p. 15.

I only proposed to stay in Nevada three months—I had not thought of staying longer than that. I meant to see all I could that was new and strange, and then hurry home to business. I little thought that I would not see the end of the three-month pleasure excursion for six or seven uncommonly long years![7]

And steamboat days were so far from being thrilling and colorful to him by the time of his journey westward that he was immeasurably bored by the six-day trip on the Missouri River from St. Louis to St. Joseph. The boat trip was to him so dull and sleepy and uneventful that when he wrote of it ten years later it had left no more impression on his mind than if it had lasted six minutes instead of that many days. He writes sarcastically of the dull monotony of snags, reefs, and bars and the boat trip as a whole.[8] Is this not evidence that for Sam Clemens the glory of the river had passed in 1861?

On August 14, 1861, the Overland Stage rolled into Carson City. The last clouds of the alkali dust through which it had been plowing were floating across the desert like smoke from a burning house. The stage jerked to a stop. Two weather-worn young men climbed out and inquired for the hotel. "It was Orion Clemens, the new Territorial Secretary, and his brother, former dandified pilot, later a lieutenant of a forlorn hope, now an obscure adventurer of the frontier."[9]

It is not improper that Sam Clemens should be thought of here as secondary in importance to his brother Orion. After all, Orion was the new Territorial Secretary. To the Westerners, Sam Clemens was nobody. A change in the relative status of the two brothers was to come later.

Thus Clemens arrived in Carson City. It was the beginning of his adventures in the communities of the frontier West. Carson was his first glimpse of a real Western community:

It was a "wooden" town; its population two thousand souls. The main street consisted of four or five blocks of little white frame stores which were too high to sit down on, but not too high for various other purposes; in

---

[7] *Ibid.*, p. 16. [8] *Ibid.*, p. 17.
[9] Paine, *A Short Life of Mark Twain* (Harper & Bros., 1920), p. 73.

fact, hardly high enough. They were packed close together, side by side, as if room was scarce in that mighty plain. The side-walk was of boards that were more or less loose and inclined to rattle when walked upon. In the middle of the town, opposite the stores, was the "plaza" which is native to all towns beyond the Rocky Mountains—a large, unfenced, level vacancy, with a liberty pole in it, and very useful as a place for public auctions, horse trades, and mass meetings, and likewise for teamsters to camp in. Two other sides of the plaza were faced by stores, offices, and stables. The rest of Carson City was pretty scattering.[10]

This is the impression of Carson City that Mark Twain had ten years later, and it is an accurate picture. But let us look also at the picture of Carson City, and the plains, and the mining country generally as he gave it shortly after his arrival. In September or October, 1861, he writes to his mother, Mrs. Jane Clemens, in St. Louis:

MY DEAR MOTHER,—I hope you *will* all come out here someday. But I shan't consent to invite you, until we can receive you in *style*. But I guess we shall be able to do that, one of these days. I intend that Pamela shall live on Lake Bigler until she can knock a bull down with her fist—say, about three months.

"Tell everything as it is—no better, and no worse." Well, "Gold Hill" sells at $5,000 per foot, cash down; "Wild Cat" isn't worth ten cents. The country is fabulously rich in gold, silver, copper, lead, coal, iron, quicksilver, marble, granite, chalk, plaster of Paris, (gypsum), thieves, murderers, desperadoes, ladies, children, lawyers, Christians, Indians, Chinamen, Spaniards, gamblers, sharpers, coyotes (pronounced Ki-yo-ties), poets, preachers, and jackass rabbits. I overheard a gentleman say, the other day, that it was "the d—dest country under the sun."—and that comprehensive conception I fully subscribe to. It never rains here, and the dew never falls. No flowers grow here, and no green thing gladdens the eye. The birds that fly over the land carry their provisions with them. Only the crow and the raven tarry with us. Our city lies in the midst of a desert of the purest—most unadulterated, and compromising *sand*—in which infernal soil nothing but the fag-end of vegetable creation, "sage-brush," ventures to grow. If you will take a lilliputian cedar tree for a model, and build a dozen imitations of it with the stiffest article of telegraph wire—set them one foot apart and then try to walk through them, you'll understand (provided the floor is covered 12 inches deep with sand), what it is to wander through a sage-brush desert. When crushed, sage brush emits an odor which isn't exactly magnolia and equally isn't exactly polecat—but it is a sort of compromise between the two.

[10] Mark Twain, *Roughing It*, pp. 169–70.

It looks a good deal like greasewood, and is the ugliest plant that was ever conceived of . . . . the Carson [is] a river, 20 yards wide, knee-deep, and so villainously rapid and crooked, that it looks like it had wandered into the country without intending it, and had run about in a bewildered way and got lost, in its hurry to get out again before some thirsty man came along and drank it up. I said we are situated in a flat, sandy desert—true. And surrounded on all sides by such prodigious mountains, that when you gaze at them awhile,—and begin to conceive of their grandeur—and next to feel their vastness expanding your soul—and ultimately find yourself growing and swelling and spreading into a giant—I say when this point is reached, you look disdainfully down upon the insignificant village of Carson, and in that instant you are seized with a burning desire to stretch forth your hand, put the city in your pocket, and walk off with it.

As to churches, I believe they *have* got a Catholic one here, but like that one the New York fireman spoke of, I believe "they don't *run* her now." . . . . And up "King's Canon," (please pronounce can-yon, after the manner of the natives,) there are "ranches," or farms, where they say hay grows, and grass, and beets and onions, and turnips, and other "truck" which is suitable for cows—yes, and even Irish potatoes; also cabbages, peas and beans.

The houses are mostly frame, unplastered, but "papered" inside with flour-sacks sewed together,—and the handsomer the "brand" upon the sacks is, the neater the house looks.[11]

This letter is important as showing Sam Clemens' reaction to the frontier West. He is enthusiastic, spirited. The newness of this land—strange, strong, manly—fascinates him. It has its hardships, but they in themselves are fascinating. He is thrilled with his widening horizon. In this letter there is, as Paine says, "Something of the 'wild freedom of the West,' which later would contribute to his fame."[12] The letter has the Western tang, the tall-story atmosphere, the masculine exuberance of the frontier. It is different from any previous Sam Clemens letter extant.

In the letter just quoted Clemens writes of Lake Bigler and of his desire that Pamela, his sister, should benefit by staying at the lake three months. A trip to Lake Bigler was, in fact, his first definite project or activity in the West. He had been "hanging around" Carson City, studying human nature, mixing with West-

[11] Paine, *Mark Twain's Letters* (Harper & Bros., 1917), I, pp. 53, 54, 55.
[12] *Ibid.*, p. 56.

ern characters, principally just loafing around the streets of the town. He had become fascinated by the curious new country, and had concluded to put off his return to "the States." He writes:

> I had grown well accustomed to wearing a damaged slouch hat, blue woolen shirt, and pants crammed into boot-tops, and gloried in the absence of coat, vest, and braces. I felt rowdyish and "bully," (as the historian Josephus phrases it, in his fine chapter upon the destruction of the Temple). It seemed to me that nothing could be so fine and so romantic.[13]

Brooks sees something ominous in this change of costume to conform with frontier fashions:

> The artist in him had lost its guiding-line; he was "broken down" again, just as he had been after his father's death; his spirit had become plastic once more. He was ready in a word, to take the stamp of his new environment.[14]

Of course, he was ready to take the stamp of his new environment, but what connection can this have with artistic frustration? Samuel Clemens was no freak; he was a normal young man acting as any other normal young man would have acted who came from Missouri to Carson City in the days of the frontier. "Merely, you imagine, the natural change in dress that any gold-seeker would have made?" asks Brooks.[15] The answer, not according to Brooks, is decisively "Yes."

In his position of private secretary to the Secretary there was nothing for Sam Clemens to do, and there was no provision for payment for these non-services. He marveled at and enjoyed for himself the easy-going freedom of life on the frontier. He made friends of Carson men, and he would tell stories of the Mississippi River to interested listeners around the stove in Orion's office during chilly fall evenings. On the streets of Carson City perhaps more notice was taken of this individual with the great mass of bushy auburn hair, the sharp eyes, and the lounging walk than of the average newcomer; but there is no reason to believe that he

[13] Mark Twain, *Roughing It*, p. 180.

[14] Van Wyck Brooks, *The Ordeal of Mark Twain* (E. P. Dutton & Co., rev. ed., 1933), p. 99.

[15] *Loc. cit.*

became conspicuous. The feeling among some of the older residents around Carson City today is that, from what they have heard and remembered, Sam Clemens was not particularly conspicuous but, like many another of the male residents of that frontier town, was lazy and indifferent and did not always take the long way around to avoid the saloons and the poker table.

Probably Sam Clemens was outwardly very much like any other average Carson male resident of the early days, particularly after he had been in the town for a few weeks. He does not seem, however, to have contracted the mining fever immediately. But he did, finally, look about him for something definite to do. The opportunity came with the possibility of locating a timber claim on Lake Bigler.

With John D. Kinney, a young man from Cincinnati, Sam Clemens went to Lake Bigler—now Lake Tahoe—in August 1861. The two had heard of the great forests around the lake and had decided to stake out a rich timber claim. Although the trip to Lake Bigler lasted only a few days, it is significant in Mark Twain's Western development. Previous to this trip he had not been particularly impressed with the desirability of staying in the West. It was a new and fascinating country; but was it worth living in? In the letter to his mother previously quoted we find Sam Clemens repeating the language of the gentleman who had called it "the damnedest country under the sun." No rain, no dew, no flowers—not a green thing to gladden the eye: The birds finding it necessary to carry their own provisions with them. Only the crow and the raven in the midst of a sandy desert where nothing but sagebrush, the fag end of vegetable creation, will venture to grow. The odor of crushed sagebrush, which is a compromise between magnolia and polecat. Not a promising picture—hardly one designed to hold a young man away from home for any length of time, even though many of the crudities and hardships of the man's life on the frontier did appeal to him.

Then Clemens came to Lake Tahoe! The glory of the lake and the mountain fastness was overpowering. The two young men had been climbing for seemingly endless miles up the mountain range from Carson City to the lake, with packs on their backs. They had been told that the distance to the lake was eleven miles, but after tramping endlessly on the level through sagebrush and greasewood and then climbing a thousand miles straight up they looked over and found no lake yet. Being gritty and determined young men, they toiled upward a couple of thousand miles more, and then looked over. Still no lake. Not being swearing men themselves, they sat down and hired a couple of transient Chinamen to cuss for them. Thus refreshed, they trudged on again, and finally the lake burst upon them:

—a noble sheet of blue water lifted six thousand three hundred feet above the level of the sea, and walled in by a rim of snow-clad mountain peaks that towered aloft full three thousand feet higher still! It was a vast oval, and one would have to use up eighty or a hundred good miles in traveling around it. As it lay there with the shadows of the mountains brilliantly photographed upon its still surface I thought it must surely be the fairest picture the whole world affords.[16]

It was a sight that Mark Twain was never to forget. In his letters, in *Roughing It,* in his *Autobiography,* in *Innocents Abroad,* in his newspaper correspondence he was to mention the glories of Lake Tahoe many times during his later years. The only other lake in the world which he was ever to find comparable with Lake Tahoe was Lake Como, and even then he was to prefer the former.

When Sam Clemens and John Kinney came to Lake Tahoe on that August day in 1861 they came to a virtually uninhabited wilderness. The only sign of human activity was a small group of workmen at a sawmill three miles down the lake shore. There probably were not more than fifteen other human beings anywhere near the lake. There was inspiration in this blue-green mountain lake, twenty-one miles long and twelve miles wide, mirroring the lofty peaks of the Sierra Nevada. Its endless bays made a picturesque shoreline of about one hundred miles.

[16] Mark Twain, *Roughing It,* p. 181.

One can be sure the two young men were travel-weary when they finally reached the borders of Lake Tahoe. They found a small skiff belonging to friends in Carson City, and they set out across the bend of the lake to the camp they were looking for. "I got Johnny to row," writes Mark "—not because I mind exertion myself, but because it makes me sick to ride backwards when I am at work. But I steered."[17] After a three-mile pull they arrived at the camp, tired and hungry. They found provisions and utensils cached among the rocks. Despite his great fatigue, Sam was still man enough to sit down on a boulder and superintend the job while his companion gathered wood and cooked supper. Many a man, Mark writes later, would have wanted to rest after going through what Mark had gone through.

The sojourn at Lake Tahoe was a glorious experience for Sam Clemens. "As the darkness closed down and the stars came out and spangled the great mirror with jewels, we smoked meditatively in the solemn hush and forgot our troubles and our pains."[18] The life in the mountain air was so invigorating, and the sleep out of doors so refreshing that it would have restored "an Egyptian mummy to his pristine vigor." Johnny and Sam made a survey of the lake shore, and about three miles from camp they were so impressed with the attractiveness of a spot that they claimed three hundred acres of timber by putting their notices on a tree.

The dense forest of yellow pine that made up their claim had to be fenced in order that they might hold their property. Accordingly they did some desultory tree-cutting. Next came the house-building, which finally narrowed down to the construction of a flimsy brush affair. "We did not sleep in our 'house.' It never occurred to us, for one thing; and besides, it was built to hold the ground, and that was enough. We did not wish to strain it."[19] They never found any difficulty in going to sleep at night. "At the first break of dawn we were always up and running foot-races to

[17] *Ibid.,* p. 182.   [18] *Loc. cit.*
[19] *Ibid.,* p. 189.

tone down excess of physical vigor and exuberance of spirits. That is, Johnny was—but I held his hat."[20]

Though Mark Twain writes in *Roughing It* of living on the timber ranch for two or three weeks, the two young men probably were actually at the lake itself only four days, as is indicated in a letter by Sam to his brother shortly after the sojourn at the lake.

Sam is recalling some of the promises he had made to his mother when he left home for the West:

But first and foremost, for *Annie's,* Mollie's, and Pamela's comfort, be it known that I have never been guilty of profane language since I have been in this Territory, and Kinney hardly ever swears.—But *sometimes* human nature gets the better of him. On the second day we started to go by land to the lower camp, a distance of three miles, over the mountains, each carrying an axe. I don't think we got *lost* exactly, but we wandered four hours over the steepest, rockiest and most dangerous piece of country in the world. I couldn't keep from laughing at Kinney's distress, so I kept behind, so that he could not see me. After he would get over a dangerous place, with infinite labor and constant apprehension, he would stop, lean on his axe, and look around, then behind, then ahead, and then drop his head and ruminate awhile. Then he would draw a long sigh, and say: "Well—could any Billygoat have scaled that place without breaking his ——— neck?" And I would reply, "No,—I don't think he could." "No— you don't think he could—(mimicking me,) "Why don't you *curse* the infernal place? You know you *want* to.—*I* do, and *will* curse the ——— thieving country as long as I live." Then we would toil on in silence for awhile. Finally I told him—"Well, John, what if we *don't* find our way out of this today—we'll know all about the country when we *do* get out." "Oh stuff—I know enough—and *too much* about the d—d villainous locality already."[21]

In the light of a wider acquaintance with Mark Twain, the reader of this letter today will be permitted to draw his own conclusions as to which of these two young men was doing the most of the swearing around the shores of Lake Bigler in those pioneer days. Can it be possible that Sam Clemens was already telling tall stories, even in his letters back to the folks at home?

He had already picked up some useful Western information. He had learned how to play faro:

[20] Mark Twain, *Roughing It,* p. 187.   [21] Paine, *Letters,* I, 57–58.

W. H. CLAGGET, S. L. CLEMENS, A. S. SIMMONS

From Cyril Clemens' *Mark Twain
Wit and Wisdom* (Stokes, 1935)

After supper we got out our pipes—built a rousing camp fire in the open air—established a faro bank (an institution of this country) on our huge flat granite dining table, and bet white beans till one o'clock, when John went to bed.[22]

When provisions began to run short, Sam and Johnny went back to the old camp down the lake for a new supply. Tired and hungry, they reached home about nightfall. While Johnny was carrying provisions from the boat, Sam took some food ashore, then lighted a fire for cooking supper. He left the fire to go back to the boat for a frying pan, and in those few moments the forest carpet of dry pine needles became ignited and the sheet of flame was tearing away through the chaparral and into the forest of pine. Sam describes the fire in a letter to his mother, and later in *Roughing It*. It was truly an awesome spectacle:

The mighty roaring of the conflagration, together with our solitary and somewhat unsafe position (for there was no one within six miles of us) rendered the scene very impressive. Occasionally, one of us would remove his pipe from his mouth and say,—*"Superb! magnificent!* Beautiful!—but—by the Lord God Almighty, if we attempt to sleep in this little patch tonight, we'll never live till morning!—for if we don't burn up, we'll certainly suffocate." But he was persuaded to sit up until we felt pretty safe as far as the *fire* was concerned, and then we turned in, with many misgivings. When we got up in the morning, we found that the fire had burned small pieces of drift wood within six feet of our boat, and had made its way to within 4 or 5 steps of us on the South side. We looked like *lava* men, covered as we were with ashes, and begrimed with smoke. We were very black in the face, but we soon washed ourselves white again.[23]

Habitation, fence, and considerable timber on the claim were destroyed by the fire. So there was nothing to do but go back to Carson City.

Thus ends the first phase of Mark Twain's Western development. The trip to Lake Tahoe has the significance of having reconciled Sam Clemens to the "damnedest country under the sun." His first impression of Nevada had, no doubt, been one of uncertainty as to the pleasure or advisability of living in this rough

[22] *Ibid.*, p. 58.   [23] *Ibid.*, pp. 56–57.

Western land. Gradually, there developed in him the feeling that there was a

bravado in mingling with these bearded men and living in a frame shack papered inside with flour sacks. Then the desert began to exert its influence. The mountains became an acceptable substitute for the Mississippi. Soon he climbed to Lake Tahoe, which "throws Como in the shade." Thereafter one hears no more about desolation.[24]

The West had exerted its influence. Homesickness had been overcome. Sam Clemens was imbued with the spirit of the frontier. He was no longer certain that his stay would be only temporary.

[24] Bernard De Voto, *Mark Twain's America* (Little, Brown & Co., 1932), p. 117.

CHAPTER 3

SILVER MINER

AFTER his first impact with the frontier and a two-month period of trying to adjust himself, to determine just what course he should take in the roaring life of the new West, Samuel Clemens was on the threshold of his third profession, that of silver miner. He had been a printer and a river pilot; now he was about to adopt the career favored in the new environment. As a miner, he entered another stage of his Western development.

For about two months after coming to Carson City, Clemens was able to withstand the exposure to the mining fever. At the end of that period, after his trip to the timber lands of Lake Tahoe, he succumbed. On his arrival at Carson City he apparently had only a casual interest in the mining excitement in the town, and, during the first weeks of his sojourn there, though he was in association continuously with those who were wild with the turmoil of silver and gold, he still had not shown more than a passing curiosity, at least outwardly. Friends with mining claims urged him to take part in their enterprises. The talk of great strikes in the mining fields buzzed continually in his ears. But he had decided to try out first the timber-claim enterprise.

When upon returning from the Lake Tahoe journey Clemens did finally decide to go into the mining activity, his enthusiasm burst out in a flood, as though the very damming up of interest in mining had filled a tremendous reservoir of energy behind his repression. Stories of sudden and fabulous wealth had had their effect, and there was evidence that was more material than the wild tales told on the streets and printed in the newspapers:

Wagonloads of ore, sometimes even of gold and silver bricks, drove through the streets of Carson City. As Paine says: "No wonder Samuel Clemens, with his natural tendency to speculative optimism, yielded to the epidemic and became 'as frenzied as the craziest.' "[1]

The Tahoe timber claim was soon forgotten. True, years later, in a letter of October 25, 1861, to his sister Pamela, Sam informs his sister that he has laid a timber claim for her husband, Mr. Moffett, and the claim can now be considered by Mr. Moffett to be better than bank stock. A sawmill is to be moved there in the spring by a Mr. Jones. The claim is two miles in length by one mile in width, and is in the names of Sam L. Clemens, Wm. A. Moffett, Thos. Nye, and three other persons. Situated on "Sam Clemens Bay," which has been so named by Captain Nye, the claim is so beautiful that Sam feels that he would be happy to go there and die. "I'll build a county seat there one of these days that will make the Devil's mouth water if he ever visits the earth."[2] But this is the last correspondence concerning the timber claims.

In a previous letter, to his mother and his sister, Sam had included a statement that showed his first awakening interest in mining activities. He had spoken of going back to Lake Tahoe to build another cabin and fence, "and get everything in satisfactory trim before our trip to Esmeralda about the first of November."[3] This reference to a trip to Esmeralda could mean only one thing—that Clemens had at last entered into the mining excitement. Esmeralda was the scene of one of the frenzied campaigns for ledges. He had visited the Esmeralda district and had been given fifty feet in the "Black Warrior," an unprospected claim. The follow-up of this incident is typical of his mining activity. The young man who had given him the fifty feet in the Esmeralda claim wrote that he had gone down eight feet on the ledge and had found an eight-foot ledge of pretty good rock; that he could take out rock now if there were a mill to

[1] Albert Bigelow Paine, *Mark Twain: A Biography* (Harper & Bros., 1912), I, 182.
[2] Paine, *Letters*, I, 60.   [3] *Ibid.*, I, 58.

ESMERALDA (AURORA), GHOST TOWN OF NEVADA TERRITORY

LAKE BIGLER (NOW LAKE TAHOE)

crush it but that the four mills were all engaged and probably it would be best to suspend work until spring. Sam answered that the claim could be left alone at present; in the spring he would go down himself to work on it, and there would then be twenty stamp mills running in the Esmeralda district.

Sam and his brother Orion were now purchasing feet in various claims, and prospects were growing bright. Sam wrote to his sister that he and Orion had confidence enough in the mining country to think that if the war would let them alone they could make themselves and their relatives rich. "This is just the country for Cousin Jim to live in," he writes to Pamela. "I don't believe it would take him six months to make $100,000 here, if he had 3,000 dollars to commence with."[4]

The folks at home heard no more from Sam for three months after this letter was written. In the meantime, instead of going to the Esmeralda district immediately, he made a midwinter prospecting trip to the Humboldt country, a newly opened mining region two hundred miles from Carson City. Though there were many trying experiences during the expedition across the alkali desert to Unionville in the Humboldt country, and the search for a promising claim was unavailing, this expedition seems to have served only to make the young miner even more anxious to succeed in his new vocation.

Sam's companions on the Humboldt excursion were two young lawyers, A. W. Oliver and W. H. Clagget, and an older man, a blacksmith named Tillou. Sam had known Clagget as a law student in Keokuk. Tillou had had considerable experience in mining, and appears to have contributed a level head and good judgment to the venture. The other members of the party were the two rather dilapidated old horses which drew the wagon filled with supplies, and two nondescript dogs. Sam wrote, in a letter to his mother, that the wagon contained, besides the provisions and mining tools, certain luxuries, including ten pounds of killikinick,

---

[4] *Ibid.,* I, 62. The "Cousin Jim" referred to here is Cousin Jim Lampton, who is later to become the Colonel Sellers of *The Gilded Age.*

Watts's *Hymns,* fourteen decks of cards, *Dombey and Son,* a crib-bage board, one small keg of lager-beer, and the "Carmina Sacra."[5] The story of the venture is told in *Roughing It.*

About the only pleasant phase of the expedition to Unionville was the unstudied picturesqueness of the vocabulary of good old Mr. Ballou [Tillou], the blacksmith, according to the account in *Roughing It.* Mr. Ballou observed, while the prospecting party was dragging its way over the barren Great American Desert, that the coffee made with alkali water was "too technical"[6] for him and that the two ancient horses trying their level best to drag along the overloaded wagon were "bituminous from long deprivation."[7]

After the difficult experiences of several weeks in the Humboldt country, Sam returned to Carson City, still looking for mining prospects. The winter hardships of desert snowstorms and extreme cold had not unnerved him. He was not a quitter. Where there was still some prospect of success in mining enterprise he had the fortitude to stand the hardships as well as other men of the frontier. Perhaps if there had been less of this tenacity and fortitude in the face of disappointments he would have been considerably better off in the long run. For certainly many enterprises of his in later life would not have been such tragic failures if he had given them up sooner than he did. This tendency to face difficulties and to work hard to overcome them, even when better judgment would call for abandonment, very probably can be traced back to the training and experience of Sam Clemens in his ventures in the frontier West.

Next follows a comparatively long period of prospecting and mining in the Esmeralda district.[8] Sam had acquired feet in this territory and was determined to make something of prospects

---

[5] Paine, *Biography,* I, 183.   [6] Mark Twain, *Roughing It,* I, 221.   [7] *Ibid.,* I, 218.

[8] That Aurora, in the Esmeralda country, was a lively mining camp in its boom days is indicated by the letter of a correspondent a few years later in the *Sacramento Union.* In the letter, published on May 22, 1866, the writer notes that three years previously Aurora had had a population of 5,000, a city government, two daily papers, two fire companies of 60 men each, with their machines, and two military companies "uniformed and equipped in every particular with their commodious and comfortable armories; also a brass band of nine pieces."

there. The return to Carson City was at the end of January 1862. With his own funds almost exhausted after the Humboldt trip, Sam turned to his brother for financial help. Paine tells us: "The brothers owned the Esmeralda claims in partnership, and it was agreed that Orion, out of his modest depleted pay, should furnish the means, while the other would go actively into the field and develop their riches."[9] Orion may not have been, as Miss Brashear suggests, "the greatest single influence in Mark Twain's life,"[10] but he certainly was an important influence in Mark Twain's career during the days in the frontier West.

In February Sam was in camp in the Esmeralda district, feverish with enthusiasm in the spirited search for mineral wealth. Now for seven months his delirium of mining prospects was to run its course. Mining in the Esmeralda district, Sam camped at various times with four different companions: Horatio Phillips, whom he writes about as Raish and Ratio; Bob Howland, who became known as the most fearless man in Nevada Territory while he was city marshal of Aurora; Calvin H. Higbie, to whom *Roughing It* was later to be dedicated; and Dan Twing.

Bob Howland, nephew of Governor Nye, had been a friend of Sam's in Carson. Paine writes:

It was the same Bob Howland who would be known by and by as the most fearless man in the Territory; who, as city marshal of Aurora, kept that lawless camp in subjection, and, when the friends of a lot of condemned outlaws were threatening an attack with general massacre, sent the famous message to Governor Nye: "All quiet in Aurora. Five men will be hung in an hour."[11]

The association with Higbie, especially, was to be pleasantly remembered by Mark Twain in later years. A happy inspiration led him to change his first plans for the dedication of *Roughing It*. In a letter to Elisha Bliss of Hartford, which Mark Twain was to write from Elmira, New York, on May 15, 1871, the following suggested dedication for *Roughing It* appears:

[9] Paine, *Biography*, I, 193.
[10] Brashear, *op. cit.*, p. 106.   [11] Paine, *Biography*, I, 176–77.

To the Late Cain
This Book Is Dedicated

Not on account of respect for his memory, for it merits little respect;
not on account of sympathy with him, for his bloody deed placed him without the pale of sympathy, strictly speaking: but out of a mere human com-
miseration for him that it was his misfortune to live in a dark age that knew
not the beneficent Insanity Plea.[12]

Can the reader of *Roughing It* doubt the greater appropriate-
ness of the dedication that was finally chosen?

To Calvin H. Higbie of California, an honest man, a genial comrade,
and a steadfast friend, this book is inscribed by the author in memory of
the curious time when we two were millionaires for ten days.

The Esmeralda days represent, it is true, a wild seeking for
wealth. Samuel Clemens wanted to be rich. Brooks sees something ominous again in this: The artist has lost his guiding-line;
he is beset with fears that he cannot fulfill great family obliga-
tions; he must recover the prestige that was his as a Mississippi
River pilot and regain his position as an important personage;
if he had any awareness of the demands of his creative instinct he
certainly could not fulfill them now, as he must fulfill his craving
for wealth and prestige; he must acquiesce in the repression of
his individuality; he must become rich. "Mark Twain was not
merely obliged to check his creative instinct; he was obliged to
do his level best to become a millionaire."[13]

Was the desire to find silver and gold, to become rich, something freakish, abnormal, in those frontier days? Has it not
occurred to Brooks that thousands of other perfectly normal
American young men were as excited as twenty-seven-year-old
Samuel Clemens?

Extravagant letters from Esmeralda to his mother and sister
tell the story of the wild hopes of the young miner. Sam and
Orion had acquired some feet in claims in the district, but when
Sam arrived to look over the claims he found them worthless and
threw the feet away. He writes of the Horatio and Derby ledge

[12] Paine, *Letters*, I, 188.
[13] Brooks, *The Ordeal of Mark Twain* (E. P. Dutton & Co., 1933), p. 105.

and of the value of water at the mines. Letters to Orion at Carson City go into excited detail: The work, Sam writes, is hampered by snow. He wants the "Live Yankee" deed, but not by the "damned Express." He expects that Gebhart will die—he was shot defending a claim. He wants $40 or $50 by mail immediately. The "Pugh" has been thrown away, will not be re-located. Snow prevents work on the "Red Bird" tunnel. The "Farnum" is doubtful. The "Governor" is under snow. The "Douglas" and the "Red Bird" have both been recorded. Orion is enjoined, by letter, to stir himself as much as possible and to lay up $100 or $150 subject to Sam's call. Orion is not to send any money home, as Sam will have Orion's next quarter's salary spent before he can get it. Sam owns one-eighth of the new "Monitor Ledge, Clemens Company," and he will not sell a foot of it because he knows it to contain a fortune. He owns interests in the "Flyaway" discovery and its extensions; workmen bring in some fine specimens. He is becoming dubious about glittering prospects, he writes, and has decided to be in only on the sure thing.

"Feet" were being acquired now and then by Orion on his own responsibility while Sam was in Esmeralda. Sam did not trust his brother's judgment, and was usually impatient and irritable at any miscellaneous buying that Orion indulged in:

"Eighteen hundred feet in the C. T. Rice's Company!" Well, I am glad you did not accept of the 200 feet. Tell Rice to give it to some *poor* man.

But hereafter, when anybody holds up a glittering prospect before you, just argue in this wise, viz: That, if all spare change be devoted to working the "Monitor" and "Flyaway," 12 months, or 24 at furthest, will find all our earthly wishes satisfied, so far as money is concerned—and the more "feet" we have, the more anxiety we must bear—therefore, why not say "No— d—n your 'prospects,' I wait on a *sure* thing—and a man is less than a man, if he can't wait 2 years for a fortune"?[14]

In another letter he is even more irritated at Orion's activities in buying more mining feet:

You have *promised* me that you would leave all mining matters, and everything involving an outlay of money, in my hands.

[14] Paine, *Letters,* I, 73–74.

Sending a man fooling around the country after *ledges,* for God's sake! when there are hundreds of feet of them under my nose here, begging for owners, free of charge. *I don't want* any more feet, and I won't *touch* another foot—so you see, Orion, as far as any ledges of Perry's are concerned, (or *any other* except what I examine first with my own eyes,) I freely yield my right to share ownership with you.[15]

In one instance, Orion did, however, convince his brother that he had bought into something worth while. Sam and Raish examined a specimen which Orion sent, found fine gold inside, tested the specimen thoroughly. "If you have actually made something by helping to pay somebody's prospecting expenses it is a wonder of the first magnitude, and deserves to rank as such," Sam writes to Orion. He says that he is well satisfied and commends his brother on the fortunate venture:

Therefore, hold on to the "Mountain House," for it is a "big thing." Touch it lightly, as far as money is concerned, though, for it is well to reserve the code of justice in the matter of quartz ledges—that is, consider them all (and their owners) guilty (of "shenanigan") until they are proved innocent.[16]

Mining details fill the pages of the letters to Orion. In his letters to his mother and to his sister, Sam Clemens is more reserved, though he occasionally breaks out into extravagant statement. There is now a gradual infusion, too, of the Western tall-story spirit that was to contribute much to Mark Twain's writing during his years in the frontier West:

And Ma says "it looks like a man can't hold public office and be honest." Why, certainly not, Madam. A man *can't* hold public office and be honest. Lord bless you, it is a common practice with Orion to go about town stealing little things that happen to be lying around loose. And I don't remember having heard him speak the truth since we have been in Nevada. He even trys to prevail upon *me* to do these things, Ma, but I wasn't brought up in that way, you know. You showed the public what *you* could do in that line when you raised me, Madam. But then you ought to have raised me first, so that Orion could have had the benefit of my example. Do you know that he stole all the stamps out of an 8-stamp quartz mill one night, and brought them home under his over-coat and hid them in the back room?[17]

---

[15] Paine, *Letters,* I, 80.   [16] *Ibid.,* p. 77.   [17] *Ibid.,* p. 68.

Eight stamps would have weighed about 4,800 pounds. The predilection for the Western style of humor was showing itself.

Brooks has made much[18] of a supposed mother-complex which exerted a powerful influence on Sam Clemens and his literary career. Yet certainly there is no evidence of this psychological factor during Clemens' Western years. Samuel Clemens' letters during the first year in the West, and, in fact, during the whole five and one-half years of his Western period, are anything but intimate love letters. They are rough, businesslike, only moderately informal letters, addressed rather generally to the folks, or to his mother and sister—occasionally to "My Dear Mother"—full of boisterousness, slapstick, good and bad humor, with the ordinary amount of information a normal boy would write. It requires a lively imagination to find any mother-complex in the Western Mark Twain.

The Esmeralda letters to his mother and sister reveal golden promises, naturally, and Sam hopes that he may some day be able to help them out in a material way. He is unselfish enough to want all his relatives to share in his good fortune, and he does not confine himself to thinking only of the welfare of his mother and his sister.

Trying experiences and hard manual labor were the main ingredients of the Esmeralda days. Young Sam Clemens was learning the fine points of mining by association with experienced men and by working the ground to the point of physical exhaustion. Money was always scarce, that which was supplied by Orion being spent as fast as it arrived, for supplies or for more "feet." For a long period the snow and the ice and the extreme cold made it difficult or impossible to work the claims. But there was always some bright prospect just about ready to pay, and for the young miner "the mountains were banked with nuggets and all the rivers ran gold."[19]

The excitement of the mining camp was so intense that Sam

[18] Brooks, *The Ordeal of Mark Twain,* p. 52.
[19] Paine, *A Short Life of Mark Twain* (Harper & Bros., 1920), p. 78.

Clemens hardly noticed a desperate border warfare that was waging, in his own district, between the territory of Nevada and the state of California. The warfare concerned a boundary dispute; several lives were lost in the battles; but the only mention Sam makes of this warfare is in an Esmeralda letter of April 13, 1862, to Orion:

Wasson got here night before last "from the wars." Tell Lockhart he is not wounded and not killed—is altogether unhurt. He says the whites left their stone fort before he and Lieut. Noble got there. A large amount of provisions and ammunition, which they left behind them, fell into the hands of the Indians. They had a pitched battle with the savages some fifty miles from the fort, in which Scott (sheriff) and another man was killed. This was the day before the soldiers came up with them. . . . . Col. Mayfield was killed, and Sergeant Gillespie, also Noble's colonel was wounded. The California troops went back home, and Noble remained, to help drive the stock over here. And, as Cousin Sally Dillard says, this is all I know about the fight.[20]

That Sam was favorable to the Nevada side of the controversy is indicated in a letter to Orion demanding an explanation for the failure of a deputy sheriff's commission to arrive for the benefit of Samuel Clemens, silver miner:

And ask Gasherie why the devil he don't send along my commission as Deputy Sheriff. The fact of my being in California, and out of his country, wouldn't amount to a d—n with *me*, in the performance of my official duties.[21]

Just how much of Clemens' mining operations were in Nevada Territory and how much in California it is difficult to determine. At the time he was in the Esmeralda district the boundary was not satisfactorily defined; the border disputes were not settled until later.[22]

Food was scarce, and hard to get—at any price. Flour went up to $100 a barrel, and finally could not be obtained. For a month

---

[20] Paine, *Letters*, I, 70–71.　　　[21] *Ibid.*, p. 81.

[22] A two-story brick building now standing in Aurora has an interesting history. The structure was built originally as the county courthouse of Mono County, California. When the California-Nevada boundary disputes were finally settled, it was discovered that the California county courthouse was actually in Nevada. The building was, therefore, turned into a hotel called The Esmeralda.

Frasher Photo

VIRGINIA CITY, NEVADA, BONANZA TOWN OF THE COMSTOCK LODE

the Esmeralda miners lived on barley, beans, and beef. Sam went to work in a quartz mill; but the chemicals nearly poisoned him, and he contracted a severe cold. He remained on this job as a common laborer a week and then went back to prospecting.

Incidents at Esmeralda furnished the material for the "blind lead" story of *Roughing It,* when Clemens and Higbie were "millionaires for ten days." The story, though partly fiction, is somewhat of a composite picture of incidents in which the setting, the local color, and the glittering prospects that the miners always had before them are realistic enough.

One incident that contributed to the "blind lead" story concerned rival miners who, armed with revolvers, took possession of Sam's Monitor claim and refused to give up possession. The law provided that unless claim jumpers used force they could not be legally ejected. Embroiled in the Monitor controversy, Sam understood now the reason for the shooting affray in which Gebhart was killed, and the Clemens Company was determined to resort to arms if necessary.

Another of the "blind lead" incidents concerns a spur of the Wide West claim. Two hundred of the four hundred feet of the spur were owned by Sam and Raish. The shaft of the spur was about one hundred feet from the Wide West shaft. Sam and his partner sublet fifty feet to a workman and furnished powder and sharpening tools. Hopes went skyrocketing for a time; but finally the Wide West claim was forfeited.

The Monitor and Wide West claims thus furnished the material for the "millionaires for ten days" story of *Roughing It.* According to this account, Sam and his companion, after some prospecting around in the hills near the town of Aurora, struck a "blind lead," a lead or ledge of ore that does not crop out above the surface of the ground. In this case it was a subsidiary lead branching out unnoticed from an already established claim. Sam and his companion were about to become wealthy!

But from the heights of potential good fortune the two young miners were soon fallen to despair. Through a misunderstanding, they failed to do the required work of improvement on their claim, and at the end of the ten-day period allowed by law for holding a claim without improvement they found that their potential wealth was lost to them forever. The blind lead had been relocated at the end of the ten days—by someone else. New owners were in command.

> It was enough. I sat down sick, grieved—broken-hearted, indeed. A minute before, I was rich and brimful of vanity; I was a pauper now, and very meek. We sat still an hour, busy with thought, busy with vain and useless self-upbraidings, busy with "Why *didn't* I do this, and why *didn't* I do that," but neither spoke a word. Then we dropped into mutual explanations, and the mystery was cleared away. It came out that Higbie had depended on me, as I had on him, and as both of us had on the foreman. The folly of it! It was the first time that ever staid and steadfast Higbie had left an important matter to chance or failed to be true to his full share of a responsibility.[23]

Thus the blind lead had been relocated by rival miners because Sam had gone out of town to nurse his friend, Captain Nye, who was dangerously ill, and Higbie had gone to Mono Lake in answer to an urgent call to investigate a cement prospect.

Inaccuracy in the *Roughing It* account, in addition to the fact of its being a composite rather than a precise single incident, is shown in the fact that the letters about the two claims referred to above point to Horatio Phillips as Sam's partner at that time rather than Higbie. As it turned out, the claims did not pay as well as had been expected; but since the value of a prospect in those feverish days was not necessarily based upon the intrinsic worth of the silver or gold ore in the location, the two young miners might very well have made considerable money by selling their claims for the "paper" value. At any rate the incidents are typical of the wild mining life that Clemens was leading in the Esmeralda country. The pace was so fast that the most authentic accounts would seem exaggerated to those not familiar with life in the diggings. As De Voto writes:

[23] Mark Twain, *Roughing It*, p. 322.

The yarn is true to the mining career of Sam Clemens in that febrile spring and summer of 1862. "Millionaires!" The image flickers along the mind's horizon as ceaselessly as the undulations of the heat mirage above Washoe.[24]

The disappointments of the Monitor and the Wide West claims pointed to the end of Sam's confidence in the Esmeralda prospects or in any other mining ventures. Even the Horatio and Derby was going stale. Sam was pleased to learn from Orion that feet in this ledge were worth from $30 to $50 in California, because if the ledge proved to be worthless it would be pleasant for him to reflect that others were beaten worse than themselves. He writes:

Raish sold a man 30 feet, yesterday, at $20 a foot, although I was present at the sale, and told the man the ground wasn't worth a d—n. He said he had been hankering after a few feet in the H. and D. for a long time, and he had got them at last, and he couldn't help thinking he had secured a good thing. We went and looked at the ledges, and both of them acknowledged that there was nothing in them but good "indications." Yet the owners in the H. and D. will part with anything else sooner than with feet in these ledges. Well, the work goes slowly—*very* slowly on in the tunnel, and we'll strike it some day. *But*—if we "strike it rich,"—I've lost my guess, that's all.[25]

This is, indeed, a tone entirely different from anything that had appeared in letters to Orion or to the folks back in Missouri. But even more decisive is a later paragraph in the same letter to Orion:

When you receive your next ¼ yr's salary, don't send any of it here until after you have told me you have got it. Remember this. I am afraid of that H. and D.

Sam is finally losing faith in the Esmeralda claims. And for the first time he is not calling for every cent that Orion can spare. The summer of 1862 thus sees the waning confidence in the mining prospects. Except for a cement prospecting trip to Mono Lake with Calvin Higbie, the career of the young miner, Sam Clemens, is over.

Significant incidents occurred, however, during the later

---

[24] Bernard De Voto, *Mark Twain's America* (Little, Brown & Co., 1932), p. 119.

[25] Paine, *Letters*, I, 80.

months of Clemens' sojourn at Esmeralda that have to do with his development as a writer. In a letter to Orion, dated Esmeralda, May 11, 1862, Sam asks his brother if he has seen his "letters in the *Enterprise*." It appears that on days spent in camp, probably when bad weather made it impossible to work the claims, Sam had written burlesque sketches and had sent them to the *Territorial Enterprise* of Virginia City, Nevada Territory. He had signed the sketches "Josh." Evidently a strong impulse to write was stirring in him, since he was at the time still filled with the mining excitement and had probably no idea of deserting mining as a career, at least for a year or two. But he had written some things for his brother's papers back in Missouri and in Iowa, and the urge to write had not left him.

The "Josh" letters to the *Enterprise* are not extant, but it is understood that they were crude burlesques written in a manner designed to meet the requirements of frontier humor. One was a take-off on a speech delivered by an egotistical lecturer who was given the name "Professor Personal Pronoun." The report ended with the statement that the lecture could not be printed in full, as the printer had run out of capital I's. Another was a burlesque Fourth of July oration which began with this sentence: "I was sired by the great American Eagle and foaled by a continental dam." Stock patriotic phrases were employed throughout the sketch. It was rough humor; but it struck the fancy of Joseph T. Goodman, owner and editor of the *Enterprise,* and Samuel Clemens' mining days were about to come to an end.

Orion had taken some pride in the fact that the "Josh" letters of his brother were being printed in the *Enterprise,* and he did not hesitate to make the identity of the writer known to the newspaper's staff members. We have no way of knowing what were Sam's motives when he first began writing the "Josh" letters, but his personal correspondence reveals that later he was thinking of newspaper work in terms of its economic advantages. The financial situation in the diggings was a serious one, and Sam had about reached the end of his patience in trying to cope with it. He writes to Orion that his debts are greater than he had thought and he does not see "how in the h—l" he is going to live on a little over $100 until October or November. He feels that he must have lucrative work of some kind very soon:

Now write to the Sacramento Union folks, or to Marsh, and tell them I'll write as many letters a week as they want, for $10 a week—my board must be paid. Tell them I have corresponded with the N. Orleans Crescent, and other papers—and the Enterprise. California is full of people who have interests here, and it's d—d seldom they hear from this country. I can't write a specimen letter—now, at any rate—I'd rather undertake to write a Greek poem. Tell 'em the mail and express leave three times a week, and it costs from 25 to 50 cents to send letters by the blasted express. If they want letters from here, who'll run from morning till night collecting materials cheaper. I'll write a short letter twice a week, for the present, for the "Age," for $5 a week. Now it has been a long time since I couldn't make my own living, and it shall be a long time before I loaf another year.[26]

True to newspaper tradition (still in vogue), Clemens did not hesitate to use his imagination a bit in stating his qualifications as a newspaper correspondent. Actually his previous experience was meager, his few newspaper contributions in the Middle West having been scarcely more than the most amateurish juvenilia, and the "other papers" being extremely limited in number except as he had worked on them as a printer, not as a writer. But he was more than willing to stretch a point now with respect to qualifications, for he was desperately in need of employment, and he felt that newspaper work was what he would like, and offered the best opportunity for him.

The "Josh" sketches fitted nicely into the *Enterprise* picture. They had the tone of humor that was popular in the silver-boom town of Virginia City. The business manager of the *Enterprise*, Barstow, persuaded Goodman to urge "Josh" to join the staff. In a letter to Orion, dated July 30, Sam informs his brother that Barstow has offered him the post of local reporter on the *Enterprise* at a salary of $25 a week. Sam had informed Barstow that he would let him know his decision by the next mail, if possible.

[26] Paine, *Letters*, I, 82.

Samuel Clemens' hesitancy to abandon his mining ventures and become a frontier newspaper reporter has been the subject matter of considerable psychological theorizing. Paine sensed a reluctance on the young man's part to become a low-down "camp scribbler": "He did not care to sign his own name. He was a miner who was soon to be a magnate; he had no desire to be known as a camp scribbler."[27] Brooks sees the artist in Samuel Clemens making a final futile struggle against the degradation of becoming a newspaper reporter and writing humor:

Somehow, in this new call, the creative instinct in Mark Twain failed to recognize its own but actually foresaw some element of danger. What, indeed, did *The Enterprise* mean for him? He had been sending in his compositions; he had been trying his hand, experimenting, we know, in different styles, and only his humor "took."[28]

There is no evidence whatever to show that Clemens had any reluctance, on artistic grounds, to becoming a reporter on the *Territorial Enterprise*. Like any other young man in the boom days of El Dorado he naturally felt that right at the moment silver and gold constituted the main chance. Why should he not be hesitant to abandon the bright prospects of fabulous wealth, possibly in the next ledge, the suddenly discovered outcropping, the rich blind lead? Here is no reason for suspecting a young man of having abnormal mental reservations, soul conflicts, or tremendous reactions of artistic sensitiveness. At any rate, Samuel Clemens did, in August 1862, become a reporter on a frontier newspaper. That a man could stoop so low is virtually beyond the comprehension of Brooks and Paine.

Before he left Esmeralda Sam spent some time in trying to decide just what to do. His hopes in the mining ventures had been destroyed. Naturally his disappointment was great; but his energies and his ambitions had been higher than those of the average miner. He hesitated to give up mining as a lost cause, particularly since he had spent such a comparatively long time and so much

[27] Paine, *Biography,* I, 194.
[28] Brooks, *op. cit.,* p. 110.

(of his brother's) money chasing the will-o'-the-wisp of silver and gold.

His letter of August 7, to Orion, virtually announces the end of the young miner's faith in his hectic silver career:

> Now, I shall leave at mid-night tonight, alone and on foot for a walk of 60 or 70 miles through a totally uninhabited country, and it is barely possible that mail facilities may prove infernally "slow" during the few weeks I expect to spend out there. But do you write Barstow that I have left here for a week or so, and in case he should want me he must write me here, or let me know through you.

For a week, it appears, Sam Clemens went somewhere away from the Esmeralda mining claims, to reflect, to contemplate his destiny. Paine says that he "had gone into the wilderness to fight out his battle alone."[29] Here again is the suggestion of reluctance on Sam's part to go into that low profession of frontier newspaper reporting. Actually there is nothing to show just what Sam Clemens did during the week—where he went, or what was his motive in going. De Voto, misinterpreting the letter to Orion, assumes that the walk of sixty or seventy miles is a part of the trip to the *Enterprise* offices:

> Sam walked sixty miles of the way from Esmeralda to Virginia City. No reason for the hike is mentioned in his letters, which merely announce it and direct Orion to tell the *Enterprise* that he is coming, and it may be that Sam was only saving stage fare.[30]

The letter to Orion does not direct the brother to tell the *Enterprise* that Sam is coming. In fact, after the mysterious week of contemplation, wherever and however it was spent, we find Sam back in Esmeralda, writing a letter to his sister, dated August 15.

In the last Esmeralda letter to Orion, before the "Week," Sam writes a final paragraph of disillusionment dedicated to the barren Esmeralda hills, where sweating miners, bearded and determined, wielded their picks and shovels in the hectic search for mineral fortune:

---

[29] Paine, *Biography*, I, 204.
[30] De Voto, *Mark Twain's America* (Little, Brown & Co., 1932), p. 120.

Bully for B.! Write him that I would write him myself, but I am to take a
walk tonight and haven't time. Tell him to bring his family out with him.
He can rely upon what I say—and *I* say the land has lost its ancient desolate appearance; the rose and the oleander have taken the place of the departed sage-brush; a rich black loam, garnished with moss, and flowers,
and the greenest of grass, smiles to Heaven from the vanished sand-plains;
the "endless snows" have all disappeared, and in their stead, or to repay us
for their loss, the mountains rear their billowy heads aloft, crowned with
a fadeless and eternal verdure; birds, and fountains, and trees—tropical
trees—everywhere!—and the poet dreamt of Nevada when he wrote:

> "and Sharon waves, in solemn praise,
> Her silent groves of palm."

and today the royal Raven listens in a dreamy stupor to the songs of the
thrush and the nightingale and the canary—and shudders when the gaudy-
plumaged birds of the distant South sweep by him to the orange groves of
Carson. Tell him he wouldn't recognize the d—d country. He should
bring his family by all means.[31]

Only those who have seen the desolate and barren hills of Esmeralda can appreciate the irony of that passage.

The final letter from Esmeralda is dated August 15, and is to
his sister Pamela—Mrs. Moffett of St. Louis. The disillusioned
miner has returned to the diggings. He wants it understood that
no matter how things stand in Nevada certainly he is not interested
in returning to a pilot's job on the Mississippi. He writes:

> What in thunder are pilot's wages to me? . . . . I never have *once*
> thought of returning home to go on the river again, and I never expect to
> do any more piloting at any price. My livelihood must be made in this
> country. . . . . Do not tell any one that I had any idea of piloting again at
> present—for it is all a mistake.[32]

The many elaborate passages of theorizing about Mississippi
River piloting being Sam Clemens' first, great, and only love, and
of his reluctance and pain at having to abandon it, are not justified
by the sentiments expressed during his Esmeralda days. In Esmeralda he is not longing for the Mississippi. There are too many
new excitements on the frontier, even if so many lead to disappointment and disillusionment. He writes to his sister that he

[31] Paine, *Letters*, I, 84.   [32] *Ibid.*, p. 85.

has been thinking of going home but has given up that notion and is planning to spend the winter in San Francisco. He is cabining with Dan Twing and Dan's dog before leaving for an uncertain destination. He still has the fortitude, however, to joke about the "domestic" roof of their ten-by-twelve mansion, the dog's catching flies, the taking turns at cooking, Dan's attendance at a funeral in an amazing costume, and the wise and severe things that the two miners had said about the vanity and wickedness of high living.[33]

It is the last letter from Esmeralda. It is the end of Samuel Clemens' mining career. Another phase of Mark Twain's Western development is completed. Next he will be seen on the Comstock Lode, come to take his place in the ranks of those lusty and vigorous newspaper writers who gave life and sparkle to what might have been a drab frontier canvas. He will appear then as a candidate for the job of reporter-at-large for the *Territorial Enterprise* of Virginia City, Nevada Territory.

[33] Paine, *Letters,* I, 86.

CHAPTER 4

THE COMSTOCK LODE

On a hot, dusty August afternoon in 1862, a weather-worn stranger appeared at the office of the *Territorial Enterprise* on C Street in Virginia City, Nevada Territory. His slouch hat, his blue woolen shirt, his pantaloons, which were stuffed into his boot tops, and his long beard were covered with alkali dust. Slung to his belt was a revolver. On his back he carried a heavy roll of blankets.

One of the proprietors of the *Enterprise,* Denis E. McCarthy, was in the office. He inquired of the visitor what his mission might be. Having thrown the pack from his shoulders and dropped wearily into a chair, the wanderer replied:

"My starboard leg seems to be unshipped. I'd like about one hundred yards of line; I think I am falling to pieces." Then he added: "I want to see Mr. Barstow, or Mr. Goodman. My name is Clemens, and I've come to write for the paper."

It was the master of the world's widest estate come to claim his kingdom.[1]

Tradition says that Samuel Clemens walked the one hundred and thirty miles from Aurora, in the Esmeralda country, to Virginia City; it is improbable that he did so. There was plenty of transportation between the two mining towns in those days—more than there is now. And the route from Aurora to Virginia lay through Carson City.

Here, at any rate, now began one of the most important periods in his life, one of the most significant in his literary development; and in this wild town where bearded miners were setting

[1] Albert Bigelow Paine, *Mark Twain: A Biography* (Harper & Bros., 1912), I, 205.

the stage for the big bonanza he came to choose a definite life career and to build its crude but substantial foundation.

So significant in Mark Twain's Western development is the Comstock Lode that some knowledge of the history of the Lode is necessary to an appreciation of the influence it could exert on one who took part in its colorful life. Although the California gold rush of 1849 in some ways eclipses it in dramatic interest, the enterprise known as the Comstock Lode is one of the most sensational highlights of the frontier West. And certainly in its economic aspects it was of tremendous significance.[2]

When Clemens came to the Comstock Lode his first impression must have been one of amazement at the degree of unconventionality and recklessness which prevailed. There were the miner, the gambler, and the Virginia City rough. There was the wild boisterousness of a community where the two leading enterprises were hard-rock mining and saloon-keeping. It was a life new and fascinating, a loud and convivial bachelor mining camp with a predilection for "rough stuff" and coarse humor. There was a strange commingling of races, some living in indolence, some striving recklessly for acquisition, others preferring the prodigal life. There were Indians, Chinese, Mexicans, Germans, Englishmen from Cornwall, Irishmen from Cork, and miscellaneous Americans.

[2] There are several accounts of the history of the famous Nevada silver lode, but authorities worth studying narrow down to a very few. Probably the best account of the early days on the Comstock Lode is by William Wright, the "Dan De Quille" of the Virginia City *Territorial Enterprise*. De Quille, despite the fact that he wrote many tall stories as jokes in the *Enterprise*, for the edification of the rough population of Virginia City, nevertheless was unusually accurate in his stories about the mines. He was considered by H. H. Bancroft to be the real authority in this field. Bancroft felt that De Quille's book, *The Big Bonanza*, was the authoritative book on the history of the Comstock Lode. He says (*History of Nevada, Colorado, and Wyoming*, p. 95) of Wright and his book: "William Wright, whose *nom de plume* as a popular writer on Nevada journals was Dan De Quille, was reporter on the Virginia City *Territorial Enterprise* for 16 years, and had the best facilities for acquiring historical facts. His book is made popular by the introduction of facetious anecdotes, and a style of raillery much in vogue in writing of mining affairs, with no better reason than that in early times one or two humorous journalists set the fashion, which few have been able to follow with similar success. Wright's book is, however, a storehouse of information, generally correct, on current events connected with the mining history of Nevada, which gives it a permanent value among my authorities."

The "honest miner," the leading character in the life on the Comstock Lode, was boisterously active in his work and in his play. He moved in a setting of strange contrasts, replete with grotesque exaggerations. Great expectations were frequently followed by equally great disappointments. Small wonder that the careers of all of the original developers of the Comstock Lode ended quickly and violently.

The average intelligence and education of those who emigrated to the mining camps from the East was surprisingly high, one remarks on first thought. But the element of surprise disappears when one considers the great hardships and the cost involved in the migration to the remote Western land of El Dorado.

When Clemens came to Virginia City, the Comstock Lode was only in its early years of operation. The first newspaper notice of the discovery of silver ore on the Comstock was given in the columns of the *Nevada Journal* of Nevada City on July 1, 1859.[3] Back of this is the story of the discovery of the Lode by the Grosch brothers—E. Allen and Hosea B., from Reading, Pennsylvania. The brothers, having previously prospected in the Gold Canyon placers below what was later to be Virginia City, returned to the diggings from California in 1853. "In Gold canyon," says Bancroft, "they found what they called 'carbonate of silver,' which they described as a 'dark gray mass, tarnished probably by sulphuric acid in the water. . . . . Other ore of silver we have found in the canyon.' "[4]

The Grosch brothers were back in the Washoe country in 1857, living in a stone cabin in American Flat ravine. They had been prospecting in various districts of the Nevada valleys and mountains and had come back to renew their investigation of the Washoe diggings. They had identified the first silver in the region, but their disclosures had not caused any excitement. "Silver was a new idea to the miners of the time and place, but one

[3] Theodore H. Hittell, *History of California* (N. J. Stone & Co., San Francisco, 1898), III, 158.

[4] H. H. Bancroft, *History of Nevada, Colorado, and Wyoming* (The History Company, 1890), p. 96.

which the Grosh[5] brothers were capable of entertaining," says C. B. Glasscock in writing of the discovery. "The gold-miners had made the same discovery but believed the metal to be lead, and threw it away with curses and contempt. Not so the Groshes. They continued to prospect for silver ore, and traced veins which their diagrams, drawn at the time, indicate were the south end of the great Comstock deposits."[6]

While the Grosch brothers were laboring away with their gold rockers trying to earn enough money to develop their silver claims, Hosea injured his foot with a pick. Blood poisoning set in, and within a month he was dead. Allen decided to go to California to raise capital. He and a companion were caught in a snowstorm in the Sierra, and wandered about in the mountains, suffering terrible hardships. They were compelled to kill and eat their pack mule. Finally, with their feet frozen, the two stumbled upon the snowbound cabin of a Mexican miner on the west slopes of the Sierra. Refusing to submit to amputation, Allen died in a delirium twelve days after reaching the cabin. His companion, broken in health, returned to Canada, whence he had come to the mining country.

When Allen Grosch left for California on his fatal journey into the snows of the Sierra, he left his cabin in charge of Henry T. P. Comstock, a miner, who, since 1856, had been prospecting in what was then western Utah Territory and who had been actively engaged in the Gold Canyon diggings for some time. Upon the death of Allen Grosch, Comstock came into possession of the Grosch brothers' books and papers. Historians differ as to the ethics of Comstock's handling of the Grosch brothers' claims. Bancroft has this to say:

How much or how little Comstock knew of the plans of the Grosch brothers previous to coming into the possession of their books and papers through the death of Allen Grosch is uncertain; but probably he had never been admitted to their confidence further than to engage his services, and to explain to him what the consideration would be, with assurances of the

[5] Glasscock and Hittell spell it "Grosh"; Wright and Bancroft, "Grosch."
[6] C. B. Glasscock, *The Big Bonanza* (Bobbs-Merrill Co., 1931), pp. 33–34.

prospective value of their mining claims. The total disappearance of their books and papers, with all the evidence of their company and individual rights, is strong presumptive evidence against Comstock as the person in charge. Whatever knowledge he had he kept to himself, and with equal care removed the traces of their claims, which might lead to identification by either of the companies,[7] or by the heirs of the Grosch brothers.[8]

Hittell disagrees with those who would assign to Comstock unethical practices in his handling of the Grosch brothers' claims. He insists that "whatever connection . . . . Comstock may have had with the Grosh brothers, there does not appear to be a particle of truth in the attempted slur cast upon him by the friends of Grosh."[9]

Comstock kept his information to himself. He became so busy with his prospecting that the miners, observing that he would not take time to bake bread, gave him the sobriquet of Old Pancake. Wright relates that "even as, with spoon in hand, he stirred up his pancake batter, it is said that he kept one eye on the top of some distant peak, and was lost in speculations in regard to the wealth in gold and silver that might rest somewhere beneath its rocky crest."[10]

Another miner in the Washoe country at the time was James Fennimore, whom Bancroft describes as an

intemperate Virginian, without either brains or education, who for some breach of lawful etiquette committed elsewhere, had found it convenient to remove to Carson valley in 1851, where he had remained ever since, digging his season's wages out of the earth to pour it down his throat in bad whiskey during his leisure months.[11]

When Fennimore first came to Washoe he called himself Finney, but he later acknowledged his true name. The miners, however, choosing what they thought was a name which suited his characteristics, called him "Old Virginia," and the appellation clung to him for the remaining years of his life.

---

[7] Friends of the Grosches had formed two companies—one in the East and one partly in El Dorado County, California, and partly in Carson Valley.

[8] Bancroft, *op. cit.,* pp. 98–99. [9] Hittell, *op. cit.,* III, 157.

[10] William Wright, *History of the Big Bonanza* (American Publishing Co., Hartford, Conn.; A. L. Bancroft & Co., San Francisco, 1876), p. 41. [11] Bancroft, *op. cit.,* p. 99.

In January 1859, Comstock, Fennimore, John Bishop, and other miners staked out claims at the head of Gold Canyon and called the place Gold Hill. Fennimore discovered and claimed also a spring of water that could be brought to the claims.

In the meantime, two miners—Peter O'Riley and Patrick McLaughlin—were prospecting at the head of Six-Mile Canyon. One day they dug into earth that looked strange to them. On that very day Comstock, who had been out searching for a horse and was riding it back to Gold Hill, came upon the two miners. "You've struck it, boys!" he shouted, and, according to Glasscock's account, "promptly declared himself in. 'The only trouble is that you've struck it on my land. You know I bought this spring from Old Man Caldwell. And I took up one hundred and sixty acres here for a ranch.' "[12]

"This exclamation," says Bancroft, "has been taken as proof that Comstock knew of this deposit, or at least that he recognized its value from knowledge obtained from the contents of the Grosch cabin, such knowledge not being possessed by the other miners."[13]

Despite the protestations of O'Riley and McLaughlin, Comstock won his point—though it was established on a feeble foundation—and was soon decidedly "in" on the claim. Thus Peter O'Riley and Patrick McLaughlin, cleaning their first rocker of rich ore which came from the top of the mine that was later to become the world-famous Ophir, were in fact the discoverers, in a practical sense, of the Comstock Lode, although its fame went to Henry T. P. Comstock.

Mining activity began in earnest on the Comstock Lode after the news of rich silver discoveries made its way to the outside. Comstock was a good bluffer. Without doing much work as a miner he took on an air of dignified proprietorship, and with much talking assumed a certain degree of importance on the Lode. Wright describes Old Pancake's procedure, which today would be called "muscling in" or "chiseling":

[12] Glasscock, op. cit., pp. 39–40.   [13] Bancroft, op. cit., p. 101.

Once Comstock got into the Ophir claim he elected himself superintendent and was the man who did all the heavy talking. He made himself so conspicuous on every occasion that he soon came to be considered not only the discoverer but almost the father of the lode. As it was all Comstock for a considerable distance round the Ophir mine, people began to speak of the vein as Comstock's mine, Comstock's lode, and the lead throughout its length and breadth came to be known as the Comstock lode, a name which it bears to this day; while the names of O'Riley and McLaughlin, the real discoverers, are seldom heard, even in the city that stands on the spot where they first opened to the light of the sun the glittering treasures of the vein.[14]

A town soon was erected on the site where Comstock had claimed 160 acres of land. At first it was called the village of Ophir, then Pleasant Hill, then Mount Pleasant Point—referring to the mountain on whose slopes it was situated, now Mount Davidson—then Winnemucca. Finally, however, "Old Virginia" went on a happy spree—or, rather, another happy spree—and this time, falling near his cabin and breaking a whiskey bottle, he waved the bottle in the air and shouted, "I baptize this ground Virginia Town!" The "town" part of the name was not used, however, the camp simply going by the name Virginia, until later, when it came to be called Virginia City.[15]

Soon after the establishment of Virginia City there was great excitement in the camp. With a hundred miners at work, quartz was being broken in fifteen arrastras. At Gold Hill, about a mile away, there was also great industry, although the eight or ten arrastras in use there were grinding quartz for the gold it contained, not for the silver. It seems that the Californians were moving in on the diggings and, realizing the value of the silver deposits at Gold Hill, were keeping information under cover as much as possible until they could buy in at low prices.

With the coming in of the Californian moneyed interests, the oldtimers on the Comstock began losing out. The story of the original discoverers and developers of the Comstock Lode is

[14] Wright, *op. cit.*, p. 55.

[15] The new camp was hardly "on the public highway to California," as Paxson suggests in his *History of the American Frontier*, p. 450. Carson Valley was on the Overland route, but it is a long, hard pull from there up to Virginia City, several thousand feet up the mountain.

Frasher Photo   WELLS FARGO BUILDING, VIRGINIA CITY

consequently short and severe. McLaughlin was soon rid of the little he received for his share of the claim and in 1875 was working as a cook at the Green Mine in San Bernardino, California, at $40 a week; he died a pauper. O'Riley erected a hotel in Virginia City, lost his money in stock-gambling, became insane, and died in a sanitarium at Woodbridge, California, about 1874.

Old Virginia's violent death is described by Bancroft:

Fennimore, who is much paraded by all the historians of Nevada, without any discoverable reason, unless a fondness for whiskey may be accounted a distinguished as well as a distinguishing trait, was killed at Dayton in July, 1861, being thrown from his horse while intoxicated, and suffering a fracture of the skull.[16]

Comstock went into the merchandising business in Carson City, but the venture soon failed and he left Nevada in 1862. After some years of mining and road-building in Oregon and Idaho he went to Montana. He was a member of the Big Horn expedition in 1870; and on his return in the same year he committed suicide near Bozeman, Montana, by shooting himself in the head. Bancroft declares that Comstock's mind was "ill balanced, or if not so naturally, he had suffered so many shocks of fortune that the last years of his life were but the record of a feeble struggle against advancing dementia."[17]

With others on the Comstock Lode, fortune dealt more favorably, though fortunes made were frequently lost as quickly. The year 1863 was considered the flush year of the early years of the Lode, but it was not until the big bonanza[18] of the Consolidated Virginia and the California mines had been discovered that production began to approach the peak. The discovery of the great bonanza in 1873 sent production up to $35,254,507 worth of bullion for the year.

When Samuel Clemens came to Virginia City, the camp was, of course, being run on a smaller scale than it would be in the

---

[16] Bancroft, op. cit., p. 108. [17] Ibid., p. 98.

[18] Virginia City Territorial Enterprise, June 14, 1866. The Mexican miners had brought in the Spanish word bonanza, signifying fair weather at sea, prosperity, good fortune in mining.

days of the big bonanza, but it was a feverish camp, nevertheless, and it was to enjoy its first big flush year in 1863, when Mark Twain was still one of its distinguished personalities. He found here on the Comstock a rough, crude, coarse, robust town. Are we to infer from this that he was shocked, that he was repelled, that his artistic sensibilities suffered prostration? On the contrary, Virginia City completely satisfied Clemens at first glance, and the thrill of his experiences there never wore off.

Probably the element that has contributed most to the myth that Clemens' artistic sensibilities met virtual disaster in Washoe is the idyllic picture that has been painted of his life as a pilot on the Mississippi during the years immediately preceding his departure for the West. Romancers have made much of this picture. One is even asked to believe that the artist in Mark Twain would have reached consummation on the River. Miss Brashear believes that "the emphasis placed by some of his biographers and critics upon his four pilot years has been out of proportion, that while, during those years, he first attained to a fuller and more nearly satisfactory life for himself than he had found up to that time, they were, after all, *Wanderjähre*—a period of taking stock of the world and of himself."[19] Of course, in a very real sense, all the years of Mark Twain's life were *Wanderjähre*.

The pilot years, though unquestionably significant in Mark Twain's development, must be examined on the basis of information in addition to that contributed by those who have romanced on Twain's own romancing about the River. Some biographers and critics have obviously taken their cue from Twain himself, and have thus been led astray, particularly by *Life on the Mississippi,* which De Voto feels ignores the conception of the steamboat age:

There is, for instance, no hint of the squalid venery of the steamboats, which were consistently a habitation for the loves of travelers, river rats, and frontiersmen. Harlots of all degree, New Orleans courtesans in the grand manner as well as broken-down yaller gals no longer useful to river-

[19] Brashear, *op. cit.,* p. 194.

side dives, were habituees of the boats. They and their pimps and all the machinery of bought protection, of display and sale, of robbery and murder were a constant in the trade. The book makes no mention of them. It probably would have made none in any case, since the amenities of literature in its time forbade, but its whole drift forbids also. There is no mention, either, of the parasitism that was also constant in the trade. The skin games, the frauds, the robberies, the gambling, the cozenage, the systematic organization of the sucker trade are wholly absent from its pages. To read the autobiography of George Devol is to perceive at once that the river as it was is not the river of Mark Twain.[20]

Could Samuel Clemens have been a pilot on the Mississippi without coming into contact with the crude, the coarse, the sordid side of river days in the steamboat age? Hardly. Hence we can assume that his artistic sensibilities had built up a fairly effective resistance before he came West. What he had not encountered during his journeyman printer days he certainly learned about during his four years on the River. Indeed, one can be safe in saying that when Clemens came to Washoe he knew the realities of life.

Nevertheless the Comstock was different, colorful, fascinating. To Samuel Clemens there was adventure in its very roughness. He enjoyed the robust life. He was never one to go in for delicate refinements; for example, up to a few months before his death he could not, though he liked music, bear to have a professional pianist play the piano for him especially. He would have preferred to have his leg amputated.[21] Samuel Clemens, in Virginia City and throughout his whole life, could withstand a remarkable amount of roughness without wincing; there are those who say that he even enjoyed it.

Moreover it would be inaccurate to say that life on the Com-

[20] Bernard De Voto, *Mark Twain's America* (Little, Brown & Co., 1932), p. 110.

[21] In a letter to Paine, from Bermuda, he writes: "It is 2:30 in the morning & I am writing because I can't sleep. I can't sleep because a professional pianist is coming tomorrow afternoon *to play for me*. My God! I wouldn't allow Paderewski or Gabrilowitsch to do that. I would rather have a leg amputated. I knew he was coming, but I never dreamed it was to play for *me*. When I heard the horrible news 4 hours ago, be d——d if I didn't come near screaming. I meant to slip out and be absent, but now I can't. Don't pray for me. The thing is just as d——d bad as it can be already" (Paine, *Biography*, IV, 1561).

stock Lode was one great rough drama. On the contrary, to balance the tough, boisterous aspect of the community there was its artistic and cultural life, the theater representing one phase of it, though not always perhaps in as refined a manner as the more delicate sensibilities might demand.

On the rough side of Virginia City life there were the saloons with their crystal ornaments, their bawdy sculptures in ivory and marble, and their mahogany and ebony bars; and there were the dance halls, the parlors, the melodeons, and the cribs. It was a "noisy, violent, incredible city. Elsewhere in the West the miner labored in inaccessible gulches and, for a bust, made infrequent pilgrimages to the big town—Denver, San Francisco, Helena. But here hard rock and the big town met in one continuous bust. The West consummated itself."[22]

In the barrooms flourished separate arts for the amusement of the hard-rock miner. There was the genius of the mahogany who compounded a multiplicity of refreshing drinks for the edification of the thirsty; there was the artist who worked his craftsmanship in mosaics, frescoes, or oils; and there was the fine wizardry of the gambling table. The "ladies of the evening" came to Virginia City on the first wave of prosperity. De Voto writes:

They constituted, no doubt, a deplorable source of gambling, pleasure and embroilment. They were not soft-spoken women, their desire was not visibly separable from the main chance, and they would have beheld Mr. Harte's portrayal of them at Poker Flat with ribald mirth. But let them have a moment of respect. They civilized the Comstock. They drove through its streets reclining in lacquered broughams, displaying to male eyes fashions as close to Paris as any then current in New York. They were, in brick houses hung with tapestries, a glamour and a romance, after the superheated caverns of the mines. They enforced a code of behavior: one might be a hard-rock man outside their curtains but in their presence one was punctilious or one was hustled away.[23]

On the better side, relatively, there were the several playhouses which flourished on the Lode. Drama, melodrama, burlesque, grand opera, and an astounding variety of other attractions were

[22] De Voto, op. cit., p. 123.   [23] Ibid., p. 124.

offered in these playhouses, not counting the less refined entertainments presented in the saloons and the cribs. Piper's Opera House was the most noteworthy theater in Virginia City. During its years of spirited enterprise it offered a notable list of attractions, never lacking in variety from one week to the next: Jenny Lind, the Swedish nightingale; the humorous lecturer, Artemus Ward; Adah Isaacs Menken, "The Menken," who, coming from the Gaietie in Paris, had scored a success in San Francisco before she came to Virginia City to present her classic Lady Godiva exhibition entitled "The Mazeppa," and who, we shall see, was to add Mark Twain to her numerous train of distinguished admirers. Other Piper's Opera House attractions ranged from Shakespearean repertoire to wildcat and bulldog fights and a battle between a bull and a bear. Imagine how the bearded miners must have sat enraptured at "The Montgomery Queen's Great Show, with an African Eland, an Abysinnian Ibex, Cassowaries, and the Only Female Somersault Rider in the World!"

To this drama of the frontier being enacted on the eastern slope of Mount Davidson, Samuel Clemens was added as a member of the dramatis personae. For two years as a newspaper reporter for the *Territorial Enterprise* he was to take an active part in the energetic spectacle of the Comstock Lode. After three apprenticeships in fields that he had abandoned, he was to choose here his life profession of authorship. Here on the Comstock Lode, robustly conscious of the great drama of the frontier, Mark Twain was born.

CHAPTER 5

REPORTER ON THE
TERRITORIAL ENTERPRISE

[August 1862 - October 1863]

WHEN Samuel Clemens joined the staff of the *Territorial Enterprise* of Virginia City he came into association with journalists who were to have much to do with his development as a writer on the Comstock Lode. During his two years as reporter for the *Enterprise* he was constantly associated, both professionally and personally, with Joseph T. Goodman, editor and proprietor of the *Enterprise;* Dan De Quille [William Wright], reporter; Steve Gillis, printer; Rollin M. Daggett, associate editor; and Denis E. McCarthy, part owner of the paper.

The *Territorial Enterprise* was a morning daily when Clemens joined its staff in 1862. The paper had been established as a weekly, by William L. Jernegan and Alfred James, the first number having been issued at Genoa, the first town in Nevada, on Saturday, December 18, 1858. It was the first printed newspaper in Nevada. An editorial in the paper, some years later, referred to the *Enterprise* as "the oldest journal in the State, having been established in Carson Valley while Nevada was an almost unpeopled portion of Utah Territory."[1] The paper was established a year before the discovery of silver in Nevada, when Genoa was a stage route town of about two hundred inhabitants.

[1] *Territorial Enterprise*, April 4, 1866.

In November 1859 the office of publication was moved to Carson City, the first issue printed there being that of November 12, 1859.[2] Jonathan Williams purchased the interest of Alfred James after the paper was moved to Carson City, and the firm name became W. L. Jernegan & Co. By October 1860 Williams had obtained sole ownership of the *Enterprise,* and in October or November, 1860, the paper was moved to Virginia City. At this time I. B. Wollard became co-publisher with Williams. Joseph T. Goodman and Denis E. McCarthy became partners of Williams on March 2, 1861;[3] D. Driscoll succeeded Williams in a short time. Goodman and McCarthy became sole proprietors on October 28, 1863. McCarthy sold his interest to Goodman on September 15, 1865, and Goodman continued as sole proprietor of the *Territorial Enterprise* until February 1874.

Dan De Quille describes the early days of the paper:

> The office in which the *Enterprise* was first published in Virginia City, was a small, one-story frame building with a shed or lean-to on one side, and was a queerly arranged establishment. The proprietors had the shed part fitted up as a kitchen and dining and lodging-place. Bunks were ranged along the sides of the room, one above another, as on shipboard, and here editors, printers, proprietors, and all hands "bunked" after the style of the miners in their cabins. A Chinaman, "Old Joe," did the cooking, and three times each day the whole crowd of "newspaper men" were called out to the long table in the shed to get their "square meal." The "devil" went for numerous lunches between meals, and often came flying out into the composition-room with a large piece of pie in his mouth, and the old Chinaman at his heels.[4]

The *Enterprise,* published under these conditions, became a journal of comradery—a lively, fresh, rugged, vigorous, fearless, picturesque, distinctive, masculine expression of the energetic life on the Comstock Lode. The chief factor in making it this kind of a newspaper was its ownership and editorship. With Joe Good-

[2] Douglas Crawford McMurtrie, *A Bibliography of Nevada Newspapers, 1858 to 1875 Inclusive* (Mainz, Gutenberg Jahrbuch, 1935), p. 7.

[3] Myron Angel, editor, *History of Nevada* (West Publishing Co., Oakland, 1881), p. 317.

[4] William Wright, *History of the Big Bonanza* (American Publishing Company, Hartford, Conn.; A. L. Bancroft & Co., San Francisco, 1876), p. 218.

man at the helm, as editor-in-chief, the newspaper's staff members were given a free hand, so long as they could make the paper's content interesting, and provided that matters that were to be presented as serious news were actually based on fact. Goodman had been a miner, explorer, printer, and contributor to journals before he took over the *Enterprise*. He was a skillful craftsman in the field of writing, being equally effective at composing fine poetry and at writing editorials with a punch. His reputation was not confined to the Comstock Lode. A correspondent who wrote for the *San Francisco Call* had this to say:

> Goodman, of the *Enterprise*, is a clever young man in more than one sense of the word. As a newspaper writer, he has few equals, and no one who knows him can for a moment doubt his sincere loyalty. His printing establishment is among the finest on the Pacific coast, and he is a universal favorite.[5]

Samuel Clemens owed much to Joe Goodman, whose kindly guidance, skillful tutorship, and understanding friendship followed Mark Twain beyond the Comstock into later years.

Goodman believed in forceful, interesting journalism. He was a younger man than Clemens, but he had rare gifts which the new reporter soon came to appreciate. When Sam began his work on the *Enterprise*, Goodman gave him this advice:

> Never say we learn so and so, or it is rumored, or we understand so and so; but go to headquarters and get the absolute facts; then speak out and say it *is* so and so. In the one case you are likely to be shot, and in the other you are pretty certain to be; but you will preserve the public confidence.[6]

Dan De Quille was Sam Clemens' fellow reporter on the *Enterprise*. They worked together and played together. De Quille, whose real name was William Wright, had greater writing ability than Sam Clemens in that day and showed much more promise of success as a writer. Even Joe Goodman, whose judgment was unusually keen, felt that De Quille would be the more successful of the two. De Quille's specialty as a serious writer was information on mines and mining activities. In his lighter moments—and there were many of these—he set the pace for other

[5] *San Francisco Call*, December 18, 1863.   [6] Paine, *Biography*, I, 206.

Frasher Photo

GOLD HILL, NEVADA

journalists of the region in the writing of hoaxes, ironical sketches, and droll humor, gaining wide notoriety on the Pacific Coast. For more than thirty years, Dan De Quille was a writer for the *Enterprise* and a contributor to many other newspapers and magazines of the West. Describing De Quille, with whom he was associated for several years on the staff of the *Enterprise,* C. C. Goodwin writes:

> He had a quaint irony through which he could make fun of his fellow-man's idiosyncracies, which everyone would recognize at a glance, but he never offended anyone.
>
> Daggett, with his intellectual cleaver, would chop a man to pieces. Mark Twain, with his droll humor, would lead his victim up to the shambles he had in waiting for him, and the unconscious creature would never suspect what was going to happen until the ax fell.
>
> But Dan had a softer way. The intended victim would know all the time after the first ten lines that he was going to be sacrificed, but he was under a spell, enjoyed the process, and laughed after he was downed. . . . . His solar armor story was one of his best ones.[7]

De Quille's solar-armor story concerned an invention which was supposed to be effective in protecting a person from the heat of summer. It consisted of an India rubber suit, a small air compressor, and a battery. With his rubber suit on, the wearer could turn on the compressor, which was concealed within. One button started the compressor, another turned it off. De Quille's story told of how the inventor put on the armor and started out across Death Valley with the temperature 117° in the shade. He disappeared in the sun, and did not return that night. A searching party went out the next morning and found the man's body a few miles out on the floor of the valley. The daring inventor had given his life for science. He had started the compressor but had been unable to turn it off, and had frozen to death. The machine was still running when the body was found. Pendant from the nose of the unfortunate scientist was an icicle eighteen inches long. This story is typical of the kind of hoax story Dan De Quille and Mark Twain wrote for the *Enterprise*. The follow-up of such

[7] C. C. Goodwin, *As I Remember Them* (Salt Lake Commercial Club, Salt Lake City, 1913), pp. 213–16.

an item was frequently amazing. Some time after the publication of the solar-armor story, De Quille received a marked copy of the London *Times,* in which a British writer who had read the story suggested that British soldiers in India be equipped with the armor.

Another *Enterprise* staff member was Rollin M. Daggett, who had come to California to mine for gold, had made his stake, and had gone to San Francisco to establish the *Golden Era,* a literary weekly which built up a fine reputation in the West and was the early workshop of many famous writers. In the late 'fifties, Daggett sold his interest in the *Golden Era* and went to Virginia City to become associate editor of the *Territorial Enterprise.* Daggett was a forceful writer, never hesitant to express his views in print. As De Voto says:

He gave himself freely the pleasures of this world, but alcohol did not soften the edge of his satire. He hurled the *Enterprise* at villainy and corruption in high places. Men went looking for him armed; he gave public notice of his office hours.[8]

C. C. Goodwin, who served with Daggett on the *Enterprise* in those days of silver, tells this incident which is typical of Daggett's personality as a newspaper man:

He and I were quietly at work one afternoon when a man came in unannounced, walked straight to him, and presenting a folded *Enterprise,* said: "Daggett, that is a shame. My cows are as well fed as any man's, and the milk I sell is rich and sweet."

Daggett took the paper, looked at the heading: "Swill Milk," swiftly glanced it over and knew that one of the reporters had been writing up the man's dairy in not very complimentary terms. Turning upon the man an indignant face, he said: "You are a pretty fellow to come to me. I was down by your corral night before last;"—he had not been there in three years;—"as I walked along the high-board fence I heard your cows gnawing bones, and when I turned the corner they looked up at me and growled like dogs." The man dropped his hands, exclaiming: "Well, by —!" turned and left the office.

"That was all on the square, I suppose?" I said.

"That was necessary," was the response. "That son of a gun will not bother us again for eighteen months."[9]

[8] Bernard DeVoto, *Mark Twain's America* (Little, Brown & Co., 1932), p. 136.
[9] Goodwin, *op. cit.,* p. 188.

Daggett had a high courage that led him to stand for justice and fair play. His satire was an effective weapon when the *Enterprise* engaged in its many noteworthy controversies with individuals, groups, or rival newspapers. Samuel Clemens learned from Daggett many valuable lessons in the job of fighting, with the printed word, corruption in high places.

Steve Gillis, ninety-five pounds and every pound a fighter, was a printer on the *Enterprise*. He became Sam Clemens' companion on many ventures. He was the king jokester of a tribe of Comstock joking giants. He brewed tricks continuously and worked them off on his closest friends with great glee. Sam was the target more than once, but Steve repaid any injury which might have been done by a thousand acts of friendship. He was to be Mark Twain's second at the famous duel which ended a Comstock career; he was to go with Mark to San Francisco; finally, it was Steve Gillis who brought Mark Twain to the significant interlude at Jackass Hill.

Denis McCarthy, who was part owner of the *Enterprise* when Clemens joined the staff, later became Mark Twain's business manager on the lecture tour in 1866.

Coming to the *Enterprise* was surely a significant event in the career of Samuel Clemens when one considers this group of men with whom he was to be associated. These were men who believed in a robust, lively, interesting journalism; they believed in giving full play to rough humor, which was an essential in the colorful life on the Comstock Lode. But the fundamental basis of their journalism was honesty, fair play. They could jest on occasion, but when principles were at stake their satire and irony invariably worked in the cause of justice, tolerance, loyalty to ideals. Associated with such men as these, and writing for a newspaper as powerful and as honest as the *Enterprise,* Clemens developed those qualities which were inherent in him. It was the first real opportunity he had enjoyed to express himself freely against sham, hypocrisy, humbug. He fitted easily and naturally into the *Enterprise* fraternity.

De Quille and Twain came to be boon companions, so much so, in fact, that a rival paper, the *Gold Hill Daily News,* wrote satirically: *"To Be Married.—*Dan de Quille and Mark Twain are to be married shortly. About time."[10] De Quille was better equipped for writing stories which demanded exact facts and figures than was Sam; so the two frequently divided up the items as they covered the town in common. The feature material was handled by Sam, the straight news by Dan.

Shortly after Clemens came to the *Enterprise,* De Quille left for a trip East. This expected absence of De Quille was, in fact, one reason for the *Enterprise* having offered Sam a position. When De Quille returned after an absence of nine months on the Plains and in the States, he found Virginia City almost wiped out by the big fire of 1863. He wrote later of the conditions he found on the Lode:

> Thus I "resumed business at the old stand" in the thick of red-hot times—in the midst of flames and war.[11] It was also in the midst of the cutting and shooting days—the days of stage robberies, of mining fights, wonderful finds of ore, and all manner of excitements. As may be imagined Mark and I had our hands full, and no grass grew under our feet. There was a constant rush of startling events; they came tumbling over one another as though playing at leap-frog. While a stage robbery was being written up, a shooting affray started; and perhaps before the pistol shots had ceased to echo among the surrounding hills, the firebells were banging out an alarm.
>
> The crowding of the whole population into that part of town which had escaped the fire led to many bloody battles. Fighters, sports and adventurers, burned out of their old haunts, thronged the saloons and gaming houses remaining, where many of them were by no means welcome visitors.[12]

After De Quille returned to Virginia City he and Mark roomed together. By this time they were making it a practice to "slam" one another in print as frequently as possible. Much of this badi-

[10] *Gold Hill Daily News,* April 18, 1864.

[11] There had been a bloody battle among the volunteer firemen, and many had been killed and wounded.

[12] Dan De Quille, "Reporting with Mark Twain," *Californian Illustrated Magazine,* Vol. IV (1893), p. 170.

nage occurred in the pages of the *Enterprise,* but some of it was published in other newspapers. In the *Golden Era* of San Francisco, De Quille wrote:

> We (Mark and I) have the "sweetest" little parlor and the snuggest little bedroom (and it's only three floors from the ground) all to ourselves. Here we come every night and live—breathe, move and have our being, also our toddies. As Mark has already hinted to the world in his modest way, through the columns of the *Territorial Enterprise,* that "our furniture alone cost $28,000, in Europe," I need only add that our upholstery, etc. cost $15,000 more, in—a horn. We have a very good dodge for getting wood, we leave our door open when we go out . . . . and the fellows that are hired to carry up wood to the rooms, make a mistake nearly every day and pile a lot in our parlor. I never have seen the fellow making these mistakes, but Mark assures me that the wood all gets into our parlor that way. I suppose he was right—it looks very plausible, but lately I've been thinking that it was rather strange that the fellow quit making these mistakes the very day that Mark went down to Carson to report the proceedings of the Constitutional Convention, and hasn't made a single mistake since.[13]

When he began his work as reporter on the Comstock Lode, Samuel Clemens saw that the spirit of the mining camp demanded a lively treatment of news. Routine matters, he was pleased to note, were of little interest to the editors of the *Enterprise.* Even a murder, if it was just an ordinary murder, was tossed off in a line or two. He had some trouble at first finding items, but Editor Joe Goodman mentioned that sometimes they made news out of the haywagons that came into town from the Truckee River. Sam, according to his own account, searched through the town and found one dilapidated haywagon creaking down the street. He used it profusely, multiplying the wagon by sixteen, bringing it into town from sixteen different directions, and making sixteen separate items out of it. Showing such remarkable aptitude, he was well on his way to becoming a qualified reporter in Comstock journalism.

But the big opportunity came when a desperado killed a man in a saloon. Sam went to cover the story. He was profuse in his thanks to the murderer:

[13] *Golden Era,* December 6, 1863.

"Sir, you are a stranger to me, but you have done me a kindness this day which I can never forget. If whole years of gratitude can be to you any slight compensation, they shall be yours. I was in trouble and you have relieved me nobly and at a time when all seemed dark and drear. Count me your friend from this time forth, for I am not a man to forget a favor."[14]

Writing up murders was almost routine work for *Enterprise* reporters. This may sound like another one of the many exaggerated Wild West stories, but one need only look into the files of Washoe newspapers of the 'sixties to verify the statement. Crimes of violence were of daily occurrence. The rough element predominated. Sam was sitting in his room one night writing a letter to his mother and sister when he heard pistol shots down the street. He made a notation in his letter: "P.S. I have just heard five pistol shots down street—as such things are in my line, I will go and see about it." He went out to investigate, returned, and added these lines: "P.S. No. 2—5 A.M.—The pistol did its work well—one man—a Jackson County Missourian, shot two of my friends, (police officers), through the heart—both died within three minutes. Murderer's name is John Campbell."[15] Residents on the Comstock said in that day that the first twenty-six graves in the Virginia City cemetery were occupied by murdered men. This would not have been particularly astonishing to the miners.

Crime conditions on the Comstock furnished Mark Twain material for his *Roughing It* protest against the American jury system. It became the subject matter of some of his earliest social criticism. The jury system, he felt, put a ban upon intelligence and honesty and rewarded ignorance, stupidity, and perjury. He believed that the system should be altered to give men of brains and honesty an equal chance with fools and miscreants. Thus while he wrote lightly enough about the doings of desperadoes of Virginia City, he was experiencing a growth of resentment against the injustice of certain aspects of the social system, and we shall find that on the Comstock little by little he developed the

[14] Mark Twain, *Roughing It,* p. 21.
[15] Paine, *Letters,* I, 89.

ability to fight these evils with humor, satire, irony, hoax stories, and other manifestations of his growing skill as a writer.

Not long after he joined the staff of the *Enterprise,* Clemens wrote the first of his hoax stories which were to give him much notoriety on the Pacific Coast. Some time early in October 1862, when he had been on the newspaper only a few weeks, he wrote the story of "The Petrified Man." It is the first of his *Enterprise* stories extant. A few weeks had sufficed to impress upon Clemens the kind of material that would be readable for the "honest miner" and the Virginia City rough. An official named Sewall, at Humboldt, a coroner and justice of the peace, had been too independent in the matter of furnishing news to the *Enterprise.* Sam felt the power of the newspaper that employed him; he had no intention of allowing anyone to seem to disdain that power; he resolved to "show up" the man of Humboldt. Thus his first big Washoe joke related how a petrified man had been found in the mountains south of Gravelly Ford. The limbs of the mummy were reported as being in perfect condition, not excepting the one-time wooden left leg of the hardened defunct. The writer went on to describe the peculiar position of the mummy:

The body was in a sitting posture and leaning against a huge mass of croppings; the attitude was pensive, the right thumb resting against the side of the nose; the left thumb partially supported the chin, the forefinger pressing the inner corner of the left eye and drawing it partly open; the right eye was closed, and the fingers of the right hand spread apart.(!) This strange freak of nature created a profound sensation in the vicinity, and our informant states that, by request, Justice Sewall or Sowell of Humboldt City at once proceeded to the spot and held an inquest on the body. The verdict of the jury was that "deceased came to his death from protracted exposure," etc. The people of the neighborhood volunteered to bury the poor unfortunate, and were even anxious to do so; but it was discovered, when they attempted to remove him, that the water which had dripped upon him for ages from the crag above, had coursed down his back and deposited a limestone sediment under him which had glued him to the bed rock upon which he sat, as with a cement of adamant, and Judge S. refused to allow the charitable citizens to blast him from his position. The opinion expressed by his Honor that such a course would be little less than sacrilege, was eminently just and proper. Everybody goes to see the stone man, as many as 300 persons having visited the hardened creature during the past five or six weeks.[16]

Since no file of the *Territorial Enterprise* for this period is extant, one must depend on reprinting in other newspapers for the text of the hoax story. In its republishing of the story, the *San Francisco Bulletin* used the heading "A Washoe Joke," and prints the following introductory statement: "The *Territorial Enterprise* has a joke of a 'petrified man' having been found on the plains, which the interior journals seem to be copying in good faith." If journals outside of Virginia City were copying this story in good faith, that fact added much to the amusement of the miners on the Comstock. It was the sort of humor that Washoe could appreciate; the story had an immediate appeal when it impounded in solid rock the age-old gesture of derision. The story was a "scoop" in Comstock newspaper realism.

It probably is a mistake to credit Dan De Quille with any influence, or his solar-armor story[17] with any incentive, for the writing of the "Petrified Man" hoax. De Quille left for the East as soon as Clemens joined the staff, and was away for nine months. The "Petrified Man" hoax was printed in the *Enterprise* some time before October 15, 1862, the date of the reprinting of "The Petrified Man" in the *San Francisco Bulletin*. One may reasonably assume that when Clemens came to join the staff of the *Territorial Enterprise* he was pretty well acquainted with the spirit of Washoe and the temper of its humor, and that he needed no instruction in this phase of his work. Besides, he had, without a doubt, a predilection for this tone of writing; he had shown it previously. He could write with a tang without undergoing a treatment of forced feeding, as the career of the humorist before and after his days on the Comstock Lode amply testifies.

Clemens developed on the *Enterprise* an appreciation of the

---

[16] *San Francisco Bulletin,* October 15, 1862. Reprinted from the *Territorial Enterprise.*

[17] De Voto (*Mark Twain's America,* p. 137) suggests that the solar-armor story probably produced the "Petrified Man."

value of names in the day's news. His sketches almost invariably deal with persons; events are important only as they deal with definite individuals. In a letter to his sister Pamela, written a few months after he joined the *Enterprise* staff, he stresses this point. He informs Pamela that she would never do for a local reporter because she does not appreciate the interest that attaches to names. He writes:

> An item is of no use unless it speaks of some *person,* and not then, unless that person's *name* is distinctly mentioned. The most interesting letter one can write, to an absent friend, is one that treats of *persons* he has been acquainted with rather than the public events of the day.[18]

Clemens' local items, hoaxes, satires, editorials, and travel letters of the Western period show that he had faith in the appeal of persons over the appeal of events.

Notoriety was not long in coming to Clemens under the liberal policy which the *Enterprise* followed with respect to its staff. The "Petrified Man" story was widely reprinted. But a few months later came a new development which was to prove of much greater significance in making Clemens known as one of the bright men of the *Enterprise*. One evening, late in 1862, as Goodman and Clemens were at dinner—they frequently had "hours of quiet association together"[19]—Sam suggested that he be permitted to report the coming proceedings of the territorial legislature at Carson City. He was not familiar with that sort of work, but he desired an out-of-town assignment and felt that he could find something interesting in the doings of the legislature. A man named Gillespie, who had become clerk of the House, had previously covered the legislative news for the *Enterprise*. The opening was there; Goodman decided that Sam Clemens was the man for the job.

Thus, early in 1863, Clemens, arrayed in a long broadcloth cloak, a starched shirt, and polished boots, arrived in Carson City. He was returning now as a person of distinction, come to report

---

[18] Paine, *Letters*, I, 89.　　　　　[19] Paine, *Biography*, I, 216.

the news of the territorial legislature for one of the most widely known and influential journals in the West. No longer was he merely another bewildered miner rushing feverishly from one claim to another and making wild splurges in fantastic "feet." He went to live with Orion's family. He was pleased to learn that Orion's wife was by this time the social leader of the capital. He himself soon took a position of importance in the life of Carson City.

Members of the legislature soon discovered in Sam Clemens a man of enthusiasm and ability. He made himself known by his wit, his assurance, and his keen insight into the problems of the day. Some of his early letters to the *Enterprise* are said to have contained some curious blunders concerning the legislative proceedings, but he was given instruction in parliamentary matters by Gillespie, clerk of the House, and soon was able to write accurately of technical matters. But the technical matters were of little concern to him. What he liked to do was to write letters that sparkled, that had life, force, interest. Clement T. Rice, legislative reporter for the *Virginia City Union,* poked fun at what he considered crudities in Clemens' first letters from Carson. Paine writes:

> But this was a mistake. Clemens in his next letter declared that Rice's reports might be parliamentary enough, but that they covered with glittering technicalities the most festering mass of misstatement, and even crime. He avowed that they were wholly untrustworthy, dubbed the author of them "The Unreliable," and in future letters never referred to him by any other term. Carson and the Comstock and the papers of the Coast delighted in this burlesque warfare, and Rice was "The Unreliable" for life.
>
> Rice and Clemens, it should be said, though rivals, were the best of friends, and there was never any real animosity between them.[20]

Two friends of Clemens made it possible for him to increase the accuracy and interest of his reports by giving him inside information concerning the workings of the political machinery. These two, who made up the Humboldt delegation, were Jack Simmons, speaker of the House, and Billy Clagget, who had been one of

[20] Paine, *Biography,* I, 220.

Sam's companions on the prospecting trip to Unionville. Simmons, Clagget, and Clemens became the conspicuous figures of the legislative session.

Letters from the Carson correspondent of the *Enterprise* were being quoted and copied in other newspapers. Clemens was building up a reputation. But he was not satisfied. He wanted to make himself better known as a writer; he desired to place himself as a personality before the reading public. He discarded several possible names before he finally hit upon the one which he thought would be suitable. It was presumably the pen name that had been used back on the Mississippi by Captain Isaiah Sellers, whom Clemens had so cruelly lampooned in the New Orleans *True Delta* in 1859. He had deeply regretted the affront to the old man, and he felt that now he had an opportunity to compensate, in part, at least. He went to Virginia City, conferred with Goodman, and on February 2, 1863, a Carson dispatch in the *Territorial Enterprise* appeared over the signature, "Mark Twain." Paine says:

In all the nomenclature of the world no more forceful combination of words could have been selected to express the man for whom they stood. The name Mark Twain is as infinite, as fundamental as that of John Smith, without the latter's wasting distribution of strength. If all the prestige in the name of John Smith were combined in a single individual, its dynamic energy might give it the carrying power of Mark Twain. Let this be as it may, it has proven the greatest *nom de plume* ever chosen—a name exactly in accord with the man, his work, and his career.[21]

Writing of Clemens' choice of a pen name, Paine is more enthusiastic about the role of reporter on a frontier newspaper than he is in writing of Sam's reluctance to become a "camp scribbler," and of his "unwillingness to surrender."[22] Brooks sees, however, in the choice of a pen name, another ominous sign of disintegration of the artist:

In short, he wanted a trade-mark in order to sell what he instinctively regarded as merchandise; and the fact that the pen-name was the fashion of the time—in pioneer circles, especially, observe—simply argues that all the other writers in the West were in a similar case. The pen-name was a

[21] *Ibid.*, p. 222.   [22] Paine, *Letters*, I, 82.

form of "protective coloration" for men who could not risk, in their own persons, the odium of the literary life, and it is an interesting coincidence that "Mark Twain," in the pilot's vocabulary, implied "safe water." . . . . He instinctively thought of his writing as something external to himself, something of which he was proud only because it paid.[23]

In this sweeping gesture, Brooks becomes psychological monarch of all he surveys. The whole group of frustrated Western authors is thrown into a single hamper: Frontier authors, we are led to believe, chose pen names because they were to become prostitutes in the outlawed business of authorship. Frontier citizens objected to high achievement or special vocations, especially in the field of writing. Writers were prohibited, on pain of social extinction, from expressing themselves. Creative lives were stunted and thwarted. Sensitive, artistic souls were shanghaied into false careers, or concealed themselves behind the screen of the nom de plume. In the case of Mark Twain all this is especially applicable.

This is, of course, entirely according to Brooks. Yet a glance through the files of newspapers and magazines of the frontier West of the 'sixties will dispel any illusions one might have as to the attitude of Western pioneers toward literature and writers. The publications are loaded down with literary writings, perhaps not of the highest standards but certainly not entirely bad. There is a riot of fanciful pen names. The writers adopt authorship joyously, write humor as often as they feel like it, and show absolutely no sign of being victims of a literary pogrom carried on by those big, bad, rough, and tough Westerners. One may reasonably infer that Clemens, like other Western authors, became a writer because he liked to write, and chose a nom de plume because he took a certain pride in his profession of authorship. One must search for a greater freak of human nature than the Western Samuel Clemens for the application of psychological theories of arrested development, lack of inner control, undeveloped genius, spiritual miscarriage, and megalomania.

[23] Van Wyck Brooks, *The Ordeal of Mark Twain* (E. P. Dutton & Co., 1933), p. 113.

Recent examination of the log of Captain Isaiah Sellers[24] reveals entries so badly written as immediately to raise doubt that Sellers ever wrote anything himself for the newspapers. Also it is doubtful, from an examination of the journal, that Captain Sellers ever used the nom de plume "Mark Twain." The entries have to do primarily with Mississippi River navigation data, and Captain Sellers makes several claims concerning the origination of various steamboating practices, particularly those connected with the work of the leadsman. Neither the name "Mark Twain" nor a single reference to Samuel Clemens occurs in the log. Clippings pasted in the journal are stories written by others—newspaper reporters—in which rather routine river data, signed by I. Sellers, are included. The entries of this type of information in the log show how necessary it was for the newspapers to edit Captain Sellers' material.

The following entry, dated June 1, 1857, is typical of Sellers' writing in the logbook:

RULES MARCH 1826

the Rule for tapen the Bell for the Deck hands to heave the lead wars enterduced by me in the Spring of 1826 on Board of the Steamer Genl. Carrall [Carrol], James Gordan Master and George Cares & Isac Adams wars Pilots I wars Pilot up the Cumberland Rivar and Starsman in the lower River before that time the Pilots wold Sing out from the Pilot Hous heav that Stabord lead and when he wars dun with it he wold Sing out lay in that lead and Soon though the trip.
In the Spring of 1847. I enterduced the tapin of the Bell as a Signal for the Pilots to pass to the wright or left and it wars adopted.
In the Spring of 1852. I proposed to extend it to Day as well as night and it went without enney opisetion.
In the winter of 1852. the Supervise inspectors enterduced the whisel as a Signal for metin and pasen Boats I wars a pose to it. but after a time com over & am in favor of the whisal and hope it will prove yousfull.

---

[24] The Sellers logbook was made available for scholarly examination for the first time recently, by its owner, Mrs. Mollie Young Mueller, of Los Angeles, grandniece of Captain Sellers. It contains entries from February 1825 to November 22, 1862. Willis Wager of New York University, at whose suggestion the present writer located and examined the logbook, is preparing for publication detailed information about the journal.

In 1836 I Bilt the first State Room Caben Steam Boat that ever com to St. Louis She wars cald the Prairie and She had a Rail Road in the hold to Carry fraight fore and aft it wars yoused on a good meney Boats up to this Day I saw it on the Champion as yet. In 1843. I enterduced the first Iron Racke for the Deck hands to stand in on the gards of the Boats to heav the lead out off and it has bin in youse eversence.

I. SELLERS.

The owner of the Sellers log, Mrs. Mollie Young Mueller, a descendant of the Hood branch of the Sellers family, has in her possession the old Hood family Bible also. In this Bible, birth and death entries show that Captain Sellers was born on October 5, 1803, and died on March 6, 1864. He died of smallpox in Memphis, Tennessee. The date of his death is further authenticated by a newspaper story pasted by someone in the smaller journal. Since Captain Sellers did not die until 1864, Paine is in error in saying that Samuel Clemens did not adopt the nom de plume "Mark Twain" until the Captain's death, for several items over the signature of Mark Twain were printed in Nevada and California newspapers in 1863.

At any rate, Samuel Clemens did choose a pen name, and ominous as the choice may have been in his career, he seems to have borne his cross with admirable fortitude. His Carson dispatches took on new significance. He became more widely known than ever and does not seem to have shrunk from the spotlight. We have no evidence that he attempted to hide his identity as an author in that low Comstock crowd! On the contrary, he seems to have been proud of the fact that he was now attracting some real attention. Friends and acquaintances now call him "Mark" instead of "Sam." He is happy in his position of importance on the *Enterprise*. His letters home are full of gaiety, youth, inspiration, contentment.

We next hear of Mark Twain in San Francisco on one of the several trips he took to the metropolis while he was a reporter on the *Enterprise*. As evidence of the fact that editorial badinage between rival newspapers did not necessarily result in personal animosity, we find that Clement T. Rice, "The Unreliable," the

Virginia City Union reporter, was Mark's companion. The blasts which Mark had set off in his Carson letters, with Rice as a target, had been followed up by others in the *Enterprise,* one of which offered "The Unreliable" advice on how to conduct himself in church. But they were still friends. In San Francisco they had a glorious time. Mark naturally hated to go back to Washoe just then, since the Bay city offered many attractions in the way of dining, drinking, and making excursions by land and by sea. Mark records Rice's enthusiasm:

> Oh, no—*we* are not having any fun, Mark—Oh, no, I reckon not—it's somebody else—it's probably the "gentleman in the wagon! (popular slang phrase)." When I invite Rice to the Lick House to dinner, the proprietors send us champagne and claret, and then we *do* put on the most disgusting airs. Rice says our calibre is too light—we can't stand it to be noticed![25]

This visit took place in the early summer of 1863, and we have remaining of the writing he did during this sojourn one sketch entitled "All About the Fashions." This sketch was dated June 19, and was sent as correspondence to the *Territorial Enterprise.* Files of the *Enterprise* of that period are not extant, but the story was reprinted in the *Golden Era* of September 27, 1863. The weekly runs as an introduction to the sketch a letter from a Washoe "widow," "A Lady at the Lick House," who writes about the Lick House ball she had attended and how Mark Twain, who is such a favorite, was there. She sends the *Golden Era* a clipping of the *Enterprise* story which Mark Twain had written about the ball and sent from San Francisco. The Washoe "widow" writes:

> EDRS. *Golden Era*—We are all delighted with the letter describing the brilliant Ball at Mr. Barron's. I am a Washoe widow, was among the favored few, and went. Sarah Smith skipped me in the toilettes. I suppose I wasn't very stunning, although Brigham & Co. said I looked "swell," and that Bobergh couldn't get up anything better. Some months ago when my spouse, now at Reese River, first brought me down from Virginia City to stop in San Francisco, I arrived in the nick of time to attend one of those charming reunions which are all the rage in the Pacific Metropolis. We have had several soirees since that, but nobody gave any account of them to the papers. It's too bad. Now we are eagerly looking forward to the next

[25] Paine, *Letters,* I, 91.

soiree, expecting the *Golden Era* to tell all about it. One of our boarders says she knows Florence Fane, and means to invite her; but I can't for the life of me get her to tell me the real name of your charming feuilletonist. I hope she'll come. And may-be Mark Twain will stay in town, to be there too. There is some talk of getting up a special gathering in compliment to him. He's such a favorite—stops here for his health—hoping to find out how to cure a cold. I am going to wear a new dress, made precisely after the pattern of one of those sweet Paris Fashion Plates in the *California Magazine*. That Ball Dress in the May number—I think it was—I've kept it in my boudoir ever since. Then if Mark Twain is only there to see; how happy, how happy, I shall be. (I don't mean that for poetry—Like what you put in the *Golden Era*.) (To take that license I am free—I write with such facility.) But I have not told you what I wanted. Mark Twain was at our party, last June, and sent the *Territorial Enterprise* an account of the affair. My husband enclosed me the paper in which it appeared. I cut it out and you can copy it. Please do. I've been bothered to death to let everybody see it, and it's dreadfully tattered and torn.[26]

From this letter we learn that Mark Twain was on another visit to San Francisco in September, and that by the summer of 1863 he was attracting attention in the metropolis. Twain opens his June 19 letter to the *Enterprise* by telling how he has just received a sweet little note from the Comstock:

VIRGINIA, June 16.

Mr. MARK TWAIN:—*Do* tell us something about the fashions. I am dying to know what the ladies of San Francisco are wearing. Do, now, tell us all you know about it, won't you? Pray excuse brevity, for I am in *such* a hurry.   BETTIE.

P.S. Please burn this as soon as you have read it.

Mark goes on to comment on this letter. He conjectures what he should do if he had a wife, but decides not to borrow trouble by following this line of reasoning. He assures Bettie that he appreciates the compliment she has paid his critical and observing eye and his varied and extensive information, which a mind less balanced than his "could scarcely contemplate without excess of vanity." He is only too glad to tell about the fashions:

I will, Bettie—you better bet you bet, Betsey, my darling. I learned these expressions from the Unreliable; like all the expressions which fall

[26] *Golden Era,* September 27, 1863.

from his lips, they are frightfully vulgar—but then they sound rather musical than otherwise.

A happy circumstance, the Lick House ball, given by the proprietors on the occasion of Mark's paying up his board bill, makes it possible for him to give a good account of the current fashions. Describing the fashions of the ladies at the ball, Mark writes of Mrs. B., arrayed in a superb speckled foulard, with stripes running fore and aft; of Mrs. J. B. W., who wore a "heavy rat-colored brocade silk, studded with large silver stars, and trimmed with organdie," not forgetting a "bournous of black Honiton lace, scolloped, and embroidered in violent colors with a battle piece representing the taking of Holland by the Dutch"; of Miss C., who wore "an elegant *Cheveux de la Reine* (with ruffles and furbelows trimmed with bands of guipure round the bottom), and a mohair Garibaldi shirt"; whose unique head-dress was crowned with "a graceful *pomme de terre* (Limerick French)," and who "had her hair done up in papers—greenbacks." Others wore similarly striking costumes.

Feeling that Bettie will want to know something of the style of male attire at the ball, Mark describes his own costume, which consisted of Mr. Lawlor's shirt, Mr. Ridgway's vest, Dr. Wayman's coat, Mr. Camp's hat, Mr. Paxton's boots, Jerry Long's white kids, Judge Gilchrist's cravat, the Unreliable's brass seal-ring, and Dr. Tollroad McDonald's pantaloons. About the last article of apparel, he adds to Bettie: "And if you have an idea that they are anyways short in the legs, do you just climb into them once, sweetness."

Ending the letter with a few words to the editors of the *Enterprise,* Mark suggests that it is about time he is getting back to the Comstock:

I expect I had better go home now. Well, I have been here long enough anyhow. I didn't come down to stay always, in the first place. I don't know of anything more here that I want to see. I might just as well go home now as not. I have been wanting to go home for a good while. I don't see why I haven't gone before this. They all say it is healthier up there than it is here. I believe it. I have not been very well for a week. I don't eat enough, I expect. But I would stay here just as long as I pleased though, if I wanted to. But I don't. Well, I don't care—I am going home—that is the amount of it—and very soon, too—may be sooner.

Here we have Mark Twain writing as a reporter on a roving assignment. It was what he liked best of all as a newspaper job. Definite assignments, and the writing of local items of straight news, did not appeal to him. Now we get a hint of the sort of writing he was to do in his travel letters later. Writing as a reporter-at-large, on any subject that struck his fancy, playing up the feature element and the human interest over the news angle—this is what Mark Twain preferred and what he was best fitted to do in the field of journalism. His humorous writing on fashions in the Lick House ball letter was, of course, not an original idea. Fashion writing in a humorous vein had already been done extensively by other writers. It was virtually a constant in the repertory of Western humorists. But Mark Twain had his own way of doing it, and he continued it in additional sketches later.

Returning to Virginia City and to his work on the *Enterprise,* Mark Twain began writing occasional letters for the *San Francisco Call.* The twelve letters in the series were published in the *Call* on the following dates: July 9, 15, 18, 23, 30, August 6, 13, 30, September 3, 19, and December 2, 11, of the year 1863. These letters deal with such subjects as shootings, the Fourth in Virginia City, mining news, theatricals, a judicial war, a billiard match, and an agricultural fair.

In August 1863 Mark was at Steamboat Springs, not far from Virginia City, attempting to recover from a severe bronchial cold. In a letter to his mother and sister, dated at Steamboat Springs, August 19, 1863, he complains that his mother has given his vanity a deadly thrust:

Behold, I am prone to boast of having the widest reputation, as a local editor, of any man on the Pacific coast, and you gravely come forward and tell me "if I work hard and attend closely to my business, I may aspire to a place on a big San Francisco daily, some day." There's a comment on human vanity for you! Why, blast it, I was under the impression that I could get such a situation as that any time I asked for it. But I don't want it. No paper in the United States can afford to pay me what my place on the "Enterprise" is worth. If I were not naturally a lazy, idle, good-for-nothing vagabond, I could make it pay me $20,000 a year. But I don't suppose I shall ever be any account. I lead an easy life, though, and I don't care a cent whether school keeps or not. Everybody knows me, and I fare like a prince wherever I go, be it on this side of the mountains or the other. And I am proud to say I am the most conceited ass in the Territory.[27]

The money value which Mark Twain in this letter places on his *Enterprise* position no doubt is an allusion to the practice, common in the Comstock journalism of that day, of presenting newspaper reporters with "feet" in claims when they wrote notices. These gifts were presented to the reporters even when the notices were not particularly favorable; publicity was desired, at any cost.

To the period of this Steamboat Springs sojourn probably belongs the sketch, "How to Cure a Cold," which appeared in the *Golden Era* on September 20, 1863, and was later included in *The Jumping Frog* (1867). Mark Twain and Bret Harte were not exactly twin spirits in authorship for the *Golden Era* of September 20, 1863. In that issue began Harte's longer version of *M'liss,* which, under the title of "The Work on Red Mountain," had been printed in the shorter form of four chapters in two installments, the first in the *Golden Era* for December 9, 1860, the second on December 16, 1860. The contrast of tone in the works of the two authors is probably nowhere more strikingly presented than in this issue of the *Golden Era*. On October 11, 1863, the *Golden Era* published another sketch by Mark Twain entitled "The Great Prize Fight." This sketch is reprinted in *Wit and Humor of America,* 1907.

On the Comstock Lode humor was of a vigorous, positive, elemental sort. And the staff members of the *Enterprise* had a particular flair for joke making. Mark Twain had not been on the staff long before his colleagues recognized in him a delightful target. He had shown that he enjoyed playing jokes at the expense of others but could never see any fun in being made the victim himself. So the battle was on. Mark's "keen love of the ridiculous

[27] Paine, *Letters,* I, 91–92.

placed him in the joker class, while his prompt temper, droll manner, and rare gift of invective made him an enticing victim."[28] Steve Gillis especially liked to play jokes on Mark, because the result was such a rare profanity as could amaze even a citizen of the Comstock Lode, a profanity that had started with an unusually vigorous gift of phrase and had developed strength and vitality through the journeyman printer, the River, and the mining days. To Mark Twain, profanity, in certain trying circumstances, offered a relief denied even by prayer.

A favorite trick of the *Enterprise* staff members was to arouse Mark's wrath by hiding the candle which he used in preference to a lamp while working. This usually resulted in an outburst of denunciation that shook the rafters of the none-too-substantial building. Then there was the incident of the meerschaum pipe. Several versions of this affair have been given by associates of Mark Twain on the Comstock Lode. Alf Doten, who reported with Mark on the Lode, wrote an account of the meerschaum pipe party for the *Nevada Magazine* of October 1899, in which he has the affair beginning with certain printers coming "into the local room where Dan and Mark were sitting at the table, busily writing."[29] But this story differs from the one told by Steve Gillis, the *Enterprise* printer who was a close friend of Mark Twain's and was actually the perpetrator of the pipe joke. Steve's account relates that Twain, returning from the Carson City assignment covering the meetings of the legislature, was grieved because other members of the staff had been presented with meerschaum pipes but he had been neglected. Steve felt that there would be no difficulty in taking care of the situation.

Soon the other staff members were informed of the plot to present Mark with an imitation meerschaum. The party took place late one night in the saloon under the opera house. Mark Twain made a speech of appreciation in all sincerity, and, after the drinks had been generously quaffed, the plotters went home

---

[28] Paine, *Biography*, I, 213.

[29] The account is in the *Nevada Magazine*, October 1899, pp. 182–84.

feeling a bit sheepish. The next day Mark found that the pipe would not color. Then came comprehension. It was a cruel joke because it had been too well planned. Probably this incident more than any other—though a fake holdup of Mark Twain on the Comstock later during his lecture tour also greatly annoyed him—contributed to the resentment he expressed in later life against the jokesters of the Comstock Lode. The cruelty of the pipe trick had been increased by the confiding statement of Dan De Quille to Mark in private beforehand that he was to be given a fine pipe by his friends. Mark, therefore, had worked hard on his speech. After the fine words of presentation, Mark made his beautiful address of appreciation. Steve Gillis, telling of the incident to Paine, said:

Sam's reply, which was supposed to be impromptu, actually brought the tears to the eyes of some of us, and he was interrupted every other minute with applause. I never felt so sorry for anybody.[30]

Small wonder that Mark Twain—who admitted that he did not have a "dear and lovely disposition," that this was a feature that had been left out of him at birth and that even at seventy he had not yet acquired it[31]—was later to write feelingly against grown-up persons who indulge in practical jokes. He felt that these were persons who had lived narrow, obscure, and ignorant lives, and that they had carried over into adult life the standards and ideals of childhood.

There were many practical jokers in the new Territory. I do not take pleasure in exposing this fact, for I liked those people; but what I am saying is true. I wish I could say a kindlier thing about them instead. If I could say they were burglars, or hatrack thieves, or something like that, that wouldn't be utterly uncomplimentary. I would prefer it, but I can't say those things. They would not be true. These people were practical jokers, and I will not try to disguise it. In other respects they were plenty good enough people; honest people; reputable and likable. They played practical jokes upon each other with success, and got the admiration and applause and also the envy of the rest of the community.[32]

[30] Paine, *Biography*, I, 225.

[31] Mark Twain, *Autobiography*, II, 171.   [32] *Ibid.*, pp. 305–6.

This was written when Mark Twain was seventy-one years old, and probably on one of his bad days. It does not express his usual feeling toward the old companions of the West. He had forgotten, for the moment, possibly, that he himself was one of those Comstock practical jokers, and frequently a cruel funmaker. For many years of his life, certainly from boyhood up, he had had more than the normal person's participation in perpetrating jokes that were injurious to the other fellow. And seldom had he felt the desire to be a "good sport" when the joke was on him. He liked fun, if he himself did not have to suffer. His attitude toward criticism is somewhat analogous: "I like criticism," he wrote, "but it must be my way."[33] Alf Doten wrote in 1899: "It was well understood by all who knew him best that although he liked practical jokes on others, he did not seem to enjoy one upon himself."[34]

But Comstock journalism was not always joking. When not otherwise occupied, the Virginia City and Gold Hill papers were often carrying on editorial controversies. "Argentoro," Virginia City correspondent for the *San Francisco Call,* wrote that the papers were fighting like cats and dogs.

> The *Enterprise* and *Union* denounce the *Bulletin* as "insignificant," "contemptible," "stupid," etc., while the *Bulletin* retorts in like manner. A few days since the *Union* unequivocally charged the *Bulletin* with having sold itself for five hundred dollars, and boasted that it could name the parties who paid the money, and dared the *Bulletin* to seek redress in a suit for libel.

The *Union* and the *Bulletin,* both Virginia City dailies, carried on a long and bitter editorial battle over this matter of the alleged acceptance of money in a political campaign. There were many other similar editorial controversies in Virginia City, with Mark Twain taking an active part.

Of all the writing that Mark Twain did for the *Territorial Enterprise,* the one story that attracted the most attention and was remembered the longest on the Comstock was his "Empire City

[33] Mark Twain, *Autobiography,* II, 247.

[34] *Nevada Magazine,* October 1899, p. 183. Cf. also Twain's reaction to a fake holdup and to the letter episode, in chapter ix, below, pp. 150–51.

Massacre." This hoax story was published in the *Enterprise* on October 28, 1863. There are many stories in Mark Twain's writings that will testify to the unusual delight he sometimes seems to have taken in composing sketches of bloody violence, but the story of the massacre at Dutch Nick's tops them all. The piece is hard to explain; probably it was just one of those things that result when a temperament has been too long restrained and the rusted safety valve has finally opened.

The story, as reprinted in the *San Francisco Bulletin* three days after its publication in the *Enterprise,* narrates how a man named Hopkins, living in a log house at the edge of a pine forest between Empire City and Dutch Nick's with his wife and nine children, went berserk and, armed with an ax, a knife, and a club, killed the mother and seven of the children, and dangerously wounded the two other children. With blood, and brains, and gore strewn about the house, Hopkins severed his wife's head from her body and went for a horseback ride.

About 10 o'clock on Monday evening Hopkins dashed into Carson on horseback, with his throat cut from ear to ear, and bearing in his hand a reeking scalp from which the warm, smoking blood was still dripping, and fell in a dying condition in front of the Magnolia saloon. Hopkins expired in the course of five minutes, without speaking. The long red hair of the scalp he bore marked it as that of Mrs. Hopkins.[35]

The massacre story, as published in Appendix C[36] of Paine's biography of Mark Twain, shows editing which goes beyond the customary changes made for consistency in typographical style. The following changes in the Paine version indicate that Mark Twain did some editing of the story after its *Enterprise* publication:[37] "we learn" for "we have learned"; "visiting in Carson" for

---

[35] *San Francisco Bulletin,* October 31, 1863.

[36] Mark Twain, in "My Bloody Massacre," *Sketches New and Old,* adds some facts not included in Paine's version of the massacre story or in the *Bulletin* reprint. Two miners, reading the story in a Virginia City restaurant, are horrified. "Jim," says one, "he b'iled his baby, and he took the old 'oman's skelp. Cuss'd if *I* want any breakfast." Since there is no baby-boiling in the *Bulletin* reprint, and none in Paine's version, it is safe to say that there was none in the original story.

[37] A Mark Twain scrapbook in the possession of the Willard S. Morse estate, Santa Monica, California, shows how Mark Twain edited his Western writings for later use in the East.

"visiting Carson"; "eyes" for "gaze"; "declare" for "state"; "no one had ever heard" for "we had never heard"; "our game" for "the game"; "invested an immense amount" for "invested to an immense amount." The *Bulletin* story can probably be taken as authentic, since it was printed soon after the original.

The Empire City massacre story has been explained as having two objects. One, supposedly, was the punishment of the *San Francisco Bulletin* for its adverse criticism of mining affairs on the Comstock Lode and its suggestions that money might better be invested in California resources. The other object was to take a secondary slap at the Magnolia saloon at Carson City, a saloon which, for some reason or other, had aroused Mark's resentment. The Magnolia dispensed a potent "forty-rod" whisky—it killed every time at that distance. This liquor was also known as "tarantula juice": "When the boys were well charged with this whisky it made the snakes and tarantulas that bit them very sick."[38]

Probably the Magnolia saloon did not suffer greatly from this publicity, and it is doubtful if the *Bulletin* or other California interests experienced any serious setback, although many persons, even on the Comstock Lode, took the story seriously. These credulous ones overlooked the fact that Dutch Nick's and Empire City were the same place; that there was nothing but sagebrush where the story described a pine forest; and that the lone bachelor living at Dutch Nick's had no family. Paine says:

Even when these things were pointed out many readers at first refused to confess themselves sold. As for the *Bulletin* and other California papers, they were taken-in completely, and were furious. Many of them wrote and demanded the immediate discharge of its author, announcing that they would never copy another line from the *Enterprise,* or exchange with it, or have further relations with a paper that had Mark Twain on its staff. Citizens were mad, too, and cut off their subscriptions. The joker was in despair.[39]

With respect to the *Bulletin's* having been taken in, Paine is in error, as is shown by that newspaper's reprint of the *Enterprise*

---

[38] Wright, *op. cit.,* p. 40.   [39] Paine, *Biography,* I, 230.

story. A dash at the end of the *Bulletin's* reprint is followed by these lines:

> (From the "Territorial Enterprise" of 29th October)
> I take it all back. * * * * * Mark Twain.

Obviously the *Bulletin* had not been misled by the massacre hoax.

The story did result in a serious predicament for the *Enterprise,* however, and Mark feared that he had ruined the paper. He offered to resign, but Editor Goodman would have none of this talk. He explained to Mark that the *Enterprise* could furnish its readers with the day's news but could not equip them with good sense. He predicted that the Empire City massacre story would be remembered long after other *Enterprise* writings of Mark Twain had been forgotten.

Here, certainly, Joe Goodman was put to a severe test. Where else could Mark Twain have enjoyed this editorial loyalty? The massacre story is not significant as an example of literary craftsmanship; it is a crude hoax story that could add no artistic prestige to its author. But that Mark Twain could write this crude story and still be championed by an editor of Goodman's caliber, so that there was yet left an opportunity to go on to more worthwhile achievement, is of real significance. Being severely penalized for this piece of writing might have resulted badly for Mark Twain, though this, of course, is merely conjecture. The story did have, after all, one redeeming quality, as De Voto points out:

> To its coarse and bloody details and to its fantastic exaggerations was added another quality: social reproof. Mark Twain was rebuking the practices of California speculators. Social satire thus makes its appearance at the *Enterprise* office, completely embedded in the native joke.[40]

[40] De Voto, *op. cit.,* p. 155.

CHAPTER 6

REPORTER ON THE
TERRITORIAL ENTERPRISE

[November 1863 - May 1864]

WITH a fine opera house, plenty of money, and enthusiastic audiences awaiting attractions at Virginia City, it was natural that players who came to San Francisco should make the Comstock Lode an important stopping-place on their Western circuit. Mark Twain took great delight in writing up theater news and views, and seems to have been a regular attendant at the outstanding attractions, as he also was in San Francisco when he visited there. A high point of his enthusiasm for personalities of the stage was reached when, during the theater season of 1863–64, Adah Isaacs Menken came to Virginia City to present her Lady Godiva play, *The Mazeppa*. She had already had a long run in San Francisco and had been given wide publicity. "The Menken" was a glamorous star of the 'sixties who gained an international reputation through her romantic and tempestuous love affairs and her artistic genius. Falk says of her:

Strapped to the back of "Mazeppa's" fiery steed, and attired in pink silk fleshings, "with the small end of a dimity nothing fastened to her waist," she earned a little hour of glory. Poetess, as well as stage-performer, she was the friend of Charles Dickens, Algernon Swinburne, George Sand, Theophile Gautier and Alexandre Dumas pere. In her train followed a motley host, from princelings to needy wits. While she lived no woman was more eagerly discussed, and, after her death, more mercilessly slandered.[1]

[1] Bernard Falk, *The Naked Lady or Storm over Adah* (Hutchinson & Co., Ltd., London, 1934), Preface. Claimed to be the only full-length life of Adah Menken.

The Jewish actress included in her remarkable adventures four marriages. John C. Heenan, "Benicia Boy," the prizefighter, was her second husband; Robert H. Newell (Orpheus C. Kerr), poet and dramatic critic, was her third.

In San Francisco, "The Menken" had played for sixty nights, at $500 a night, at Tom Maguire's Opera House. Praises of her performances of *The Mazeppa* echoed over the mountains to Washoe. The miners awaited her coming. Imagine their dismay, however, when, making her debut at Maguire's new theater in Virginia City on the night of March 2, 1864, Adah chose as the play for the opening night, *The French Spy*. Every seat in the house had been sold the day previous, however, as no one wanted to miss seeing the glamorous star.[2] *The Mazeppa* followed, and the Washoe miners gazed in rapture, as did also the newspaper reporters:

> Quarrying a rude vein of local journalism, Mark Twain, the moment his eyes glimpsed the astonishing vision, fell under Menken's spell. In Dante Gabriel Rossetti's memorable phrase, "she was a stunner!" What should impress his youthful imagination more than this strange woman, who united rare intelligence and most glamorous personality, with ravishing loveliness of an order rarely witnessed in those parts? . . . .
>
> To speak her praises in the Virginia City *Enterprise* became the humorist's solemn and chivalrous duty. His championship of the actress extended to the boycott of a manager who caused her offense. A final expression of his admiration was to nominate her his *Egeria*. To be honored with her judgment, he brought along his own unripe inventions, content, like Hillel at the feet of Gamaliel, to be the recipient of her superior wisdom. More crudely than we have phrased the circumstance, Mark Twain's own words put on record one of those engaging episodes:
>
> "I took it [an article] over to show to Miss Menken, the actress, Orpheus C. Kerr's wife. She has a beautiful white hand, but her handwriting is infamous; she writes fast, and her calligraphy is of the doorplate order—her letters are immense. I gave her a conundrum, thus:
>
> "MY DEAR MADAM,
>
> "Why ought your hand to retain its present grace and beauty always? (*Answer.*) Because you fool away devilish little of it on your manuscript."[3]

Other theatrical attractions occupied Mark Twain's attention

[2] *Golden Era,* March 6, 1864.   [3] Falk, *op. cit.,* pp. 67–68.

during the season of 1863–64. *Ingomar, the Barbarian,* was presented in the opera house in the autumn of 1863. Mark Twain's connection with this play proved of more than usual significance, because his critique was copied in the East, and we have the first instance of Eastern periodicals printing the Western writings of Mark Twain. The *Golden Era,* introducing its reprint of Mark Twain's *Ingomar* write-up, says that "during the Fall Season of Mr. Maguire's Dramatic troupe at his new Opera House in Virginia City, the *Territorial Enterprise* has indulged its readers with an extraordinary succession of humorous, pungent and peculiar *critiques.*"[4] Writing up *Ingomar* in a fashion which he felt the Comstock miners could appreciate, Twain presented a résumé of the play in the columns of the *Enterprise.* Mrs. Claughley is described as "a healthy Greek matron (from Limerick)," who urges her daughter to marry Polydor to save the family homestead from the sheriff. Polydor, a "wealthy, spindle-shanked, stingy old stockbroker," is refused by the Greek maiden, who speaks without a foreign accent. The Comanches capture Parthenia's father and hold him in "soak." Parthenia appeals to Polydor, who advises her to "shove out after" her parent. "She shoves!" Tableau of Comanche camp shows the Indians throwing dice and Parthenia's father, now a slave, "packing faggots on a jack." Parthenia becomes a hostage in place of her father. She falls in love with Ingomar. "The Comanches again, with Thorne at their head! He asks who enslaved the Chief? Ingomar points to Polydor. Lo! Thorne seizes the trembling broker, and snatches him baldheaded!" The chief of police makes a treaty with the Comanches, and gives them a ranch apiece. Grand tableau of Comanches, police, Pi-Utes, and citizens generally. Ingomar and Parthenia in a love scene. "The old thing."[5]

In this *Ingomar* review, Mark Twain shows a breaking away from the cruder humor that was in evidence in earlier burlesque writings. Gradually he came to depend more and more on cleverness rather than coarseness. The critique, besides being reprinted

---

[4] *Golden Era,* November 29, 1863.   [5] *Ibid.*

in the West, found its way into the columns of a monthly magazine in the East, *Yankee Notions*. In its April 1864 number, under
the heading, "The Play of *Ingomar* in California," *Yankee Notions*
introduces its reprint of the burlesque review with these words:

> The following is a résumé of the well-known play of "Ingomar," made
> by Mark Twain, of the Virginia (N.T.) *Territorial Enterprise*. We miss a
> figure if anything more thoroughly droll has been perpetrated in many a
> long year. The company playing at the Virginia City theatre, was the one
> from Maguire's Opera house, San Francisco, and the persons alluded to
> are of course the actors of that company.[6]

An event of significance in the Western development of Mark
Twain occurred when Artemus Ward [Charles F. Browne] came
to Virginia City in December 1863. There was money on the
Comstock Lode, and the town had a fine opera house and enthusiastic audiences. Ward came with the intention of lecturing
for a few days; but he remained to play, and his visit lasted three
weeks. The reason: there was also comradery on the Comstock.

Previous to Ward's coming, Mark Twain wrote a notice for
the *Territorial Enterprise* in which he welcomed to Washoe the
"Wild Humorist of the Plains":

> We understand that Artemus Ward contemplates visiting this region
> to deliver his lectures, and perhaps make some additions to his big "sho."
> In his last letter to us he appeared particularly anxious to "sekure a kupple
> ov horned todes; alsowe, a lizard which it may be persessed of 2 tales, or any
> komical snaix, and enny sich little unconsidered trifles, as the poets say,
> which they do not interest the kommun mind. Further, be it nown, that I
> would like a opportunity for to maik a moddel in wax of a average size
> wash-owe man, with feet attached, as an kompanion pictur to a waxen figger
> of a nigger I have sekured, at an large outlaye, whitch it has a unnatural
> big hed onto it. Could you alsowe manage to gobbel up the skulp of the
> layte Missus Hoppins? I adore sich foot-prints of atrocity as it were,
> muchly. I was roominatin on gittin a bust of mark Twain, but I've kwit
> kontemplatin the work. They tell me down heer too the Ba that the busts
> air so kommon it wood ony bee an waist of wax too git un kounterfit
> presentiment." We shall assist Mr. Ward in every possible way about mak-
> ing his Washoe collection and have no doubt but he will pick up many
> curious things during his sojourn.[7]

[6] *Yankee Notions*, April, 1864.

[7] *Golden Era*, November 29, 1863. Reprinted from the *Territorial Enterprise*.

The reference to the "skulp of the layte Missus Hoppins" in Ward's letter indicates that the Empire City massacre story of October 28 had been spread around on the Pacific Coast. The labored effect of Ward's humor, depending so greatly on mis-spelling, is a hint of the *impasse* Mark Twain might have come to if he had not abandoned the Snodgrass style of humor when he came West.

As a lecturer in that day, however, Artemus Ward was im-mensely popular. When he came to the Comstock Lode he was at the peak of his career. Dan De Quille, writing later of Ward's visit, said that the humorist

was then in fine health and spirits. Everything he saw called forth a joke or a quaint saying. His drollery was without effort. His fun like the quality of mercy was not strained. It was natural to him to see the comical side of everything. He teemed with waggery which on the slightest provocation expanded into a surprising flow of facetiousness—into a merry, sportive string of pleasantry. There was nothing malicious in his fun.[8]

Whatever may have been their estimate of the man in other respects, the members of the *Enterprise* staff found that Artemus Ward had "the gift of friendship. Something in his gentle madness excused the labor of his witticisms and the odium of his practical jokes. He made men glow."[9] To Joe Goodman, Dan De Quille, and Mark Twain he became a brother in the fraternity of the Com-stock. The four of them, with Denis McCarthy and E. E. Hing-ston, Ward's manager, painted Virginia City; the job required three weeks. The mines, Chinatown, the bars, and the restaurants were their workshops; they mixed the colors of the rainbow in a riot of fun. Dining at Chaumond's restaurant, the company arose for a toast in which Ward gave them Upper Canada. Joe Good-man wanted to know why he was giving away Upper Canada. "Because I don't want it myself," replied Ward. Joe Goodman had a joke, but he kept it until daybreak, when the dinner ended. It was the bill for the dinner—two hundred and thirty-seven

[8] *Californian Illustrated Magazine,* August 1893, p. 403.
[9] De Voto, *Mark Twain's America* (Little Brown & Co., 1932), p. 138.

dollars. Ward saw the joke, paid the bill. The fun was still not over. Artemus and Mark went roof-walking, and had a gay time jumping from one roof down to the other, which was not difficult even for a couple of heavy banqueteers, since Virginia was built on a steep hillside.

Another gay session ended in a private party for Artemus Ward. He writes of it in a letter from Austin, Nevada, after he has left the Comstock:

> Why did you not go with me and save me that night?—I mean the night I left you after that dinner party. I went and got drunker, beating, I may say, Alexander the Great, in his most drinkinist days, and I blackened my face at the Melodeon, and made a gibbering, idiotic speech. Goddam it! I suppose the *Union* will have it. . . . . Some of the finest intellects in the world have been blunted by liquor.[10]

The two great personalities, Artemus Ward and Mark Twain, complemented each other during those memorable three weeks in that frontier mining town. There resulted a

> rising tide of humor that could hardly be matched in the world to-day. Mark Twain had awakened to a fuller power; Artemus Ward was in his prime. They were giants of a race that became extinct when Mark Twain died. The youth, the wine, the whirl of lights and life, the tumult of the shouting street—it was as if an electric stream of inspiration poured into those two human dynamos and sent them into a dazzling, scintillating whirl. All gone—as evanescent, as forgotten, as the lightnings of that vanished time; out of the vast feasting and entertainment only a trifling morsel remains.[11]

Mark Twain was to present a picture of that happy comradeship back on the Comstock Lode to Thomas Bailey Aldrich in a letter written eight years after Ward's visit to Virginia City:

> *Scene*—private room in Barnum's Restaurant, Virginia, Nevada; present, Artemus Ward, Joseph T. Goodman, (editor and proprietor Daily "Enterprise"), and "Dan de Quille" and myself, reporters for same; remnants of the feast thin and scattering, but *such* tautology and repetition of empty bottles everywhere visible as to be offensive to the sensitive eye; time, 2:30 A.M.; Artemus thickly reciting a poem about a certain infant you wot of, and interrupting himself and *being* interrupted every few lines by pound-

[10] Paine, *Letters* (Harper & Bros., 1917), I, 93–94.
[11] Paine, *Biography* (Harper & Bros., 1912), I, 240–41.

ings of the table and shouts of "Splendid, by Shorzhe!" Finally, a long, vociferous, poundiferous and vitreous jingling of applause announces the conclusion, and then Artemus: "Let every man 'at loves his fellow man and 'preciates a poet 'at loves *his* fellow man, stan' up!—stan' up and drink it *stanning!*" (On all hands fervent, enthusiastic, and sincerely honest attempts to comply.) Then Artemus: "Well—consider it stanning, and drink it just as ye are!" Which was done.[12]

The three weeks of comradeship in Virginia City were more than merely weeks of play, however. There were serious moments, and in some of these Artemus Ward counseled Mark Twain in the ways of successful authorship. He advised him to work into the Eastern publications immediately. He promised to write a letter to the editors of the *New York Sunday Mercury* informing them of Mark Twain and his work in the West. It may be that Twain sent a sketch to the *Sunday Mercury* a short time later and that it was printed; Paine suggests that such a sketch on the subject of absurd remedies for children was printed. It is not extant. There is no doubt, however, that Ward had aroused in Twain a desire to be known beyond Washoe and the Pacific Coast. In a letter to his mother early in 1864 Mark writes that he was sometimes throwing off pearls which ought "for the eternal welfare" of his race to have a "more extensive circulation than is afforded by a local daily paper" and that Ward had suggested that he leave the sagebrush obscurity and accompany Ward to New York. Mark, however, had preferred not to burst too suddenly upon the New York public, and had decided to remain in Washoe.[13] The desire for a wider field of authorship was now definitely in Mark Twain's mind. It would not be long before he would leave Washoe for a more extensive sphere of activity.

On January 12, 1864, the two houses of the Nevada territorial legislature convened at Carson City. It was to be the last gathering of this body as a group representing a territory, since Nevada became a state on October 31, 1864. Mark Twain was again sent by the *Territorial Enterprise* to report the legislative sessions. This

[12] Paine, *Letters*, I, p. 183.   [13] Paine, *Biography*, I, 243–44.

second Carson City assignment is of great significance in Mark Twain's career, for he becomes during this reporting period a really important figure in public affairs. Now, his writings, although mostly still in a humorous vein, carry weight with the readers. There is almost invariably to be found in them some element of political or social criticism. His satire and irony are now being directed toward problems of some real importance in the life of the community. His work on the *Enterprise* had been attracting general attention by the time he went to the legislative sessions for the second time, but probably nothing he wrote had been considered more than a humorous treatment of unimportant subjects, or rather unimportant feature writing of news around the Comstock Lode. Now, in Carson City, his humor became more substantial writing, more thought-provoking, less ephemeral, and much less coarse than some of his previous writings. No doubt, the fact that he felt that he now had some real influence in public affairs had much to do with the change in content, style, and tone of his articles. He wrote later of the influence he enjoyed, as contrasted with that of his brother Orion:

> Orion was soon very popular with the members of the legislature, because they found that whereas they couldn't usually trust each other, nor anybody else, they could trust him. He easily held the belt for honesty in that country, but it didn't do him any good in a pecuniary way, because he had no talent for either persuading or scaring legislators. But I was differently situated. I was there every day in the legislature to distribute compliments and censure with evenly balanced justice and spread the same over half a page of the *Enterprise* every morning; consequently I was an influence.[14]

Writing of the affairs of the legislature and mingling with those who had been sent to represent various sections of the territory at the capital city, Twain became a respected and influential figure in the political life of the territory. Members of the legislature hoped for his commendation, feared his ridicule. He became such a power that, with his friends, Simmons and Clagget, he could control a large number of votes, and could wield a great

[14] *Mark Twain's Autobiography* (Harper & Bros., 1924), II, 307–8.

influence in the passing or rejection of bills.[15] His popularity was so great that when a burlesque "Third House" was organized, he was chosen "Governor." The first session was made a public occasion, and "Governor" Mark Twain delivered an address—not extant. On this occasion he was presented with a gold watch, inscribed with his name and title, by Judge A. W. (Sandy) Baldwin and Theodore Winters. A forceful writer representing a powerful journal was an individual to be reckoned with. "That he was fearless, merciless, and incorruptible, without doubt had a salutary influence on that legislative session," says Paine. "He reveled in his power; but it is not recorded that he ever abused it."[16] The only legislative activity in which he indulged that could possibly have had a direct personal interest to him was a bill that increased his brother's fees in connection with his work as territorial secretary. This bill, which Mark was successful in having passed, required every corporation doing business in the territory to record the full text of its charter with the secretary of the territory. The bill was entirely justified.

Mark Twain kept an eagle eye on the doings of the legislature. Members were conscious of his discerning attention; whenever a move in his estimation bad was made, there was bound to be publicity. If a bad law was passed, Mark rushed to print with a denunciation of skulduggery; if a good law cleared up a previously bad situation, he frequently had more than a casual word to say about the matter. When the legislature passed a law restricting the number of notaries public in the territory, Mark wrote a satirical sketch on conditions with respect to notaries up to that time. The sketch, entitled "Concerning Notaries," appeared in the *Enterprise* early in the year 1864 and was reprinted in the *Golden Era* on February 28, 1864. "Concerning Notaries" is a vast improvement over any previous Western writing of Mark Twain that is extant. There is more real humor without the coarseness of previous sketches. It is far removed from such strained effects as the Empire City massacre story. It is more rounded out, more complete, more

---

[15] Paine, *Biography*, I, 244 ff.   [16] *Ibid.*, p. 244.

convincing, more entertaining than earlier attempts. It still employs exaggeration, but does it in a pleasing, effective manner. It employs irony in a way that predicted the successful use of this device in later writings.

Reprinting the sketch on notaries, the *Golden Era* refers to Mark Twain as the "wild humorist of the Sage Brush Hills" who writes to the *Territorial Enterprise* from Carson City, "telling all about the Legislature, Governor Nye, and the rest of mankind at Nevada's Capital."[17] The Carson City letters of Mark Twain were obviously attracting more than a casual interest on the Pacific Coast. And the reference to Mark as the "wild humorist of the Sage Brush Hills" indicates that the Western newspapers were looking to Mark Twain as a possible equal of Artemus Ward, who had not long before been on his Western lecture tour. As reprinted in the *Golden Era,* the sketch on notaries opens with Mark being amazed at an occurrence in Carson City:

A strange, strange thing occurred here yesterday, to wit:

A MAN APPLIED FOR A NOTARY'S COMMISSION

Think of it. Ponder over it. He wanted a notarial commission—he said so himself. He was from Storey county. He brought his little petition along with him. He brought it on two stages. It is voluminous. The County Surveyor is chaining it off. Three shifts of clerks will be employed night and day on it, deciphering the signatures and testing their genuineness. They began unrolling the petition at noon, and people of strong mining proclivities began locating claims on it. We are too late, you know. But then they say the extensions are just as good as the original. I believe you.

After writing this much, Mark presumably goes out to investigate, and finds that his news wasn't so sensational, after all, as there are already seventeen hundred and forty-two applications for notaryships on file in the governor's office. "There are also as much as eleven cords of petitions stacked up in his back yard. A watchman stands guard over this combustible material—the back yard is not insured." Mark goes out to investigate some more, and runs into a "seedy, ornery, ratty, hang-dog-looking stranger" named Billson, who insists he has been yearning to meet Mark.

[17] *Golden Era,* February 28, 1864.

He said "D—n it, old Quill-driver, you must come and take a drink with me;" and says I, "D—n it, old Vermin-ranch, I'll do it." (I had him there.) We took a drink, and he told the bar-keeper to charge it. After which, he opened a well-filled carpet-sack and took out a shirt-collar and a petition. He then threw the empty carpet sack aside and unrolled several yards of the petition—"just for a starter," he said. "Now," says he, "Mark, have you got a good deal of influence with Governor Nye?" "Unbounded," says I, with honest pride; "when I go and use my influence with Governor Nye, and tell him it will be a great personal favor to me if he will do so and so, he always says it will be a real pleasure to him—that if it were any other man —any other man in the world—but seeing it's me, he won't." Mr. Billson then remarked that I was the very man; he wanted a little notarial appointment, and he would like me to mention it to the Governor. I said I would, and turned away, resolved to damn young Billson's official aspirations with a mild dose of my influence.

Ten steps farther on, Mark meets a cordial, travel-stained individual, who shakes hands so enthusiastically in greeting that Mark has to straighten his mashed knuckle joints back into place. It is Borias, from Washoe, good old Borias. They gobble cocktails in the nearest saloon. Borias mentions, just incidentally, that he wants a notaryship, and wonders if Mark can't help along a little.

Next comes J. Bidlecome Dusenberry of Esmeralda, formerly of the City of New York. He observes casually that he has a petition. And there are Chief Justice Turner, and William Stewart, and Sandy Baldwin, and scores of others, with pack trains and wagons loaded with petitions.

Mark continues down the street, examining the petition of every man he meets. It becomes a monomania with him. Finally, he stumbles upon a "pensive, travel-worn stranger, leaning against an awning-post." Mark is curious.

I went up and looked at him. He looked at me. I looked at him again, and again he looked at me. I bent my gaze upon him once more, and says I, "Well?" He looked at me very hard, and says he "Well—well what?" Says I, "Well—I would like to examine your petition, if you please." He looked very much astonished—I may say amazed. When he had recovered his presence of mind, he says, "What the devil do you mean?" I explained to him that I only wanted to glance over his petition for a notaryship. He said he believed I was a lunatic—he didn't like the unhealthy light in my eye, and he didn't want me to come any closer to him.

Mark explains the situation, and the two become friendly. The stranger swears that he has just arrived in Carson City, and doesn't want any notaryship. Mark feels that it is his turn to treat, by thunder. They enter a deserted saloon and drink up its contents.

We lay upon a billiard table in a torpid condition for several minutes, but at last my exile rose up and muttered in a sepulchral voice, "I feel it— O Heavens, I feel it in me veins!" "Feel what?" says I, alarmed. "I feel— O me sainted mother! I feel—feel—a hankering to be a Notary Public!" And he tore down several yards of wall-paper, and fell to writing a petition on it. Poor devil—he had got it at last, and got it bad. I was seized with the fatal distemper a moment afterward. I wrote a petition with frantic haste, appended a copy of the Directory of Nevada Territory to it, and we fled down the deserted streets to the Governor's office.

But I must draw the curtain upon these harrowing scenes—the very memory of them scorches my brain. Ah, this Legislature has much to answer for in cutting down the number of Notaries Public in this Territory, with their infernal new law.

Mark Twain's writings during this session of the territorial legislature gave him more favorable publicity than anything he had done previously. He was recognized now as being capable of writing more than merely coarse burlesques. He had developed a certain repression in his articles; he was experiencing for the first time the effectiveness of social satire; he was prepared to develop the new vein he had discovered in his Carson City prospecting. When he returned to Virginia City his position as a character of importance was so well established that he and Dan De Quille could safely indulge in personal badinage in the *Enterprise* without the danger of boring the readers. On May 1, 1864, the *Golden Era* remarks that "recent issues of the *Territorial Enterprise* give the particulars of a series of terrible calamities that have befallen two of the literary celebrities of Silver Land." Under the heading, " 'Mark Twain' and 'Dan De Quille,' Hors de Combat," the *Golden Era* reprints the playful controversy between the two *Enterprise* writers. Mark writes of a disastrous accident to his confrere and roommate, and describes the torn and mutilated body of Dan, that is, what was left of him after he was thrown from a horse. He adds, however, that Dan "is recovering fast, and what is left of him will be around the breweries again to-day, just as usual."[18] Dan comes back in kind, describing what happened to Mark's nose when that gentleman took a lesson in the manly art.

The next development of significance in connection with Mark Twain's work on the staff of the *Territorial Enterprise* was to be the last of his writing activities on the Comstock Lode. With startling suddenness he was engaged in an editorial controversy with a rival Virginia City newspaper. Within a few weeks, the editorial fight flared up, a duel was arranged, a warrant was signed, and Mark Twain was leaving the scene of his first two years as a writer on the frontier.

An array of varied stories has been told about Mark Twain's Comstock duel. Taking their lead from Twain himself, many narrators have allowed their imaginations to run riot, although, with respect to the duel incident, Mark was strangely silent in later years. He leaves the story out of *Roughing It,* where his version might very well have been given. Probably the newspaper files of the time are the best authority for the details of Twain's last editorial controversy on the Comstock Lode. One thing is certain: the controversy involved the "Flour Sack Sanitary Fund," which was being collected on the Comstock for the relief of wounded Union soldiers. The first meeting in Virginia City for the "Sanitary Fund" was thus announced by the *Virginia City Union:*

To-day, at 2 o'clock, the long deferred mammoth Sanitary meeting will be held at the Opera House. The announcement alone ought to fill the house, but when it is remembered that sweet singers, eloquent orators, pretty ladies, and a fine brass band will be in attendance, who can stay away? Turn out for the honor of Nevada! Turn out for the sake of loyalty and humanity. Listen to the cry of suffering from our wounded thousands on the road to Richmond, and fill the building with an eager throng of humane, generous-hearted givers.[19]

[18] *Golden Era,* May 1, 1864.   [19] *Virginia City Union,* May 15, 1864.

In an article on the following day, the *Union* told of the enthusiastic response of the people of Virginia City to the fund but condemned the mining companies for not being more generous in their donations. "The contributions of yesterday," said the *Union,* "were, with a few honorable exceptions, made by the miners, merchants, mechanics and professional men of Nevada. The great companies, which could easily have afforded to donate a quarter of a million from their coffers, were generally most shamefully indifferent."[20] But what led to serious trouble for Twain was a dispute, between the *Union*[21] and the *Enterprise,* concerning newspaper workers' donations to the fund. Joseph Goodman was away from Virginia City at the time, and Twain was in charge of the *Enterprise.* The ensuing trouble reminds one of the editorial controversy in which Samuel Clemens had engaged while his brother was away on a Tennessee trip, back in the Hannibal days. Now, on the Comstock, Mark Twain was experienced in newspaper warfare, and the strife assumed major proportions in a very short time. Files of the *Enterprise* of that time not being extant, we turn to other newspapers for reprints of Mark Twain's editorials and for the *Union's* editorials. Following up editorials in the *Enterprise,* the *Union,* thoroughly aroused, replied, under the heading, "The 'How Is It' Issue":

When last the Sanitary Commission called for aid, the publishers and employes of the Virginia *Daily Union* unostentatiously united with their generous fellow citizens and contributed the sum of five hundred and fifteen dollars.[22] We have paid that sum in gold to the Treasurer of the Sanitary Fund for Storey county. The *Territorial Enterprise* newspaper has only pretended to contribute. It has paid nothing of the contributions which it, with great self-show, promised—always in the presence of a crowd. This sort of showing off was not sufficient in itself. The *Enterprise* must contemptibly boast of its liberality over the *Union,* and, in the most unmanly manner, carry its unwarrantable assertions so far as to say that the gentlemen in the employ of the *Union* would not pay their subscriptions. We showed the utter and unprecedented meanness of the *Enterprise* in this

---

[20] *Virginia City Union,* May 17, 1864.

[21] Not the *Chronicle,* as Paine records.

[22] The editor was mistaken as to the amount, which should have been three hundred and fifteen dollars, as shown by other references.

instance, and that paper yesterday returned a string of despicable stuff knotted so full of lies that there was not left a space sufficient for the smallest thread of truth. Never before, in a long period of newspaper intercourse— never before in any contact with a contemporary, however unprincipled he might have been, have we found an opponent in statement or in discussion, who had no gentlemanly sense of professional propriety, who conveyed in every word, and in every purpose of all his words, such a groveling disregard for truth, decency and courtesy, as to seem to court the distinction only of being understood as a vulgar liar. Meeting one who prefers falsehood; whose instincts are all toward falsehood; whose thought is falsification; whose aim is vilification through insincere professions of honesty; one whose only merit is thus described, and who evidently desires to be thus known, the obstacles presented are entirely insurmountable, and whoever would touch them fully, should expect to be abominably defiled.[23]

This is the opinion that James L. Laird, editor of the *Union,* had of Mark Twain. In the same issue of the *Union* in which this editorial by Laird appeared there was published a communication, signed "Printer," in which employees of the *Union* took Twain to task:

"HOW IT IS."

Virginia *Daily Union:*—The editor of the *Daily Enterprise* has, during the last two days, in his anxiety to injure a cotemporary, seen fit to place before the public in a false light, and slander in a cowardly manner the printers of this city. We refer to his misrepresentation of the circumstance attending our donation to the Sanitary Fund. We wish it distinctly understood that we have no sympathy whatever in any issue between the proprietors of the *Union* and *Enterprise.* Nor do we entertain any feeling of rivalry toward our fellow-craftsmen employed on that paper. We consider that what redounds to our credit is equally due to them. The editor of the *Enterprise* has asserted that but for *his* promptings, the employes of the *Union* would never have paid their last contribution. In this he wilfully *lies.* The employes of the *Union* were in no way instigated to make the donation by their employers, and never contemplated repudiating it. Thursday morning's *Union* gave a full list of the men who had donated the money, and the receipt of Mr. Black, Secretary of the Sanitary Fund, attesting that it ($315) had been paid. This should have removed all doubts, if any existed, as to who were the donors. Why does not the editor of the *Enterprise* accuse Mr. George F. Jones, Mr. De Long and many other prominent citizens who subscribed repeatedly during the evening, of being influenced to do so by a spirit of rivalry toward his establishment?

[23] *Virginia City Union,* May 21, 1864.

We can only view his blackguardism as an attack upon members of our craft. In asserting that we "had not intended to pay the bill, but on secondary consideration, and for the sake of saving an entirely imaginary reputation for virtue and honesty, concluded to do so," he has endeavored to misinterpret the generous, patriotic promptings of laboring men who gave their little mite willingly; and in so doing he has proved himself an unmitigated *liar, a poltroon and a puppy.*

PRINTER.[24]

This is the opinion that the *Daily Union* printers had of Mark Twain at the moment. The communication had been prepared by J. W. Wilmington, a member of the *Union's* printing force. Twain immediately took personal offense at the two items in the *Union.* There was an exchange of personal notes between the editors. In reprinting these notes, the *Sacramento Union* observed that sharp notes had been appearing in the *Enterprise,*

between Samuel Clemens, of that paper, and J. W. Wilmington and James Laird, of the *Union* office, on account of the appearance in the latter journal of two articles which reflected somewhat severely on Clemens. Clemens demanded of Laird, one of the publishers of the *Union,* a retraction of, or satisfaction for, the alleged insults.[25]

Evidently Twain had wasted no time in sending a sharp note to Laird of the *Union,* since Wilmington, according to the Sacramento paper's reprint, replied as follows:

Office of the *Virginia Daily Union,*
VIRGINIA, May 21, 1864.

SAMUEL CLEMENS: James Laird has just handed me your note of this date. Permit me to say that I am the author of the article appearing in this morning's *Union.* I am responsible for it. I have nothing to retract.
Respectfully,
J. W. WILMINGTON.[26]

Twain replied by sending another note to Laird, in which he accused Laird of shirking responsibility. Laird, then, sent a note upholding Wilmington, who, he said, was formerly one of the proprietors of the *Cincinnati Enquirer* and, as captain of a company in the Sixth Ohio Regiment, had fought at Shiloh. He insisted that Mark must meet on the field of honor with Wilmington.

[24] *Virginia City Union,* May 21, 1864.
[25] *Sacramento Union,* May 26, 1864.   [26] *Ibid.,* May 26, 1864.

The "liar, poltroon and puppy" designation of Wilmington's note was mentioned twice in this note by Laird.

To this Mark replied that he had objected even more to Laird's editorial than he had to Wilmington's communication. "In the meantime," he wrote to Laird, "if you do not wish yourself posted as a coward, you will at once accept my peremptory challenge, which I now reiterate." Another note from Laird resulted in the following from Mark Twain:

I denounce Laird as an unmitigated liar, because he says I published an editorial in which I attacked the printers employed on the *Union,* whereas there is nothing in that editorial which can be so construed. Moreover, he is a liar on general principles, and from natural instinct. I denounce him as an abject coward, because it has been stated in his paper that its proprietors are responsible for all articles appearing in its columns, yet he backs down from that position; because he acknowledges the "code," but will not live up to it; because he says himself that he is responsible for all "editorials," and then backs down from that also; and because he insults me in his note marked "IV," and yet refuses to fight me. Finally, he is a fool, because he cannot understand that a publisher is bound to stand responsible for any and all articles printed by him, whether he wants to do it or not.

SAM. L. CLEMENS.[27]

At the end of its column of reprints of the Clemens-Laird notes, the *Sacramento Union* adds: "There was no fighting at last accounts."[28] Two days later, the *San Francisco Call,* under the heading, "The Duello in Virginia," reviews the Clemens-Laird notes and adds this comment:

It is well, perhaps, that only ink instead of blood has been shed in this affair, but it would have appeared better if neither had been spilt. The day has gone by when duels can give any man credit for bravery or honor, wisdom or truth; and to call people fools, cowards, poltroons, liars, puppies, and other flattering names, does not make them so, nor prove them so. It simply shows that passion and not good sense has been for a time the master.[29]

In addition to the controversy that Mark Twain had stirred up with the *Union,* there arose another with the ladies of Carson

[27] *Sacramento Union,* May 26, 1864.   [28] *Ibid.,* May 26, 1864.
[29] *San Francisco Call,* May 28, 1864.

City. The subject concerned was the matter of disposition of certain money collected by the ladies for the "Sanitary Fund." An editorial of Mark Twain's published in the *Enterprise* on May 18[30] had aroused the ire of the Carson ladies. They sent a note to the *Enterprise,* which made no mention of it. The note was then sent to the *Union* and was printed in the rival paper:

CARSON CITY, May 18th, 1864.

EDITORS OF THE *Enterprise:* In your issue of yesterday, you state "that the reason the Flour Sack was not taken from Dayton to Carson, was because it was stated that the money raised at the Sanitary Fancy Dress Ball, recently held in Carson for the St. Louis Fair, had been diverted from its legitimate course, and was to be sent to aid a Miscegenation Society somewhere in the East; and it was feared the proceeds of the sack might be similarly disposed of." You apparently mollify the statement by saying "that it was a hoax, but not all a hoax, for an effort is being made to divert those funds from their proper course."

In behalf of the ladies who originated and assisted in carrying out the programme, let us say that the whole statement is a *tissue of falsehoods,* made for *malicious* purposes, and we demand the name of the author. The ball was gotten up in aid of the Sanitary Commission, and *not* for the St. Louis Fair. At a meeting of the ladies, held in this city last week, no decision was arrived at as to whether the proceeds of the ball should be sent to St. Louis or New York, but one thing *was decided,* that they should go to the aid of the sick and wounded soldiers, who are fighting the battles of our country, *and for no other purpose.* . . . . the ladies having the matter in charge, consider themselves capable of deciding as to what shall be done with the money, without the aid of outsiders, who are probably desirous of acquiring some *glory* by appropriating the efforts of the ladies to themselves.

MRS. W. K. CUTLER, *President.*
MRS. H. F. RICE, *Vice President.*
MRS. S. D. KING, *Treasurer.*
MRS. H. H. ROSS, *Sec'y. San. Ball.*[31]

By this time Mark Twain was in trouble in both Virginia City and Carson City. He had been too hasty in his editorial comments. While his battle with the *Union* was going on he received the note from the Carson City ladies and was unwilling to apologize

[30] This is the date given in a note to the *Union;* May 17 is indicated in the letter below.
[31] *Virginia City Union,* May 27, 1864.

to them at that particular time because of the possible embarrassment to himself. He learned, however, that Mrs. Orion Clemens
was being snubbed by the ladies of Carson; so he wrote a letter
to Mrs. Cutler, in which he explained his difficulty with the
Union and how he had been prevented from publishing an apology
for the Carson editorial. He added:

> But my chief object, Mrs. Cutler, in writing you this note (and you will
> pardon the liberty I have taken,) was to thank you very kindly and sin-
> cerely for the consideration you have shown me in this matter, and for your
> continued friendship for Mollie while others are disposed to withdraw theirs
> on account of a fault for which I alone am responsible.[32]

The Laird-Clemens duel never did materialize, despite the
many stories told of that duel in later years by Mark Twain, Steve
Gillis, and numerous others. However, there was still trouble
enough. A new law had been passed in Nevada making it a
felony even to send or to accept a challenge to a duel. Faced with
the threat of arrest and imprisonment, Mark Twain, accompanied
by Steve Gillis, left for San Francisco at the end of May 1864: "So
ended Mark Twain's career on the Comstock. He had come to
it a weary pilgrim, discouraged and unknown; he was leaving it
with a new name and fame—elate, triumphant, even if a fugitive."[33]

The members of the *Enterprise* staff were sorry to see Mark go,
and there is reason to believe that the people generally on the Comstock Lode were also sorry. Rival newspapers on the Lode, having
felt the sting of Twain's satire, were not emotionally overcome.
The *Union* was silent concerning his departure. The *Gold Hill
News,* a mile away from Virginia City, having ridiculed the Laird-
Clemens controversy in several editorials, had this to say, among
other things, after Twain had left the Comstock:

> Is it necessary to say that we allude to the lamented Twain? That loved
> and lost journalist, tortured by a demand for "news" when it was not, did
> manufacture some that he fondly believed would satisfy the public craving.
> He filled the pine forest at Dutch Nick's with the ghastly corpses of the
> Hopkins family, and sprinkled the road to Carson with gore from the

---

[32] Paine, *Letters,* I, 98.
[33] Paine, *Biography,* I, 252.

vermillion scalp of the apocryphal mother of those mythical slain. That "news" satisfied the greedy mind of the public, and it stared itself out of countenance in frozen horror for a few brief hours, and was content. But mark the sequel: the indignation of the non-manufacturer and the dia-bolical damnation of the deceived. The fate of that unhappy man is ever before us, and warns us to avoid the rock upon which he split whenever we are asked "What's the news?"[34]

Even without the editorial troubles of May 1864 Mark Twain would not have remained on the Comstock Lode indefinitely. He had become interested in wider fields, and although he might have gone less precipitately under different circumstances, there is no reason to believe that he would not soon have been going out to seek better literary contacts and opportunities. However, the two years on the Comstock Lode as a reporter on the *Territorial Enter-prise* had definitely contributed to Mark Twain's development as a writer. From the very beginning of his connection with the *Enterprise* the newspaper had given him virtually a free rein. It would be difficult, probably, to think of any other paper as in-fluential and well-known as the *Enterprise* that would have given him similar freedom. Of course this freedom was in some respects harmful. Twain wrote sometimes with too little restraint; there was frequently a coarseness or an over-zealousness that needed ton-ing down. But this was not serious, and the good points of the sort of position he enjoyed on the *Enterprise* outnumbered the bad points.

On the *Enterprise* Mark Twain first took up writing as a career. On the *Enterprise* he adopted the pen name that was to become famous the world over. On the *Enterprise* he first attracted a read-ing public beyond his own locality, his work gaining the notice even of Eastern publications. Before coming to the Comstock Lode, Samuel Clemens had served three apprenticeships, with none of them resulting in the choice of a life work. When Mark Twain left the Comstock Lode, he had served his final apprenticeship; he had made writing his career.

[34] *Gold Hill Daily News,* June 8, 1864.

CHAPTER 7

BOHEMIA
AND JACKASS HILL

ENTERING easily into the literary company of San Francisco's Bohemia late in May 1864 required no apology on the part of Mark Twain. His work as a writer on the *Territorial Enterprise* had given him wide notoriety, and in previous visits to San Francisco he had been treated as a celebrity.[1] Twain had a wide acquaintance in San Francisco and had a good comprehension of its reputation as a literary center when he came there in May 1864.

With his companion, Steve Gillis, Mark settled down, temporarily, to a steady job. Gillis took a job as compositor on the *San Francisco Morning Call* and Mark joined the staff of the paper as a reporter. The two young men lived together, going from one lodging to another with frequency. By the time they had been in San Francisco four months they had changed their lodgings five times and their hotel twice.

From the first, it appears, Twain was dissatisfied with his position on the *Call*. The contrast with the *Enterprise* was too much for him. Under Joseph T. Goodman, and in association with other brilliant journalists in small Virginia City, he had enjoyed a literary freedom that he could never hope to command in the metropolitan journalism of San Francisco. On the *Enterprise* he had been a free spirit; he could free-lance to his heart's content. On the *Call* he was merely another staff member, and as such was compelled to follow

---

[1] See the letter from the *Golden Era*, September 27, 1863, quoted above, pp. 83–84.

the rules of the paper, particularly where the politics of the *Call* was concerned.

In this uncongenial atmosphere, Twain's literary ability was cramped, at least with respect to his contributions to the *Call*. It was a steady, regular job—too steady and too regular for his adventurous, free soul. We have no way of knowing how much he wrote for the *Call* during the time he was on its staff; of the several severely critical articles he is said to have then written, only one seems to have appeared in that newspaper.[2] Previously, while he was a reporter for the *Enterprise,* he had sent several articles to the *Call,* and these were published, evidently not being in opposition to the policies of the paper. Now, as a staff member, writing about local affairs, he found himself unable to write the sort of thing his newspaper wanted.

In San Francisco, Mark Twain's humor became more and more impregnated with social reproof, and the *Call* felt no particular obligation to publish this kind of copy. However, one item did achieve publication, probably because the *Call's* vanity had been hurt. It was a sharp denunciation of an undertaker whose establishment was conducted as a branch of the coroner's office. Writing to his mother and sister on September 25, 1864, Twain told of his controversy with the coroner's deputy:

> I have triumphed. They refused me and other reporters some information at a branch of the Coroner's office—Massey's undertaker establishment, a few weeks ago. I published the wickedest article on them I ever wrote in my life, and you can rest assured we got all the information we wanted after that.[3]

As a practical joke, someone had made a false entry on the information slate kept at the shop. The *Alta,* the *Bulletin,* and the *Flag* each published the misleading item and, upon discovering its falsity, rebuked the coroner's deputy for allowing the item to go to the newspapers. The undertaker thereupon removed the slate from his office and refused further information to reporters. In his ar-

[2] Paine, *Biography,* I, 258.
[3] Paine, *Mark Twain's Letters* (Harper & Bros.), I, 100.

ticle, captioned "A Small Piece of Spite," Twain severely criticized
Coroner Sheldon and his assistants for denying to the public this
vital information. He felt that the people would not see the propriety of the coroner's hiding the affairs of his office from them,
"in order that the small-potato malice of his employes against two
or three newspaper reporters may be gratified." As for the employes, he was distrustful of them:

> You see the dead-cart leaving the place, and ask one of them where it
> is bound, and without looking up from his newspaper, he grunts, lazily,
> and says, "*Stiff,*" meaning that it is going in quest of the corpse of some
> poor creature whose earthly troubles are over. You ask one of them a dozen
> questions calculated to throw more light upon a meagre entry in the slate,
> and he invariably answers, "*Don't know*"—as if the grand end and aim of
> his poor existence was not to know anything, and to come as near accom-
> plishing his mission as his opportunities would permit. They would vote
> for General Jackson at the "Body-snatchers' Retreat," but for the misfor-
> tune that they "don't know" such a person existed. What do you suppose
> the people would ever know about how their interests were being attended
> to if the employes in all public offices were such unmitigated ignoramuses
> as these? One of these fellows said to us yesterday, "We have taken away
> the slate; we are not going to give you any more information; the reporters
> have got too sharp—by George, they know more'n *we* do!" God help the
> reporter that don't! It is as fervent a prayer as ever welled up from the
> bottom of our heart.[4]

While he was on the staff of the *Call,* Twain came into association with many literary figures in San Francisco's Bohemia, among
whom were Bret Harte, Prentice Mulford, Charles Warren Stod-
dard, Fitzhugh Ludlow, Orpheus C. Kerr, and Joaquin Miller.
Many of the city's important literary figures gathered in the offices
of the *Golden Era,* California's first literary publication. Fraterniz-
ing with this group, Twain soon became a leading figure in the
San Francisco literary world, and, like the others, a contributor to
the *Golden Era* and the *Californian.*

Twain had already contributed two articles to the *Golden Era*
before he left Virginia City. These were "How to Cure a Cold,"
published September 20, 1863, and "The Great Prize Fight," pub-

---

[4] *San Francisco Call,* September 6, 1864.

lished October 11, 1863. Although he was later to express some dissatisfaction with the literary tone of the *Golden Era,* he no doubt welcomed the opportunity to contribute to it when he first came to join San Francisco's literary circle. The first issue of the *Golden Era* had appeared on December 19, 1852, and although it called itself "a weekly family newspaper—devoted to literature, agriculture, the mining interest, local and foreign news, commerce, education and the fine arts," it filled its columns chiefly with literary material. It was really a magazine; only in size and typography did it resemble a newspaper.

Mark Twain's first contribution to the *Golden Era* after he came to live in San Francisco was a sketch entitled "Evidence in the Case of Smith vs. Jones," a burlesque in which conflicting testimony is offered by witnesses called in an assault case. The article was published June 26, 1864.

His next contribution to the *Golden Era* was a sketch called "Early Rising, as Regards Excursions to the Cliff House." In this he attempts to show that Benjamin Franklin was wrong in advising a man to go to bed early and arise early. Mark tells how he tried out Franklin's method in Virginia City, in fact, had gone so far as to view the sunrise four times a week for a limited time on the Comstock Lode; and instead of growing healthier on account of it, he got to looking blue, and pulpy, and swelled, like a drowned man, and his relations grew alarmed and thought they were going to lose him.

They entirely despaired of my recovery, at one time, and began to grieve for me as one whose days were numbered—whose fate was sealed—who was soon to pass away from them forever, and from the glad sunshine, and the birds, and the odorous flowers, and murmuring brooks, and whispering winds, and all the cheerful scenes of life, and go down into the dark and silent tomb—and they went forth sorrowing, and jumped a lot in the graveyard, and made up their minds to grin and bear it with that fortitude which is the true Christian's brightest ornament.[5]

However, Mark had determined to give Franklin's proverb one more test, so he had gone with a friend on an excursion to the

[5] *Golden Era,* July 3, 1864.

Cliff House, starting at four in the morning. They had almost frozen to death in the bracing atmosphere, everything had smelt of horse-blankets, the fog had sometimes shut even the horse from view, and the two excursionists were human icicles when they reached the Ocean House and found no fire there. Mark reports banishing all hope, going back on his "religion," and seeking "surcease of sorrow in soothing blasphemy." Finally, they were served coffee by a melancholy individual whose gravity was so impressive and so appropriate to the surroundings that it thawed out some of Mark's better instincts, and Mark told him that "he might ask a blessing if he thought it would lighten him up any— because he looked as if he wanted to very bad—but he only shook his head resignedly and sighed. . . . . 'Put no trust'," Mark warns, " 'in the benefits to accrue from early rising, as set forth by the infatuated Franklin—but stake the last cent of your substance on the judgment of old George Washington, the Father of his Country, who said 'he couldn't see it.' " After the publication of this article, another year passed before Twain was again a contributor to the *Golden Era.*

The next important literary connection which Mark Twain had in San Francisco was with the *Californian.* Late in 1863, Bret Harte and Charles Henry Webb—"Bret" and "Inigo"—"were becoming restive at playing second fiddles for the provincial *Era,* and were considering the foundation of a larger magazine over which they would themselves have some editorial control."[6] On Saturday, May 28, 1864, the first number of the *Californian* appeared, with C. H. Webb as editor and publisher and Bret Harte as chief contributor. It was a small folio of sixteen pages, with a three-column makeup except for the last two advertising pages, which were arranged in a four-column typography. In the first number of the magazine, and at the very time that Mark Twain was leaving Virginia City and its Comstock Lode journalism for

---

[6] George R. Stewart, Jr., *A Bibliography of the Writings of Bret Harte in the Magazines and Newspapers of California, 1857–1871* (University of California Press, Berkeley, California, 1933), p. 146.

the San Francisco Bohemia, appeared a notice about Twain's controversy with Laird of the *Union:*

A belligerent correspondence has been passing between a couple of editors in Virginia City. It is none of our business, but we should regret if any hostile meeting occurred. Why should one editor desire to give another out for even a single "insertion," in the cold ground, as "leaded matter"? Bullets are not arguments, and blood never washed a stain out from any character. Duels at best are but the fooling and foolish relics of the exploded custom of a barbarous age, and the sooner the duel is permitted to lapse into desuetude, the better.[7]

On September 10, 1864, a notice in the *Golden Era* announced that Bret Harte had become editor of the magazine:

In the change of a name at the head of this paper, and of a personal influence in its columns, the undersigned trusts will hereafter be found the only essential alteration in that general character and design which have made it acceptable to its readers.

F. B. Harte.

Harte's editorship lasted until November 19, 1864; later he was again editor for a short period, December 9 to 30, 1865. It was shortly after Harte's first assumption of the editorship that Mark Twain's first contribution to the *Californian* appeared. This sketch, "A Notable Conundrum," published on October 1, 1864, was followed by other articles almost every week for more than two months, until Twain left San Francisco for the Tuolumne hills.

For a year after July 3, 1864, nothing by Mark Twain appeared in the *Golden Era.* The fact that the *Californian* was considered by many to be superior to the *Golden Era* in both typography and literary quality no doubt had much to do with this. In a letter to his mother and his sister, dated September 25, 1864, Twain writes of his preference for the newer magazine:

I have engaged to write for the new literary paper—the "Californian"— same pay I used to receive on the "Golden Era"—one article a week, fifty dollars a month. I quit the "Era," long ago. It wasn't high-toned enough. The "Californian" circulates among the highest class of the community, and is the best weekly literary paper in the United States—and I suppose I ought to know.[8]

[7] *Californian,* May 28, 1864.
[8] Paine, *Mark Twain's Letters* (Harper & Bros., 1917), I, 100.

Shortly after he arrived in San Francisco, Twain sent to the
Enterprise an article that the *Golden Era* reprinted under the
heading, " 'Mark Twain' in the Metropolis." In its introduction,
the *Golden Era* says: "The Sage-Brush Humorist from Silver-
Land, 'Mark Twain,' has come to town, and stops at the Occidental."[9]

In this article Mark writes of the Occidental Hotel as Heaven
on the half-shell, of the lively San Francisco theaters, and of Fred.
Franks, his favorite Washoe tragedian, "whose name they have
put in small letters in the programme, when it deserves to be in
capitals—because, whatever part they give him to play, don't he
always play it well? and does he not possess the first virtue of a
comedian, which is to do humorous things with grave decorum
and without seeming to know that they are funny?" Here Twain
gives an interpretation of humor which he was to repeat several
times in later writings. He goes on in the article to tell of the
birds, and the flowers, and the Chinamen, and the winds of San
Francisco, and cannot understand why the natives are always com-
plaining:

> But it is human nature to find fault—to overlook that which is pleasant
> to the eye, and seek after that which is distasteful to it. You take a stranger
> into the Bank Exchange and show him the magnificent picture of Sampson
> and Delilah, and what is the first object he notices?—Sampson's fine face
> and flaming eye? or the noble beauty of his form? or the lovely, half-nude
> Delilah? or the muscular Philistine behind Sampson, who is furtively ad-
> miring her charms? or the perfectly counterfeited folds of the rich drapery
> below her knees? or the symmetry and truth to nature of Sampson's left
> foot? No, sir, the first thing that catches his eye is the scissors on the floor
> at Delilah's feet, and the first thing he says, "Them scissors is too modern—
> there warn't no scissors like that in them days, by a d—d sight!"

The routine job of news-gathering on the *Call* soon palled on
Mark Twain. The impersonal nature of the work dampened his
enthusiasm; he felt keenly the loss of that freedom of expression
which had been allowed him when he was a reporter on the
Comstock Lode. He detested the drudgery of serving as a cog
in the *Call* machine; as he wrote later:

[9] *Golden Era*, June 26, 1864.

At nine in the morning I had to be at the police court for an hour and make a brief history of the squabbles of the night before. They were usually between Irishmen and Irishmen, and Chinamen and Chinamen, with now and then a squabble between the two races, for a change.

During the rest of the day we raked the town from end to end, gathering such material as we might, wherewith to fill our required columns; and if there were no fires to report, we started some. At night we visited the six theaters, one after the other, seven nights in the week. We remained in each of those places five minutes, got the merest passing glimpse of play and opera, and with that for a text we "wrote up" those plays and operas, as the phrase goes, torturing our souls every night in the effort to find something to say about those performances which we had not said a couple of hundred times before.

It was fearful drudgery—soulless drudgery—and almost destitute of interest. It was awful slavery for a lazy man.[10]

Probably the work on the *Call* was not as bad as this would lead one to believe, for these memories were written down many years after Twain had left the West. But certainly he did lose interest, and his connection with the newspaper became unsatisfactory both to himself and to his employer. He had previously induced the *Call* to pay him $25 a week and let him work only in the daytime, his hours then becoming from ten in the morning until five or six in the afternoon. The paper had even furnished Mark with an assistant to help him gather the news. But this had not cured Mark's indifference to his duties. Finally, an interview with George E. Barnes, one of the *Call's* editors, resulted in Twain's resignation from the paper. The *Roughing It* account is probably fanciful:

Suffice it that I so lost heart, and so yielded myself up to repinings and sighings and foolish regrets (about a mining investment), that I neglected my duties and became about worthless, as a reporter for a brisk newspaper. And at last one of the proprietors took me aside, with a clarity I still remember with considerable respect, and gave me an opportunity to resign my berth and so save myself the disgrace of a dismissal.[11]

This is merely another of the many instances of Twain's predilection for exaggerating his shortcomings. Barnes later declared that

[10] Paine, *Mark Twain: A Biography* (Harper & Bros., 1912), I, 257.
[11] Mark Twain, *Roughing It*, pp. 169–70.

Twain had resigned with great willingness. The various stories told of the supposed discharge from the *Call* have probably arisen from many different stories which Twain himself told of the incident.

Complications in San Francisco were increased for Mark Twain by certain letters he was sending to his old newspaper, the *Territorial Enterprise*. In his *Enterprise* correspondence he assailed San Francisco officials for the political corruption that existed in the city. He was specific in his references, called names, pictured the scene just as he saw it, and drew down the wrath of the city's officials. Especially were the police incensed at the ferocity of the attacks that Twain made upon them through the columns of the *Enterprise*. Finally, Martin G. Burke, San Francisco's chief of police, filed a libel suit against the *Enterprise*. But even this did not stop Mark Twain or the *Enterprise*. The San Francisco correspondent sent to the Comstock Lode a still more forceful letter, describing the police corruption in the city and the lechery that was openly permitted. Goodman published the letter in full.

At the time when Twain was having all this controversy with San Francisco's officials, Steve Gillis, his companion, got into trouble with the police. Steve while passing a saloon had observed a fight going on, had joined in it, and was soon in the hands of the police on a charge of assault with intent to kill. It happened that the big bartender whom Steve—a small but scrappy fellow— had picked for his adversary was a friend of Chief of Police Burke. Steve was released, on bail furnished by Mark, and departed for Virginia City. When the case was called, and Steve did not appear, Burke took pleasure in instituting action against the bondsman.

James N. Gillis,[12] brother of Steve, happened to be in San Francisco at the time. He invited Mark to come up to his cabin

---

[12] James Gillis is supposed to be the "Truthful James" of Bret Harte. However, William R. Gillis, brother of James and Steve, writes, in his *Gold Rush Days with Mark Twain* (p. 182), that it was not his brother who was the original of Bret Harte's "Truthful James," but J. W. E. Townsend, a well-known California newspaper worker and a teller of tall stories. Since William Gillis claims, in his book, almost every distinction in sight, one must pause to consider the very definite possibility that his brother was not Harte's "Truthful James."

in the Tuolumne hills until things cooled down in San Francisco. "In that peaceful retreat," says Paine, "were always rest and refreshment for the wayfarer, and more than one weary writer besides Bret Harte had found shelter there. James Gillis himself had fine literary instincts, but he remained a pocket-miner because he loved that quiet pursuit of gold, the Arcadian life, the companionship of his books, the occasional Bohemian pilgrim who found refuge in his retreat."[13]

On December 4, 1864, Mark Twain arrived at Jim Gillis' cabin on Jackass Hill in the Mother Lode country, a few miles from Tuttletown and Sonora. C. C. Goodwin, a Comstock Lode and California journalist of those days, describes Jim Gillis and his hermitage in the hills:

The cabin was in the big pines, the mountains rose like temples in the background and far away to the east, across the range, the setting sun was turning to purple the crest of Mount Bodie.

I did not ask him if he was ever lonely, for I knew that he was not. He had his books, his daily papers, his dogs, his rabbits, his birds and his flowers; his mine, which he worked a little daily, and the murmur of the breeze in the big pines to go to sleep by.

There was nothing of the hermit's exclusiveness about the place. There were no locks on the doors or the cupboard, all passers-by were welcome and moreover, he was an authority in that region. People brought their troubles and differences to him for advice or adjustment and there were no appeals from his decisions.

Then, too, though living there alone, he was fully abreast of all current events, as given day by day through the newspapers, and would drop shrewd remarks as he discussed them. If there was a trace of bitterness or prejudice in his soul, he kept it hid.[14]

Bret Harte had been a visitor at the Jim Gillis cabin. He had come there ragged, hungry, and discouraged. Gillis had befriended him, and had advised him to leave the hills and try the newspapers of San Francisco. He gave the young man $50 to help him on his way. When Gillis visited Harte a few months later in San Francisco, Harte snubbed him; in fact, he was offended, and could

[13] Paine, *Biography*, I, 265–66.
[14] Goodwin, *As I Remember Them* (Salt Lake Commercial Club, 1913), p. 92.

think of nothing except the money which he owed, though Gillis himself had written the loan off his books and had come only to congratulate Harte on his San Francisco success. Here was one of the many instances where Harte insisted upon considering as enemies those from whom he had borrowed money. Bret Harte became an unpleasant memory to kindly Jim Gillis, who, of all men, had not a trace of any aptitude for making enemies.

Between Jim Gillis and Mark Twain the relations were entirely different. From the time that the two first met they remained friends, and always had a good word for each other. On Jackass Hill Twain found surcease for a troubled mind. Away from the turmoil of San Francisco, in a new and peaceful environment, he could relax, he could reorganize himself. He found here also the opportunity to improve the foundation of his literary career. In the humble cabin of logs and slabs, sheltered by a giant oak, with books at hand, and a fireplace and modest comforts, Mark Twain reached another point in his literary development. Occupying the cabin, in addition to Mark and Jim, were William, a younger Gillis boy, and Dick Stoker and his cat (Dick Baker and his cat, Tom Quartz, of *Roughing It*). There had at one time been great mining activity in the region, but now there was solitude, with only an occasional pocket miner prospecting in the deposits along the Stanislaus River and in the hills of the Mother Lode.

When rainy days kept the family indoors, Jim Gillis stood before the fire and related marvelous stories in which Dick Stoker frequently was the central figure. Stoker took these stories philosophically, never objecting to their extravagance. The story of Dick Baker and his cat, the story of the Jaybird and the Acorn, and the story of the "Burning Shame" were among those which Mark Twain heard here from Jim Gillis. There were visits with other pocket miners in the hills; and romance had some share when Mark and young "Billy" Gillis called on the "Chaparral Quails," the two pretty daughters of an old couple, the Carringtons, who lived a short way from Jackass Hill.

During his interlude at Jackass Hill, Mark Twain spent much of his time pocket-hunting for gold with the Gillis boys and Stoker. When weather permitted, they made forays some distance from the cabin. On New Year's night, 1865, Twain is at Valle-cita in Calaveras County, probably on a prospecting trip, and ob-serves a "magnificent lunar rainbow—first appearing at 8 P.M— moon at first quarter—very light drizzling rain."[15] In the same month he is in Angel's Camp, on a pocket-mining trip with Jim Gillis. The coffee at the French Restaurant is bad—"day before yesterday's dish-water"—and they are served this coffee and beans for breakfast and dinner every day. The monotony of some fea-tures of these January days Mark recorded in his notes:

January 23, 1865, Angels. Rainy, stormy, beans and dish-water, for breakfast at the Frenchman's; dish-water and beans for dinner, and both articles warmed over for supper.

24th. Rained all day—meals as before.

25th. Same as above.

26th. Rain, beans and dish-water—beefsteak for a change—no use, couldn't bite it.

27th. Same old diet—same old weather—went out to the "pocket" claim, had to rush back.

28th. Rain and wind all day and all night. Chili-beans and dish-water three times today as usual and some kind of "slum" which the Frenchman called "hash." Hash be damned!

29th. The old, old thing. We shall *have* to stand the weather, but as J. says we *won't* stand the dish-water and beans any longer, by God.

30th. Jan.—moved to the new hotel, just opened—good fare and coffee that a Christian may drink without jeopardizing his eternal soul. Dick Stoker came over today from Tuttletown, Tuolomne Co.[16]

This would appear to have been a dreary existence for a man of Mark Twain's restless temperament, but it does not actually tell the whole story of Twain's days on the Mother Lode. True, the prospecting results were discouraging; there was much prom-ise, but little fulfillment, although Jim Gillis was always ready with a word of encouragement and might have been able to pro-duce results if he had been given more co-operation, and if the

[15] Paine, *Mark Twain's Notebook* (Harper & Bros., 1935), p. 6.

[16] *Ibid.,* pp. 6–7.

prospecting had lasted longer. The story of the claim that was deserted because Mark was tired of the rain and the cold, whereas Jim wanted to continue panning, is rather pretty but certainly fictitious. According to this tale,[17] two Austrians came along, observed how the rain had washed the dirt away on the deserted claim, revealing a handful of nuggets, waited for the thirty-day claim notice to expire, then posted their own notice, and took out thousands of dollars worth of gold. And Jim and Mark had failed to become rich simply because Mark refused to carry just one more pail of water for panning!

There were, however, rich claims to be prospected in the Mother Lode country, and Mark Twain realized this. After all, he had for some years now been definitely in the career of authorship. And his newspaper reporting and magazine writing experience had placed him on the alert for literary material with human interest in it. At Angel's Camp he made what was for him probably the greatest scoop of his career. For he heard Ben Coon tell about the jumping frog, and he sensed that it would make a good story. He wrote it up, and it became the foundation of his literary fame.

Most of the days at Angel's Camp were spent by Mark and Jim and Stoker in the barroom of the dilapidated tavern. Here they found themselves in the company of a frequenter of the tavern, Ben Coon, a former Illinois River pilot, "a solemn, fat-witted person, who dozed by the stove, or told slow, endless stories, without point or application. Listeners were a boon to him, for few came and not many would stay. To Mark Twain and Jim Gillis, however, Ben Coon was a delight. It was soothing and comfortable to listen to his endless narratives, told in that solemn way, with no suspicion of humor."[18] Coon himself, seemingly, did not see point in his yarns. But Mark and Jim, playing billiards in the tavern, saw real human interest in the jumping-frog story, a yarn which they seemingly had not heard of before but versions of which had been printed in California newspapers before this

[17] Paine, *Biography*, I, 272–73.   [18] Paine, *Biography*, I, 271.

time.[19] Twain recorded in his notes, around the first of February, the incident of Ben Coon's jumping-frog story:

Coleman with his jumping frog—bet a stranger $50.—Stranger had no frog and C. got him one:—In the meantime stranger filled C's frog full of shot and he couldn't jump. The stranger's frog won.[20]

Since he went to the trouble of recording these details of Ben Coon's story in his notes, it seems reasonable to infer that Twain had neither heard the jumping-frog story previously nor read versions of it which had appeared in print.

Other literary material was gathered by Twain during his sojourn in the Tuolumne hills. The germs of "The Californian's Tale," and of many other stories and sketches of later years, were found here. But the jumping-frog story from Angel's Camp proved most useful of all the material.

For variety and with a purpose in mind, Mark took Dick Stoker to dine at the Frenchman's on February 3. He wanted Dick to see how the Frenchman did things:

Had "Hell-fire" soup and the old regular beans and dishwater. The Frenchman has 4 kinds of soup which he furnishes to customers only on great occasions. They are popularly known among the boarders as "Hell-fire," "General Debility," "Insanity" and "Sudden Death," but it is not possible to describe them.[21]

The days at Angel's Camp came to an end on February 25, 1865, when Mark and Jim and Dick walked over the mountains to Jackass Hill in a snowstorm, the first Mark had ever seen in California, and he was struck by the beautiful view from the mountain tops. That night, back in San Francisco again, at the Occidental Hotel, he found letters from Artemus Ward asking him to write a sketch for Ward's new book which was soon to come out. "Too late—ought to have got the letters three months ago," he writes

---

[19] A version of the folk tale had appeared in the *Sonora Herald* on June 11, 1853. This is reprinted in Oscar Lewis' *The Origin of the Celebrated Jumping Frog of Calaveras County*. A later version, by Samuel Seabough, had appeared in the *San Andreas Independent* December 11, 1858. Another variant, "Frogs Shot without Powder," written by Henry P. Leland for the New York *Spirit of the Times* and published May 26, 1855, is reprinted in Appendix B of De Voto's *Mark Twain's America*.

[20] *Mark Twain's Notebook*, p. 7.   [21] *Ibid.*, pp. 7–8.

in his notes.[22] The letters from Ward were dated in early November. Twain answered, explaining the circumstances of his absence from San Francisco. He also prepared the "Jumping Frog" story and sent it on to New York.

When he returned to San Francisco, Twain resumed his correspondence to the *Territorial Enterprise* and also began writing again for the *Californian*. He did not, however, submit his jumping-frog story to the *Californian,* or, if he did, it was not first printed there, despite Bret Harte's story of the circumstances, which is as follows:

> He had been away in the mining districts on some newspaper assignment in the meantime. In the course of conversation he remarked that the unearthly laziness that prevailed in the town he had been visiting was beyond anything in his previous experience. He said the men did nothing all day long but sit around the bar-room stove, spit, and "swop lies." He spoke in a slow, rather satirical drawl, which was in itself irresistible. He went on to tell one of those extravagant stories, and half unconsciously dropped into the lazy tone and manner of the original narrator. I asked him to tell it again to a friend who came in, and then asked him to write it out for "The Californian." He did so, and when published it was an emphatic success. It was the first work of his that had attracted general attention, and it crossed the Sierras for an Eastern reading. The story was "The Jumping Frog of Calaveras." It is now known and laughed over, I suppose, wherever the English language is spoken; but it will never be as funny to any one in print as it was to me, told for the first time by the unknown Twain himself on that morning in the San Francisco Mint.[23]

Inaccurate as this recollection is, both Merwin, as quoted above, and Pemberton, in his *Life of Bret Harte* (page 73), show Harte to have been extremely enthusiastic over the jumping-frog story. Although Harte was not at this time editor of the *Californian,* he was still closely enough connected with it to have had great influence in bringing about publication of the sketch in the magazine. There is, of course, the possibility that Harte actually was enthusiastic about the jumping-frog story and suggested to Twain that he write it for the *Californian* but that Twain, hoping to get

[22] Paine, *Biography,* I, 274.

[23] Henry Childs Merwin, *The Life of Bret Harte* (Houghton Mifflin Co., 1911), pp. 39–40.

the story into Ward's book, had preferred to write it for New York publication. As it turned out, the "Jumping Frog" story did not appear in the *Californian* until December 16, 1865, when it was reprinted from the *New York Saturday Press,* which had published the story in its issue of November 18, 1865. The story had arrived in New York too late for Ward's book; and Carleton, Ward's publisher, had handed the sketch to Henry Clapp, editor of the *Saturday Press,* who had printed it in his publication.

The printing of the "Jumping Frog" in the East was momentous in its significance to Mark Twain. Despite the fact that it had not arrived in time to be printed in Artemus Ward's book, it nevertheless achieved wide publicity throughout the East and the Middle West. It carried the name of Mark Twain to a reader territory of tremendous importance to an aspiring author. Obviously, the Pacific Coast could offer no great inducements to the author who wished to achieve national or world-wide importance; only in the East could one expect to gain the publishing co-operation so necessary to successful authorship. Previous to the publication of the "Jumping Frog" in the *Saturday Press,* the only writing signed by Mark Twain which had achieved anything near what might be called general circulation was the review of the play *Ingomar,* a review which had been written by Twain for the *Territorial Enterprise* and which had been reprinted by *Yankee Notions* in its issue of April 1864. Certainly only a few Eastern readers were familiar with the name of Mark Twain before the *Saturday Press* printed the "Jumping Frog." Now national attention was gained, as the sketch was reprinted and quoted in many publications and "everyone who took a newspaper was treated to the tale of the wonderful Calaveras frog, and received a mental impress of the author's signature. The name Mark Twain became hardly an institution, as yet, but it made a strong bid for national acceptance."[24]

News of the great popularity of the frog story was slow in

[24] Paine, *Biography,* I, 278.

getting back to Mark Twain; but at last the enthusiastic reports arrived. Much has been made of his supposed disappointment at having this "villainous backwoods sketch" publicized in the East. All the discussion on this alleged disappointment appears to be based on a few comments Mark Twain made in a letter to his mother and sister, written from San Francisco on January 20, 1866. In this letter he writes of his "uneventful" life, of his wish to be back piloting on the Mississippi, and includes an account of the publishing of the frog story:

> To think that, after writing many an article a man might be excused for thinking tolerably good, those New York people should single out a villainous backwoods sketch to compliment me on!—"Jim Smiley and His Jumping Frog"—a squib which would never have been written but to please Artemus Ward, and then it reached New York too late to appear in his book.
>
> But no matter. His book was a wretchedly poor one, generally speaking, and it could be no credit to either of us to appear between its covers.[25]

This letter has apparently been taken at its face value by Mark Twain's biographer and by his critics. The opinion generally expressed is that Twain was keenly disappointed that this particular sketch had been the one to achieve Eastern publication rather than some other. Some of his critics would almost have one believe that he went around with a hangdog expression, was ashamed to look his friends in the face, and was virtually prostrated by this artistic miscarriage. Paine says Twain did not regard the sketch highly as literary material.[26] Brooks sees in Mark Twain's letter to his mother and sister "the bitter prompting of his creative instinct, in rebellion against the course into which he has drifted."[27] De Voto, in his enthusiasm to refute Brooks at every turn, attacks Brooks for his supposed resentment at Twain's writing of humor, but interprets the letter as showing conclusively that Twain was not proud of the story.

To the present writer, the sentiment Mark Twain expressed in the letter to his mother and sister, concerning the "Jumping

[25] Paine, *Letters,* I, 101.   [26] Paine, *Biography,* I, 277.
[27] Van Wyck Brooks, *The Ordeal of Mark Twain,* p. 116.

Frog," has this explanation: Twain was peevish and disappointed at not having achieved book publication for it. Hence, a period of fretfulness resulted in the expression of disappointment. That whatever hesitation Twain might have had in accepting the story as worth-while literary material was short-lived is shown by his reactions to the story not long after its publication and in later years. He was proud of the story when he visited the Sandwich Islands, he used its title for that of his first book and placed the sketch itself first in that book, and he referred to the story with pride in letters and speeches many times in later years.

Of course, Twain's story of the frog is not the greatest story ever written, as one would be led to believe by those who have not yet read it. But perhaps a rereading would convince those who read the story some time ago and have since been inclined to regard it lightly as literary material that it is far from being a poor piece of work. It has literary merit which has stood the test of time.

It was during Bret Harte's second period of editorship of the *Californian* that this magazine reprinted the frog story.[28] In the December 9, 1865, issue of the *Californian* appeared the name of Francis Bret Harte, Editor. In the next week's issue was published the reprint of the story, under the title, "The Celebrated Jumping Frog of Calaveras County." Preceding the story the *Californian* inserted the following comment:

The *Saturday Press* introduces this sketch in the following complimentary manner: "We give up the principal portion of our editorial space today, to an exquisitely humorous sketch—'Jim and his Jumping Frog'—by Mark Twain, who will shortly become a contributor to our columns. Mark Twain is the assumed name of a writer in California who has long been a favorite contributor to the San Francisco press, from which his articles have been so extensively copied as to make him nearly as well known as Artemus Ward."[29]

Obviously, Bret Harte at that time knew that the *Californian* was not the first place of publication of the "Jumping Frog" story.

[28] Harte was editor of the *Californian* for three periods: September 10 to November 19, 1864; December 9 to 30, 1865; April 28 to August 18, 1866.
[29] *Californian*, December 16, 1865.

It is now plain that, having struck a promising vein during his literary and philosophical prospecting in the Mother Lode country, Mark Twain came back to San Francisco prepared for more rapid advancement in his career of authorship. The interlude at Jackass Hill had given him new inspiration and a greater desire for literary achievement.

CHAPTER 8

FINAL STORY IN THE WEST

WHATEVER Mark Twain's early opinion of his frog story may have been, the popularity it gained after publication in the *Saturday Press* gave substantial impetus to his plans for going East in search of more promising fields of authorship. On his return from the interlude at Jackass Hill, he had thought over his problems thoroughly enough to know that it was time to look for possibilities of more significant literary achievement. When word of the success of the frog sketch reached him, he lost interest somewhat in his California connections.

After his sojourn in the Tuolumne hills, he contributed again to the *Californian*. The first sketch, published March 18, 1865, entitled "An Unbiased Criticism" concerned the California Art Union and "its moral effects upon the youth of both sexes carefully considered and candidly commented upon." Then there were two sketches of "Important Correspondence," one in the issue of May 6 and the other published on May 13. The correspondence was "Between Mr. Mark Twain of San Francisco, and Rev. Bishop Hawkes, D.D., of New York, Rev. Phillips Brooks of Philadelphia, and Rev. Dr. Cummings of Chicago, concerning the occupancy of Grace Cathedral."

Illustrative of the facility with which Mark Twain could now handle even the simplest theme is the sketch, "How I Went to the Great Race between Lodi and Norfolk," published in the *Californian* May 27, 1865. In this sketch Mark writes of the difficulties he encountered in trying to arrange for transportation to the ocean race course where the great contest was to be held. He went to all the livery stables and found that the teams had been engaged a week before, but that one horse remained in waiting to be attached to a dray, and another was a saddle horse, of which Mark writes:

Then they said they had a capacious riding-horse left, but all the seats on him except one had been engaged; they said he was an unusually long horse, and he could seat seven very comfortably; and that he was very gentle, and would not kick up behind; and that one of the choicest places on him for observation was still vacant, and I could have it for nineteen dollars—and so on and so on; and while the passenger agent was talking, he was busy measuring off a space of nine inches for me pretty high up on the commodious animal's neck.

It seemed to me that the prospect of going to the races was beginning to assume a very "neck-or-nothing" condition, but nevertheless I steadfastly refused the supercargo's offer, and he sold the vacancy to a politician who was used to being on the fence and would naturally consider a seat astride a horse's neck in the light of a pleasant variety.[1]

Then Mark ran into Homestead, clerk of the Incidental Hotel, who invited him to take a drink. "I cannot be positive," writes Mark, "but it is my impression that I either stated that I would, or else signified assent by a scarcely perceptible eagerness of manner common to me under circumstances of this nature." While they were drinking, Homestead remarked that he was going to the great race on Tuesday and that he had a vacancy. Mark jumped at the opportunity, wrung Homestead's hand with heartfelt warmth and cordiality, and shed tears of gratitude. He promised to be on hand at the hotel sharply at ten o'clock Tuesday morning. As it turned out, Mark arrived at the appointed time, found a crowd of one hundred and fifty men at the hotel, and learned that they were all going to the great race with Homestead; and the upshot of it all was that Homestead announced that he was going to walk and they could all go with him. "I have made a plain, simple statement of the facts connected with this outrage," Mark writes, "and they can be substantiated by every man who was present upon that occasion. I will now drop this subject forever."

Beginning June 3, 1865, Twain conducted in the *Californian* a

[1] *Californian*, May 27, 1865.

department called "Answers to Correspondents." The first printing of the column was accompanied by this announcement:

All letters for this department should be addressed to Mr. Mark Twain, who has been detailed from the editorial staff to conduct it. Courting Etiquette, Distressed Lovers, of either sex, and Struggling Young Authors, as yet "unbeknown" to Fame, will receive especial attention.[2]

It is worthy of note here that at this time someone had the opinion that Mark Twain had reached the point of successful authorship where he was in a position to offer guidance to "struggling young authors." This may, of course, have been expressed entirely in a facetious mood, and yet there probably was some seriousness behind the announcement of the *Californian*.

At the end of the second "Answers to Correspondents" column, published June 10, the conductor wrote as follows:

Note.—Several letters, chiefly from young ladies and young bachelors, remain over, to be answered next week, want of space precluding the possibility of attending to them at present. I always had an idea that most of the letters written to editors were written by the editors themselves. But I find, now, that I was mistaken.[3]

There were four more of these columns conducted by Twain in succeeding weeks' issues of the *Californian*. During the rest of the time he was in the West he wrote only nine sketches for the *Californian*, although that magazine reprinted many of his sketches —from its own columns, from the *New York Saturday Press*, from the *New York Weekly Review*, from the *Territorial Enterprise*, and from the *Sacramento Union*. The last sketch which Twain contributed to the *Californian* concerned the manner in which the Smiths and the Joneses should be written up; it was entitled "Origin of Illustrious Men," and was published September 29, 1866.

On July 2, 1865, Mark Twain began contributing again to the *Golden Era*, the publication that he had deserted a year previously in favor of the more "high-toned" *Californian*. This time his contribution, entitled "Smith Brown Jones," consists of an article announcing that the *Golden Era* has had the good fortune to secure the services of the eminent Smith B. Jones, Esq., who has

[2] *Californian*, June 3, 1865.　　　　[3] *Ibid.*, June 10, 1865.

just arrived by steamer, as a weekly contributor to its columns. Two more articles followed in the same series and with similar titles.

Following the series of "Smith Brown Jones" articles, there was no contribution by Twain in the *Golden Era* until February 25, 1866, when two sketches were published, one entitled "Mark Twain on Fashions" and the other, "Mark Twain on California Critics." In the former he writes of the uncertainty prevailing among the ladies of San Francisco regarding the wearing of hoops; in the article on critics he warns the actor, Edwin Forrest, that no matter how much praise he has won in the East and no matter how well he plays in San Francisco he will be given a drubbing by the California critics.

The new wildcat religion of the San Francisco spiritualists is adversely criticized by Mark Twain in an article in the *Golden Era* of March 4, 1866. Mark had been upset by the fact that another spiritual investigator had passed his examinations at the séances of the Friends of Progress and had been shipped, a raving maniac, to the Stockton insane asylum. He fears that the spiritualists are going too far; they should stick to the old standard religions. He does not take any credit because he never went crazy on Presbyterianism. The Presbyterians "go too slow" for that. They don't rant, and shout, and tear up the ground. They set a good example:

Notice us, and you will see how we do. We get up of a Sunday morning and put on the best harness we have got and trip cheerfully down town; we subside into solemnity and enter the church; we stand up and duck our heads and bear down on a hymn book propped on the pew in front when the minister prays; we stand up again while our hired choir are singing, and look in the hymn book and check off the verses to see that they don't shirk any of the stanzas; we sit silent and grave while the minister is preaching, and count the waterfalls and bonnets furtively, and catch flies; we grab our hats and bonnets when the benediction is begun; when it is finished, we shove, so to speak. No frenzy—no fanaticism—no skirmishing; everything perfectly serene. You never see any of us Presbyterians getting in a sweat about religion and trying to massacre our neighbors. Let us all be content with the tried and safe old religions, and take no chances on wildcat.[4]

4 *Golden Era,* March 4, 1866.

MAIN STREET, ANGEL'S CAMP, CALIFORNIA

Spiritual séances attracted the interest of Mark Twain during the winter of 1865–66. He attended many of these in San Francisco, particularly those at Mrs. Ada Hoyt Foye's. At Mrs. Foye's séances Mark was appointed a member of the investigating committee. This made the ghosts a bit nervous, according to the *Golden Era's* "Feuilleton" column of February 4. Twain wrote articles on these séances for the *Territorial Enterprise* and for the *Golden Era*. The *Golden Era* first reprinted some of the *Enterprise* articles, then presented one of its own entitled "More Spiritual Investigations by Mark Twain." In this sketch, Mark tells of happenings at a fireside séance that he had stumbled upon a night or two before. He describes some of the spirits that appeared, and concludes with a note of satisfaction:

Very well; the *Bulletin* may abuse spiritualism as much as it pleases, but whenever I can get a chance to take a dead and damned Smith by the hand and pass a joke or swap a lie with him, I am going to do it. I am not afraid of such pleasant corpses as these ever running me crazy. I find them better company than a good many live people.[5]

The last of Mark Twain's contributions to the *Golden Era* was a sketch entitled "Reflections on the Sabbath," published March 18, 1866. It expresses in a facetious way the religious skepticism that was to be the subject matter of much of Twain's writing in his later years. In this sketch he explains that he has not been to church for many months because he has been unable to get a pew, and, on occasion, has had to sit in the gallery, among the sinners. This he objects to, as he considers himself a brevet member of the Presbyterian church, having been sprinkled in infancy. He prefers the Presbyterian hell of fire and brimstone to the "heterodox hell of remorse of conscience of these blamed wildcat religions." Whereas the heaven and hell of the wildcat religions are vague and ill-defined, there is nothing mixed about the Presbyterian variety.

The Presbyterian hell is all misery; the heaven all happiness—nothing to do. But when a man dies on a wildcat basis, he will never rightly know hereafter which department he is in—but he will think he is in hell anyhow,

[5] *Ibid.*, March 11, 1866.

no matter which place he goes to; because in the good place they pro-gress, pro-gress, pro-gress—study, study, study, all the time—and if this isn't hell I don't know what is; and in the bad place he will be worried by remorse of conscience.[6]

After his sojourn in the Tuolumne hills, Mark Twain resumed regular correspondence to the *Territorial Enterprise,* in addition to his writing for the *Californian* and the *Golden Era.* Files of the *Enterprise* for that period not being extant, one must depend on reprints of these articles in San Francisco newspapers and magazines for information as to the character of the *Enterprise* correspondence.[7]

One of the *Enterprise* letters, "Mark Twain's New Year's Day," was reprinted in the *Golden Era.* In this letter, Mark relates his experiences in making the customary New Year's Day round of visits to the homes of friends and strangers. He tells how he sampled the wines and was finally successful in "coralling" a meal, and of how some of the ladies dressed "in character." He found

. . . . Faith, Hope and Charity in one house, dealing out claret punch and kisses to the annual pilgrims. They had two kinds of kisses—those which you bite and "chaw" and swallow, and those which you simply taste, and then lick your chops and feel streaky. The only defect there was in the arrangement was that you were not permitted to take your choice.[8]

Some of the frequent censure which Twain heaped on the San Francisco police department is contained in an *Enterprise* letter entitled "What Have the Police Been Doing?" reprinted in the *Golden Era* on January 21, 1866. In a series of ironical questions and assertions in this letter he rebukes the police for having permitted an assaulted prisoner to die in his cell. He also finds fault with the department for assigning four officers, at a cost of five hundred dollars a month, as nurses for a captain with a broken leg.

A typical Mark Twain "bloody" story occurs in the *Enterprise* letters of this period. It was captioned "Mark Twain's Kearny Street Ghost Story," and was reprinted in the *Golden Era* on Janu-

[6] *Golden Era,* March 18, 1866.

[7] There are also clippings of some of Mark Twain's letters to the *Territorial Enterprise* in Mark Twain's scrapbook, which is in Willard S. Morse's collection.

[8] *Golden Era,* January 14, 1866.

ary 28, 1866. It is in a class with two stories he had written previously, "The Empire City Massacre" and "The Great Prize Fight." It tells of disembodied spirits that have been on a rampage for more than a month in a San Francisco home, making it impossible for the family to keep a servant. "The moment a new and unsuspecting servant maid gets fairly to bed and her light blown out, one of those dead and damned scalliwags takes her by the hair and just 'hazes' her; grabs her by the waterfall and snakes her out of bed and bounces her on the floor two or three times." The spirits tramp about the house at dead of night. "They are a bloody lot." One of them came to the bedside of the young lady of the house one night:

> The ghost came and stood by the bed and groaned—a deep, agonizing, heart-broken groan—and laid a bloody kitten on the pillow by the girl's head. And then it groaned again, and sighed, "Oh, God, and must it be?" and bet another bloody kitten. It groaned a third time in sorrow and tribulation, and went one kitten better. And thus the sorrowing spirit stood there, moaning in its anguish and unloading its mewing cargo, until it had stacked up a whole litter of nine little bloody kittens on the girl's pillow, and then, still moaning, moved away and vanished. When lights were brought, there were the kittens, with the fingermarks of bloody hands upon their white fur—and the old mother cat, that had come after them, swelled her tail in mortal fear and refused to take hold of them. What do you think of that? What would you think of a ghost that came to your bedside at dead of night and had kittens?[9]

Several of the *Enterprise* letters concerned Mark Twain's experiences at spiritual séances. He writes of one occasion when four hundred ladies and gentlemen were present, "and plenty of newspaper people—neuters." He observed a "good-looking, earnest-faced, pale-red-haired, neatly dressed, young woman standing on a little stage behind a small deal table with slender legs and no drawers—the table, understand me," he explains. "I am writing in a hurry, but I do not desire to confound my description of the table with my description of the lady. The lady was Mrs. Foye."[10] The letter tells of the success which members of the group had in conversing with departed acquaintances.

[9] *Golden Era*, January 28, 1866.   [10] *Golden Era*, February 4, 1866.

That Mark Twain was a figure of importance in the literary circles of San Francisco by 1866 is evidenced in a statement he makes in a letter, written on January 20, 1866, to his mother and sister: "Though I am generally placed at the head of my breed of scribblers in this part of the country, the place properly belongs to Bret Harte, I think, though he denies it, along with the rest." At any rate, he was extended special honors when he was invited to be one of a party of guests to make the initial trip of the new steamer "Ajax" to the Sandwich Islands. He did not accept the invitation, as he felt he could not neglect his newspaper correspondence, but after the steamer had departed he was sorry that he had not gone on the voyage.

With the regularity of his newspaper correspondence growing monotonous, Twain considered the possibility that some California newspaper might be willing to send him to the Sandwich Islands as its correspondent to write about the life, agriculture, scenery, commerce, and other features of the islands. He was well acquainted with the publishers of the *Sacramento Union,* and arrangements were soon made with that paper. The original plan was that he should remain in the islands a month and send twenty or thirty articles back to the *Union.* Accordingly he began his first sea voyage on March 7, 1866, sailing for the Sandwich Islands on the second trip of the "Ajax."

The first four letters to the *Union* deal with incidents on the passage. During the stormy trip Twain learned some of the language of the sea, particularly when Captain Godfrey was making sail:

"Let go the main-hatch. Belay! Haul away on your tops'l jib! Belay! Clew up your to-gallants'l spanker-boom halliards! Belay! Port your gaff-tops'l sky-scrapers! Belay! Lively, you lubbers! Take a reef in the lee scuppers! Belay! Mr. Baxter, it's coming on to blow at about four bells in the hog-watch; have everything taut and trim for it. Belay!"[11]

[11] *Sacramento Union,* April 16, 1866. The Sandwich Islands letters have been reprinted as: *Letters from the Sandwich Islands,* written for the *Sacramento Union* by Mark Twain. Introduction and Conclusion by G. Ezra Dane. Illustrations by Dorothy Grover. The Grabhorn Press. San Francisco, 1937. 550 copies. See List of References, p. 162.

Mark got up at this point and started over to ask the captain if he didn't think it would be a good idea to belay a little, but the sea was too rough and Mark fell down.

In the first letter Mark begins making use of his fictitious friend Brown, whom he uses frequently in succeeding letters. When Mark finds twenty-two passengers leaning over the bulwarks he also finds Brown there. The passengers are

vomiting and remarking, "Oh, my God!" and then vomiting again. Brown was there, ever kind and thoughtful, passing from one to another and saying, "That's all right—that's all right, you know—it'll clean you out like a jug, and then you won't feel so ornery and smell so ridiculous."[12]

This was one of those less-refined passages which Twain frequently found it impossible to resist writing.

The "Ajax" arrived at Honolulu on March 18, 1866. Mark thought he saw the king sitting in a two-horse buggy alone on the wharf, with big whiskers, a leather complexion, and gold bands on his plug hat and his coat. But the speculation was wrong; it was the king's driver. Mark Twain became immediately enthusiastic over Hawaii. He found "no careworn or eager, anxious faces in the land of happy contentment—God what a contrast with California and Washoe. Everybody walks at a moderate gait but, to speak strictly, they mostly ride."[13] He met his friend Rev. Franklin S. Rising, and many other friends, who offered him Honolulu hospitality.

There is much serious information in the Sandwich Islands letters. Twain no doubt felt a sense of responsibility in furnishing the readers of the *Union* something that would make it worth their while to read the letters. He was also grateful to the proprietors of the *Union* for giving him such a splendid assignment, and wanted to do his best to see that they got something substantial for their money. However, the letters are not, by any means, weighted down by this element of serious information; there are numerous lighter passages, as Twain frequently found that to him

[12] *Sacramento Union*, April 16, 1866.
[13] Paine, *Mark Twain's Notebook*, p. 16.

the most serious things were frequently the best subject matter for humorous treatment.

By way of worth-while information, the letters deal with the living habits of the people of the Islands, with the Hawaiian legislature, with the royal family, with the whaling trade, and with the death and funeral of Her Royal Highness Victoria Kamamalu Kaahumanu, heir presumptive to the crown and sister to the king. There is also much information about the sugar, coffee, and fruit plantations, and about labor conditions, and there is a prediction that California will some day have coolie workers. Twain writes enthusiastically of California's prospects in relation to the Sandwich Islands. He feels that California is in a position to ask that the world pay tribute to her, as she

is about to be appointed to preside over almost the exclusive trade of 450,000,000 people—the almost exclusive trade of the most opulent land on earth. It is the land where the fabled Aladdin's lamp lies buried—and she is the new Aladdin who shall seize it from its obscurity and summon the genie and command him to crown her with power and greatness, and bring to her feet the hoarded treasures of the earth.[14]

Historical facts about the Islands are given in some detail in the letters. Legendary tales are likewise not overlooked. There are many fine passages of description: the Honolulu market place on a festive Saturday afternoon, the ruins of the city of refuge, the Nuuanu and Kalihi valleys, the great volcano of Kileaua. He finds the girls entrancing in their finery on Saturday afternoon, with

fine black silk robes; flowing red ones that nearly put your eyes out; others as white as snow; still others that discount the rainbow; and they wear their hair in nets, and trim their jaunty hats with fresh flowers, and encircle their dusky throats with home-made necklaces of the brilliant vermillion-tinted blossom of the *ohia;* and they fill the markets and the adjacent streets with their bright presences, and smell like thunder with their villainous cocoanut oil.[15]

The solid information in the letters is given the saving grace of Mark Twain's human-interest treatment. There are frequent humorous passages. The steed Oahu becomes the progenitor of

[14] *Sacramento Union,* September 26, 1866.   [15] *Ibid.,* May 21, 1866.

many other horses that Mark Twain is to write about. Then there is Mrs. Captain Jollopson, who describes her sad accident to Mark in the vocabulary of the whaling trade. Mrs. Jollopson had been on her way to market and "here comes a ship-keeper round the corner three sheets in the wind and his dead-lights stove in." Mrs. Jollopson saw the danger of a collision: "I backed off fast as I could, and sung out to him to port his helm, but it warn't no use; he'd everything drawing and I had considerable sternway, and he just struck me a little abaft the beam, and down I went, head on, and skunned my elbow." Mark is sympathetic:

> I said, "Bless my life!"
> And she said, "Well you may say it! My! such a jolt! It started everything. It's worse'n being pulled! I shouldn't wonder if I'd have to be hove down—" and then she spread her hand alongside of her mouth and sung out, "Susy, ahoy!" to another woman, who rounded to to wait for her, and the two fell off before the wind and sailed away together.[16]

On two occasions during the Sandwich Islands sojourn, Mark finds himself called upon to cure his friend Brown of seasickness, according to the *Union* letters. The first time, Mark experimented with a variety of remedies: "I talked to him for some time, but strangely enough, pathetic narratives did not move his emotions, eloquent declamation did not inspirit him, and the most humorous anecdotes failed to make him even smile." Finally, Mark got around to reciting a paraphrase of a passage from Shakespeare. The poem did the job, and in a minute or two Brown "felt entirely relieved and comfortable. He then said that the anecdotes and the eloquence were 'no good,' but if he got seasick again he would like some more poetry."[17] Brown did, in fact, become seasick again one night, and the captain came rushing down to Mark for assistance because Brown was calling frantically for poetry. Mark was soon on deck, groped his way to the sufferer, and recited a poem made up of alternate lines from "The Burial of Sir John Moore" and the "Destruction of Sennacherib." At the conclusion of this poem Mark could see that his efforts had not

---

[16] *Ibid.*, May 22, 1866.   [17] *Sacramento Union*, August 18, 1866.

been in vain. " 'It is enough. God Bless you!' said Brown, and threw up everything he had eaten for three days."[18] Despite the occasional inclusion of these coarse passages in his letters, Twain kept the general tone of his Sandwich Islands correspondence on a high level. Where he did admit a bit of crudity it was of the type that readers of the *Union* at that time probably thought very funny.

The high point of the Sandwich Islands letters was reached in his report of the burning of the clipper ship "Hornet" at sea. The story was dated at Honolulu, June 25, 1866. Fortunately for Twain, he had the assistance of Anson Burlingame, United States minister to China, in covering this story. Burlingame, en route to his post, had arrived in Honolulu accompanied by his son Edward and by General Van Valkenburgh, minister to Japan. Mark had just returned from a tour of the Islands and was sick in bed suffering from saddle boils when he received word that Minister Burlingame and his party were planning to visit him. Instead of waiting for the party to come to him, Twain crawled out of bed and drove to the American minister's residence, where the party was staying. Twain explains the circumstances of the visit in a letter to his mother and sister:

> Hon. Anson Burlingame, U.S. Minister to China, and Gen. Van Valkenburgh, Minister to Japan, with their families and suites, have just arrived here *en route*. They were going to do me the honor to call on me this morning, and that accounts for my being out of bed now. You know what condition my room is always in when you are not around—so I climbed out of bed and dressed and shaved pretty quick and went up to the residence of the American Minister and called on *them*.[19]

On the day this letter was written, June 21, 1866, word came to Honolulu of the arrival at the island of Hawaii of

> nineteen[20] starving wretches, who had been buffeting a stormy sea in an open boat for forty-three days! Their ship, the "Hornet," from New York, with a quantity of kerosine on board, had taken fire and burned in lat. 2 degrees north and long. 135 degrees west.[21]

[18] *Sacramento Union*, October 25, 1866.   [19] Paine, *Mark Twain's Letters*, I, 107.
[20] It turned out that there were only fifteen survivors.
[21] *Sacramento Union*, July 16, 1866.

ORIGINAL JACKASS HILL CABIN

After mention of the ship tragedy in this letter to the *Union,* Twain had hopes of covering the story more completely in a later letter. The survivors were brought to Honolulu, but Twain was still sick in bed and might never have been able to interview them if he had not received the help of Anson Burlingame. The Burlingame party came to Twain's hotel, and he was carried on a cot, escorted by the legations of China and Japan, to the hospital, where eleven of the "Hornet" survivors were being cared for. Burlingame did all the interviewing; all Mark Twain had to do was take notes.

The story of the "Hornet" disaster was written that night. Next morning the manuscript was rushed to a vessel which was just pulling away from the dock. The letter, a sensational newspaper scoop, was published by the *Sacramento Union* on July 19, 1866. Mark Twain had proved his abilities as a newspaper reporter; this letter was the most significant serious article he had written up to that time, and it added greatly to his prestige. To Anson Burlingame Mark Twain was deeply indebted, not only for the assistance in covering the "Hornet" story but also for advice and encouragement which was given the younger man. Burlingame said to Twain:

> You have great ability; I believe you have genius. What you need now is the refinement of association. Seek companionship among men of superior intellect and character. Refine yourself and your work. Never affiliate with inferiors; always climb.[22]

From a lesser man than Burlingame this advice would have been shed by Mark Twain like water from a duck's back; it probably would have struck him as being ridiculous. As it is, the effect of this advice on Twain has probably been overemphasized. He was too democratic to adopt a holier-than-thou attitude. Certainly in the West he preferred rubbing elbows with humanity to an aristocratic aloofness to the life about him. Burlingame urged Mark Twain to travel. This was advice that Mark Twain could accept with real enthusiasm. Hence, when Burlingame suggested that he

[22] Paine, *Biography,* I, 287.

come to China soon, to write up that part of the world, he promised that he would.

Although the story of the "Hornet" disaster was the high point of Mark Twain's Sandwich Islands correspondence, it was the subject matter of only one of his letters out of the total of twenty-five which he sent to the *Union*. Some subjects became recurrent in the letters. Twain never could make up his mind definitely about the missionaries; sometimes he thought they were all right and probably had done the Islands some good, whereas at other times he thought the missionaries had serious shortcomings. In his notes he writes: "More missionaries and more row made about saving these 60,000 people than would take to convert hell itself."[23] Evidently Twain had been talked about a little during his days in Honolulu, for he records in his notes:

All small villages are gossipy, but Honolulu heads them a little. They let me off comparatively easy, though I don't thank them for it because it argues that I wasn't worth the trouble of blackguarding. They only accused me of murder, arson, highway robbery and some other little eccentricities, but I knew nothing of it till the day I started. The missionary (I should say preacher) feature of insincerity and hypocrisy makes the atmosphere of the place.[24]

Toward the natives and their habits Twain expresses a variety of sentiments. There is a frankness in his notes that is not shown in the letters: "Kanakas will have horses and saddles and the women will fornicate—two strong characteristics of this people."[25] The technique of the natives in eating "poi" engaged the attention of Mark and his friend Brown:

Many a different finger goes into the same bowl and many a different kind of dirt and shade and quality of flavor is added to the virtues of its contents. One tall gentleman, with nothing in the world on but a soiled and greasy shirt, thrust in his finger and tested the poi, shook his head, scratched it with the useful finger, made another test, prospected among his hair, caught something and eat it; tested the poi again, wiped the grimy perspiration from his brow with the universal hand, tested again, blew his nose— "Let's move on, Brown," said I, and we moved.[26]

---

[23] Paine, *Mark Twain's Notebook*, p. 21.   [24] *Ibid.*, p. 23.
[25] *Ibid.*, p. 20.   [26] *Sacramento Union*, May 21, 1866.

Twain's sojourn in the Sandwich Islands came to an end on July 19, 1866, when he boarded a sailing vessel, the "Smyrniote," for San Francisco, after four months of a visit originally planned to last but one month. The vessel was becalmed a good deal of the time, and it was not until August 3 that it arrived in San Francisco.

The Sandwich Islands had been a dreamlike interlude in Mark Twain's life. Tahoe, Jackass Hill, the Sandwich Islands—many times in later years he was to look back wistfully upon the happiness of those carefree days. Back in San Francisco, he wrote:

> Aug. 13. San Francisco. Home again. No *not* home again—in prison again and all the wide sense of freedom gone. The city seems so cramped and so dreary with toil and care and business anxiety. God help me, I wish I were at sea again.[27]

But the experience had contributed to Mark Twain's development. Literary development is clearly discernible in his Sandwich Islands sojourn. His letters show a change from the lighter, less substantial writings of his previous Western experience. And there has come to Mark Twain's view now a widened horizon that gives him a longing to travel, to write on a greater variety of subjects, to win more than a local fame. He is ready now for great adventure in the field of authorship. Thus, the reporting assignment to cover the Sandwich Islands constitutes another, and virtually the final, phase of Mark Twain's Western development.

[27] Paine, *Mark Twain's Notebook,* p. 29.

CHAPTER 9

CONTRIBUTION
OF THE FRONTIER WEST

On his return to San Francisco from the Islands, Twain sensed that the time had come for him to seek greater opportunities than had so far come within his experience. The thrills of the biggest newspaper assignment he had ever had, the encouragement of Anson Burlingame, the great success of his twenty-five letters to the *Union*—all these had crystallized in his mind a plan for the immediate future: he would make a trip around the world and write on an even larger scale. This was now his whole objective; he was impatient to take care of loose ends in San Francisco and be on his way.

If Twain was despondent at this time, as he is said to have confessed,[1] it must have been because he could not find the means immediately to be off on the great adventure. But the opportunity was not far off. In the meantime, he went to Sacramento to settle accounts with the *Union,* whose proprietors were so enthusiastic about his Sandwich Islands letters that when Twain suggested a fee of $300 extra for his "Hornet" story they laughed and paid it. It was a high figure, especially since the letters had already been paid for at the regular rate, and Twain was no doubt joking when he asked for the extra $100 a column for the "scoop" story; but the *Union* proprietors were well satisfied to give him a good reward for a job well done.

During his last four months in the West Twain did little writ-

---

[1] Paine, *Mark Twain: A Biography,* I, 291.

ing. He sent one letter of news back to the *Daily Hawaiian Herald*. This letter, dated in San Francisco September 24, tells of the arrival of Queen Emma and her suite in San Francisco; of Twain being snubbed in Sacramento by Mr. John Quincy Adams (Alphabet) Warren, formerly of the Islands; and of his plan to go back to the Hawaiian Islands for the express purpose of eating Mr. Whitney, the editor of the *Commercial Advertiser,* who had said that Twain did not write the truth about the Islands and had run off with Father Damon's *History of the Islands*. Mark feels that Mr. Whitney's case is about hopeless:

> Mr. Whitney is jealous of me because I speak the truth so naturally, and he can't do it without taking the lock-jaw. But he ought not to be jealous; he ought not to try to ruin me because I am more virtuous than he is; *I* cannot help it—it is my nature to be reliable, just as it is his to be shaky on matters of fact—we cannot alter those natures—us leopards cannot change our spots. Therefore, why growl?—why go and try to make trouble? If he cannot tell when I am writing seriously and when I am burlesquing—if he sits down solemnly and takes one of my palpable burlesques and reads it with a funereal aspect, and swallows it as petrified truth,—how am I going to help it?[2]

There were only five more contributions to Western publications before Mark Twain's departure for the East. One was a "Card to the Highwaymen" in the *Territorial Enterprise,* and another was his farewell letter to the editor of the *Alta California*. The other three were "Interior Notes" written for the *San Francisco Bulletin* and published by that newspaper on November 30, December 6, and December 7, 1866; these letters were travel correspondence from Sacramento, Grass Valley, Red Dog, You Bet, Washoe, and San Jose.

Though the writing he did in his final months in the West was not extensive, there occurred one development of some consequence: he began his career as a lecturer. When he returned from the Islands he considered the possibility of using his experiences as subject matter for a lecture before a San Francisco audience. But he was hesitant and did not make up his mind definitely

[2] *Daily Hawaiian Herald*, October 17, 1866.

until he received the hearty encouragement of Colonel John McComb of the *Alta California*. He then hired Tom Maguire's new opera house, wrote the announcements himself, and made a tremendous success of his first real lecture on October 2, 1866. The gross return was $1,200, and the newspapers were enthusiastic in their praise. Mark Twain had come a long way since the time he had appeared before the Nevada legislature as "Governor of the Third House," though even then he had been enthusiastically applauded. Now his fame was coming to be something more than merely local, and he no doubt saw the possibilities before him in a wider field beyond.

The succeeding lectures that he gave in California and Nevada towns were as enthusiastically received as had been the one in San Francisco. In Washoe, excitement ran particularly high; Carson City, Virginia City, and Gold Hill welcomed him back with wild acclaim. But the boys in Virginia City saw their final chance to get back at him for the many practical jokes he had played on them a few years before. It was a bit of sentimentality they could not resist. So they staged a fake robbery on a bitterly cold night when Mark and his manager, Denis McCarthy, were returning to Virginia City from a lecture at Gold Hill. The holdup was perpetrated on the Divide between the two towns, and to Mark it was an uncomfortably real affair, although McCarthy was in on it.

The day after the fake holdup on the Divide, Twain wrote a "Card to the Highwaymen" for publication in the *Territorial Enterprise* of November 11, 1866. He wrote seriously, hoping to recover particularly the watch that had been presented to him as "Governor of the Third House" of the Nevada legislature by Judge Sandy Baldwin and Theodore Winters. In the same issue Dan De Quille had a paragraph on the robbery:

MARK TWAIN ROBBED.

After his lecture at Gold Hill last evening, Mark Twain and his agent (Mac) were coming on foot up to this city, when just as they were on the Divide, near the Montreal House, they were stopped by five highwaymen, and robbed of about $100 in coin and a valuable gold watch. Mark publishes a card on the subject in another column. This is no joke, but it is downright sober earnest. There should be a little hanging done among these rascals. This is the boldest robbery yet.[3]

When Mark discovered that it was a practical joke which the boys had played on him, he canceled the return-lecture engagement that he had planned for Virginia City and left by Pioneer Stage for California. He was angry, and did not hesitate to tell the boys what he thought of them. It was his customary reaction when the joke was not by but on him. He soon cooled down, however, and forgave his Washoe friends, though in later years he was to look back more than once with resentment at the practical jokers who had made use of him as a target.

Perhaps Mark's resentment at the Virginia City fake holdup can be attributed to some extent to the fact that just previously, near Nevada City, on the same lecture tour, he had been the victim of another practical joke. Evidently he was systematically victimized, since he writes in a *San Francisco Bulletin* letter that between Grass Valley and Nevada City "began the series of practical jokes with which I have been assailed lately."[4] The first of the series concerned a letter that Mark was to have delivered to a distinguished citizen of Nevada City. A man in the stage represented himself as the addressee, Mark was taken in by the deception, and the letter started on a circuitous route to the rightful man. Mark explains how the truth leaked out:

One of the party said, "Why that fellow in the stage was named Duell —he don't know enough to come in when it rains!" I said that that was what I thought in the first place, but after all that was as much intelligence as a practical joker requires—any idiot can tell a lie, and no practical joke is anything more than a spoken or acted deception. You can carefully analyze the best one you ever heard of and you will find that that is exactly all it consists of.

The letter had passed through some fifty hands, and when Mr. S— received it it was about worn out. However, I accepted the harmless joke, and some time or other when an opportunity offers, I will try to "get even" on the festive ass they call Duell.[4]

[3] *Territorial Enterprise,* November 11, 1866.
[4] *San Francisco Bulletin,* November 30, 1866.

Returning to San Francisco after his swing through California and Nevada towns, Twain delivered a second lecture, the final one of the series, on November 16. Of the first lecture the *San Francisco Bulletin* had said, at the end of a laudatory review:

The lecture was superior to Artemus Ward's "Babes in the Wood" in point of humor. It evinced none of that straining after effect that was manifested by the great showman, and possessed some solid qualities to which Ward can make no pretensions. As a humorous writer Mark Twain stands in the foremost rank, while his effort of last evening affords reason for the belief that he can establish an equal reputation as a humorous and original lecturer.[5]

Of the final lecture the *Alta California* said the enthusiasm with which it had been received "was a deserving testimonial to a humorist who has made his fame among us and is now about to take his departure."[6]

The *Alta California* was not only vigorous in its praise of Mark Twain but willing to back its faith in his ability. When Twain sailed from San Francisco on the Opposition steamer "America," Captain Ned Wakeman,[7] at noon on December 15, 1866, he left under commission to the *Alta California* for a series of letters during his proposed trip around the world:

"Mark Twain" goes off on his journey over the world as the Travelling Correspondent of the *Alta California,* not stinted as to time, place or direction—writing his weekly letters on such subjects and from such places as will best suit him; but we may say that he will first visit the home of his youth—St. Louis—thence through the principal cities to the Atlantic seaboard again, crossing the ocean to visit the "Universal Exposition" at Paris, through Italy, the Mediterranean, India, China, Japan, and back to San Francisco by the China Mail Steamship line. That his letters will be read with interest needs no assurance from us—his reputation has been made here in California, and his great ability is well known; but he has been known principally as a humorist, while he really has no superior as a descriptive writer—a keen observer of men and their surroundings—and we feel confident his letters to the *Alta,* from his new field of observation, will give him a world-wide reputation.[8]

Soon he would be in the East, where he could say to Howells,

[5] *San Francisco Bulletin,* October 3, 1866.   [6] *Alta California,* November 17, 1866.
[7] The Captain Ned Oakley of *Roughing It,* Captain Stormfield of "Captain Stormfield's Visit to Heaven," and Captain Hurricane Jones of "Rambling Notes of an Idle Excursion."   [8] *Alta California,* December 15, 1866.

the high priest of gentility: "When I read that review of yours [of *Innocents Abroad*] I felt like the woman who said that she was so glad that the baby had come white"; where pious Olivia Clemens could smugly polish, purify, edit her husband and his words; where Howells, Aldrich, and Mrs. Clemens could grow faint with embarrassment over the old-fashioned string-tie which was still a favorite with Mark Twain; where effete Boston could stare straight ahead in frozen horror at his blasphemous Whittier birthday speech, one of the finest things Mark Twain ever did; where Oliver Wendell Holmes, the last of the Brahmins, on being thanked by Twain for a Holmes poem in honor of Twain on his fiftieth birthday, could write with his own hand and his own conceit: "Did Miss Gilder tell you I had twenty-three letters spread out for answer when her suggestion came about your anniversary? I stopped my correspondence and made my letters wait until the lines were done."[9] How far by then would Mark Twain, son of the frontier, have wandered from his home in the West!

When Mark Twain departed from San Francisco after five and a half years in the West he had arrived at a significant point in his artistic development. At the end of those five and a half years he differed widely from the young adventurer who had come on a "three months' pleasure trip" to the silver mines of Nevada.

He had come to Nevada unknown, undecided as to his objective in life. He had previously done some writing, but all of his attempts had been amateurish, premature. There had been no sustained effort at authorship; and although he was twenty-five when he arrived in Nevada, he had not by any means decided upon authorship as a career. Examination of new material not previously available reveals that certain tendencies of his pre-Washoe writings carried over into this Western period, however. Among these were his predilection for humorous writing; his preference for writing travel letters rather than local items; his aptitude for editorial controversy, and the love of a battle of words; his tendency

[9] Paine, *Mark Twain's Letters*, II, 466.

to satirize individuals, often unjustly, for the sake of building a good story or making a point which in itself may have been justified. However, his earlier use of exaggerated dialects, misspellings, and other similar elements of style was abandoned in Nevada and California.

Before coming to Nevada, Mark Twain had served two apprenticeships, as printer and as a pilot on the Mississippi. In Nevada, after the pastoral interlude at Lake Tahoe had reconciled him to the "damnedest country under the sun," he took up the career of silver miner and stayed with it until he was thoroughly convinced that he could not be successful at it. Then he went to Virginia City to join the staff of the *Territorial Enterprise* and to take a vigorous part in the glamorous life of the Comstock Lode. Here, after three false apprenticeships, he chose authorship as his life work.

The significance of the two years on the *Territorial Enterprise* in the Western development of Mark Twain can hardly be over-estimated. He was associated with men from whom he could learn much. He was given a freedom of utterance that permitted him to try out his literary talents and thus enabled him to separate the good writings from the bad. He was not so bad a critic of his own work, despite what has been written of him, that he did not know what was worth while as contrasted with that which was flimsy, or crude, or, in his own words, "hogwash." He did not continue to write "Empire City Massacre" stories for the remainder of his days on the *Enterprise,* although Joe Goodman was so intent on giving Mark the free run of the newspaper that he might have kept on printing them indefinitely. Twain himself determined that he could and would write better things. Yet the experience he gained in trying his hand was no doubt a valuable one for such a spirit as his. Contrast this with his later experience on the *San Francisco Call,* where editorial restraint forced him to give up what many other capable newspaper and magazine writers on the Coast would have considered a very fine position.

On the *Enterprise* Mark Twain took up writing as a life career.

On the *Enterprise* he adopted the pen name that was to achieve world-wide fame. Who can estimate the ultimate significance of this one incident of choice of pen name? Surely it must be given a major rating among the varied elements of Twain's literary development. That there was no "original Mark Twain" other than Samuel Clemens himself is revealed by the present writer's study of Captain Isaiah Sellers' logbook, made available for the first time for scholarly examination. Five months after Clemens' nom de plume appeared first in the *Enterprise* it appeared in the *San Francisco Call*. On July 9, 1863, the *Call* printed the first article, either reprinted or directly contributed, with Mark Twain's signature, to appear in any known publication outside of the *Territorial Enterprise*. Then came the first Eastern notice of Mark Twain, when *Yankee Notions* reprinted from the *Enterprise* his review of *Ingomar, the Barbarian*. Establishment of this point was made possible by the present writer's discovery of the April 1864 issue of *Yankee Notions* in the Willard S. Morse collection.

It was in Virginia City, in December 1863, that Mark Twain first met Artemus Ward. This suggests the question of Ward's influence on Twain. There is little evidence that Artemus Ward influenced Twain except in an indirect way. By the time the two met, Twain had already made a reputation for himself on the Coast. The present writer's investigation shows that Twain had written a series of letters for the *San Francisco Call* and articles to the *Golden Era,* and that many of his *Enterprise* articles had been reprinted by San Francisco publications. He was well enough known for the *Golden Era,* on September 27, 1863, to give its reprint of an *Enterprise* article the heading "Mark Twain—More of Him." When Ward came with the label, "Wild Humorist of the Plains," a similar title, "The Wild Humorist of the Pacific Slope," was conferred upon Twain.

But this title did not stick. Twain did not have the mind, the manner, the method, or the temperament of Artemus Ward. They were two different spirits. Twain had one thing in common with Ward, as he had in common with John Phoenix, Josh Billings, and Petroleum V. Nasby: he was, at the time, chiefly concerned with humorous writing. There were certain conventional subjects and certain extravagant and burlesque treatments of these subjects which were conventional in newspaper humor of the time. Twain indulged in these to a small degree, but that he soon deserted the traditional devices in favor of his own style of presentation no doubt explains why, of the many humorists who flourished in his day, only Mark Twain remains. That any of these writers had any rubber-stamp influence on Twain cannot be admitted when one makes a comparison of their works with the writings of Twain during his Western period. If, occasionally, he borrowed an inspiration, from whatever source, he usually had the artistic aptitude to improve on it.

Some indirect influence by Artemus Ward has significance, however. Ward had the gift of friendship, and when he came to Virginia City the members of the *Enterprise* staff found in him a congenial companion. Twain enjoyed the comradeship immensely, and was therefore willing to take advice from Ward, who, instead of setting himself above Twain, encouraged him as a brother humorist. Twain felt then, no doubt, that he could follow in the footsteps of this man who was winning popular acclaim. A chain of linked circumstances then continues from their Virginia City companionship to the publication of the "Jumping Frog" story and to Twain's beginnings on the lecture platform.

There has been widespread acceptance of the fiction of Bret Harte's influence on Mark Twain. This appears to be based generally on a passage in a Twain letter to Thomas Bailey Aldrich dated January 28, 1871:

> But I did hate to be accused of plagiarizing Bret Harte, who trimmed and trained and schooled me patiently until he changed me from an awkward utterer of coarse grotesquenesses to a writer of paragraphs and chapters that have found a certain favor in the eyes of even some of the very decentest people in the land—and this grateful remembrance of mine ought to be worth its face, seeing that Bret broke our long friendship a year ago without any cause or provocation that I am aware of.[10]

[10] Paine, *Mark Twain's Letters* (Harper & Bros., 1917), I, pp. 182–83.

This was indeed extravagant praise of the man who was dropping his Western friends right and left, usually on the basis of his having borrowed money from them. And what did Twain have to thank Harte for? Just one thing: Harte was either editor of, or star contributor to, the *Californian* while Twain was in San Francisco and was helpful in getting many Twain sketches into the magazine. This, however, does not prove influence. It was probably the *Californian,* a high-quality publication, that had an effect in toning Twain's articles and increasing their literary excellence, rather than the influence of any individual. Twain was shrewd enough to play up to both Harte and the *Californian* in order to achieve publication in what was undoubtedly the finest literary journal in the West at that time.

Whatever Harte's alleged influence may have been, it was in actuality not strong enough to keep Twain from writing the "Kearny Street Ghost Story," or other sketches that were not submitted to the *Californian* and that no doubt offended Harte's finer sensibilities, if he read these sketches. This less-refined writing, much of it in the Sandwich Islands letters, came after the fictitious influence allegedly began. Nor was this influence strong enough to prompt Harte to see that the jumping-frog story was published first in the *Californian,* although he had heard it told by Twain before it was submitted to Eastern publishers.

From what has been written about the influence of Harte on Mark Twain, one might suppose that there was a sudden and violent change in Twain's writing immediately after he came in contact with Harte. No such sudden change is evident in the Western writings; there is simply a normal development whereby Twain broadened his scope and improved by degrees the quality of his writing style. That Harte should have sought Twain's articles for the *Californian* is not remarkable; it is not unusual for editors to seek the work of good writers for their publications, with no question of personal feelings or influence involved.

Although Twain no doubt felt under some obligation to Harte during the California days, his estimate of Harte, outside of the "influence" passage, was not a high one. There is a likelihood that Twain, like other Westerners, had Harte pretty well labeled from the beginning as an impossible person but played up to his position rather than to the man. And Twain never could take even the good advice of a person whom he did not respect, whereas he seldom hesitated to take bad advice from his friends. In later years, away from the possibility of enjoying any practical benefit through Harte's benevolence, Twain was realistic enough in his judgment of the man. On one occasion when Frank Harris praised Harte, Twain "denounced him and told a story about how he had cheated his publishers. 'I told the publishers,' he said, 'that they ought to have him put in prison. A man should be honest, above everything.' "[11] Harte had no enthusiasm for the success of others; he was envious, covetous of honors bestowed even upon those who considered themselves to be his friends.

Finally, though personal friendship is not necessarily a test of literary influence, it may possibly be relevant to note that in the 515-page volume of *The Letters of Bret Harte,* assembled and edited by Geoffery Bret Harte, there is not a single letter to Mark Twain. So much for Harte's influence on Mark Twain, an influence which was probably not equal to that of many another of Twain's friends and editorial associates in Nevada and California.

Regardless of Bret Harte's relationship to Mark Twain, however, the *Californian* did play a major part in Twain's literary development during his Western period. But it was still only one of the several channels through which Twain's writings reached the public. There were also the *Territorial Enterprise,* the *San Francisco Call,* the *Golden Era,* the *Napa County Reporter* (three San Francisco letters in the winter of 1865), the *Sacramento Union,* the *Hawaiian Herald,* the *San Francisco Bulletin,* and the *Alta California.* These publications and many others also carried reprints of numerous Twain items.

An important factor in Mark Twain's Western development

[11] Edward Wagenknecht, *Mark Twain: The Man and His Work* (Yale University Press, 1935), p. 165.

was his growth as a personality. He had not been long on the streets of Carson City, after his arrival by Overland Stage in August 1861, before he was standing out as one distinct from the crowd. On the *Enterprise* he was given complete freedom to develop this individuality; for this the East took revenge, later, by shanghaiing him into gentility. When he adopted his nom de plume, the name Mark Twain immediately had a personality behind it; it was not simply another writer's pen-name. The name was no doubt a good one, but what would it have amounted to without the personality behind it? Its effectiveness lay chiefly in the dynamic spirit whose individuality it expressed. From the very earliest Western days Twain became the chief figure in groups with which he became associated. His was an eager, vigorous, enthusiastic, dynamic spirit that could not serve as mere background.

That Mark Twain enjoyed the position of importance that he occupied soon after he came West is shown particularly in his letters. As early as August 1863 he wrote home that he was "prone to boast of having the widest reputation, as a local editor, of any man on the Pacific Coast."[12] And his writings from the first were highly personal. He lived close to his material, received his subject matter and his inspirations from realities about him. He made himself an important actor in the drama of the West. It is a vital factor in the growth of Mark Twain as a writer and as a man that he had the opportunity to live in the frontier West, where for five and a half years that vigorous personality was permitted to develop in its own way.

Had Mark Twain been only a humorist in the West, there would have been no odium attached; he was capable of writing humor—good humor. But from the beginning he was more than a humorist. During the Western period he became an accomplished social satirist, and with a gradually broadening scope he wrote artistically with a variety of effects, from the coarsest bur-

[12] Paine, *Letters*, I, 91.

lesque to fine descriptive and informational articles. That much of his life's work was in embryo in the West is shown by a study of a quantity of previously unreprinted material.

Many of the cruder writings of Mark Twain in the West he wrote in the role of a debunker. Some he wrote just because he felt that way, just as he did when he called Laird a "cowardly sneak," a "craven carcass," an "unmitigated liar," and an "abject coward" in the duel correspondence which was discovered by the present writer reprinted in the *Sacramento Union,* although stories discovered in newspapers of the time indicate that no duel was actually fought. The frontier West probably did not draw him out in the writing of coarseness any more than did other parts of the world. He was pretty well away from the West, with its "Doleful Ballad of the Rejected Lover," which he and Steve Gillis intoned in San Francisco's byways, when he wrote *1601* and when he made his speech to the Stomach Club in Paris. Paine's suggestion that Twain's taste was so unreliable that he needed the editing assistance of Mrs. Clemens and W. D. Howells is not verified in the Western record. Twain could have kept on in the West with the cruder type of writing, but his artistic sense pointed the better way. Yet, after all, the cruder products of Mark Twain's pen are so small a part of his total output that they must be given a distinctly minor place in an appraisal of his work.

In the West, Mark Twain was a journalist. Gradually it became more and more evident that he was throwing off "pearls which ought for the eternal welfare" of his race, "to have a more extensive circulation than is afforded by a local daily paper,"[13] as he himself wrote. In December 1866, the Coast no longer offering him the best opportunities, he went to examine the larger field, though even then he was on assignment for the *Alta California* and intended to return to San Francisco after a trip around the world. The innocent went abroad, however, and stayed. The West lost its son; but the world, including the West, gained by the loss.

---

[13] Paine, *Biography,* I, 243–44.

LIST OF REFERENCES

NEWSPAPER and magazine files have been consulted at the following libraries: Nevada State Library, for *Territorial Enterprise;* University of Nevada Library, for *Territorial Enterprise, Gold Hill Daily News, The Nevada Magazine;* Bancroft Library of the University of California, for *Territorial Enterprise, Virginia City Union, San Francisco Call, San Francisco Bulletin, Alta California, Golden Era, Californian, Sacramento Union;* University of California Library, for *Golden Era;* Willard S. Morse's collection, for miscellaneous items; the Clarke Library, for *The Californian;* the California State Library, for *Californian Illustrated Magazine* and *Golden Era.* The Hillcrest edition of the writings of Mark Twain has been used for works not separately listed in the bibliography.

ANGEL, MYRON (Ed.). *History of Nevada.* Thompson & West, Oakland, California, 1881

ARMSTRONG, C. J. "Mark Twain's Early Writings Discovered," *Missouri Historical Review,* Vol. XXIV, July, 1930

BANCROFT, H. H. *History of Nevada, Colorado, and Wyoming. Works.* Vol. XXV. The History Company, San Francisco, 1890

BLISS, WALTER. *Twainiana Notes from the Annotations of Walter Bliss.* Edited with introduction by Frances M. Edwards. The Hobby Shop, Hartford, Connecticut, 1930

BRASHEAR, MINNIE M. *Mark Twain, Son of Missouri.* University of North Carolina Press, Chapel Hill, N.C., 1934

BROOKS, VAN WYCK. *The Ordeal of Mark Twain.* E. P. Dutton & Co., rev. ed., New York, 1933

BROWNELL, GEORGE H. "Mark Twainiana," *American Book Collector,* Vol. III, March, 1933

CLEMENS, CLARA. *My Father Mark Twain.* Harper & Brothers, New York, 1931

CLEMENS, CYRIL (Ed.). *Mark Twain Anecdotes.* Mark Twain Society, Webster Groves, Missouri, 1929

CLEMENS, S. L. *The Adventures of Thomas Jefferson Snodgrass.* (CHARLES HONCE, Ed.) Pascal Covici, Inc., Chicago, 1928

———. *The Celebrated Jumping Frog of Calaveras County.* JOHN PAUL (pseud.). C. H. Webb, New York, N.Y., 1867

CLEMENS, S. L. *Letter to the California Pioneers.* Dewitt & Snelling, Oakland, California, 1911

————. *Mark Twain's Autobiography.* With an Introduction by ALBERT BIGELOW PAINE. 2 vols. Harper & Brothers, New York, 1924

————. *Mark Twain's Letters.* Arranged with Comment by ALBERT BIGELOW PAINE. 2 vols. Harper & Brothers, New York, 1917

————. *Mark Twain's Notebook.* Harper & Brothers, New York, 1935

————. *Mark Twain's Speeches.* With an Introduction by WILLIAM DEAN HOWELLS. Harper & Brothers, New York, 1910

————. *What Is Man?* Harper & Brothers, New York and London, 1917

CLEMENS, WILL M. *Mark Twain: His Life and Work.* Clemens Publishing Co., San Francisco, 1892

CUMMINS, ELLA STERLING. *The Story of the Files.* Issued by World's Fair Commission of California Columbian Exposition, San Francisco, 1893

DANE, G. EZRA (Ed.). *Letters from the Sandwich Islands Written for the "Sacramento Union" by Mark Twain.* The Grabhorn Press, San Francisco, 1937

————. *Letters from the Sandwich Islands . . . . by Mark Twain.* Photolith reprint, Stanford University Press, Stanford University, California, 1938

DE QUILLE, DAN (WILLIAM WRIGHT). "Artemus Ward in Nevada," *Californian Illustrated Magazine,* IV (August, 1893), 403–6

————. "Reporting with Mark Twain," *Californian Illustrated Magazine,* IV (July, 1893), 170–78

DERBY, CAPT. GEORGE HORATIO (JOHN PHOENIX). *Phoenixiana.* 2 vols. The Caxton Press, Chicago, 1897

DE VOTO, BERNARD. *Mark Twain's America.* Little, Brown & Co., Boston, 1932

DOTEN, ALF. "Early Journalism in Nevada," *The Nevada Magazine,* Vol. I, No. 3 (Winnemucca, Nevada, October, 1899), 182–84

FALK, BERNARD. *The Naked Lady or Storm over Adah.* Hutchinson & Co., Ltd., London, 1934

FISHER, HENRY W. *Abroad with Mark Twain and Eugene Field. Tales They Told to a Fellow-Correspondent.* Nicholas L. Brown, New York, 1922

GILLIS, WILLIAM R. *Gold Rush Days with Mark Twain.* Albert and Charles Boni, New York, 1930

————. *Memories of Mark Twain and Steve Gillis.* The Banner, Sonora, California, 1924

GLASSCOCK, CARL B. *The Big Bonanza.* Bobbs-Merrill Co., Indianapolis, 1931

GOODWIN, C. C. *As I Remember Them.* Salt Lake Commercial Club, Salt Lake City, 1913

HARTE, GEOFFREY BRET. *The Letters of Bret Harte.* Houghton Mifflin Co., Boston, 1926

HAZARD, LUCY LOCKWOOD. *The Frontier in American Literature.* Thomas Y. Crowell Co., New York, 1927

HENDERSON, ARCHIBALD. *Mark Twain.* Duckworth & Co., London, 1911

HITTELL, THEODORE H. *History of California,* Vol. III. N. J. Stone & Co., San Francisco, 1898

HOWELL, JOHN (Ed.). *Sketches of the Sixties: by Bret Harte and Mark Twain.* John Howell, San Francisco, 1926

HOWELLS, W. D. *My Mark Twain.* Harper & Brothers, New York, 1911

JAMES, G. W. "How Mark Twain Was Made," reprinted from *National Magazine,* February, 1911

————. "Mark Twain and the Pacific Coast," *Pacific Monthly,* XXIV (1910), 115–34

JOHNSON, MERLE. *A Bibliography of the Work of Mark Twain, Samuel Langhorne Clemens.* Harper & Brothers, New York and London, 1910

LAWTON, MARY. *A Lifetime with Mark Twain.* Harcourt, Brace & Co., New York, 1925

LEACOCK, STEPHEN. *Mark Twain.* D. Appleton & Co., New York, 1933

LEWIS, OSCAR. *The Origin of the Celebrated Jumping Frog of Calaveras County.* The Book Club of California, San Francisco, 1931

LORCH, FRED W. "A Source for Mark Twain's 'The Dandy Frightening the Squatter,'" *American Literature,* III (1931), 309–13

LYMAN, GEORGE D. *The Saga of the Comstock Lode.* Charles Scribner's Sons, New York, 1934

McMURTRIE, DOUGLAS. *A Bibliography of Nevada Newspapers, 1858 to 1875 Inclusive.* Gutenberg-Jahrbuch, Mainz, 1935

————. *A History of California Newspapers.* Plandome Press, New York, 1927

MEINE, FRANKLIN J. *Tall Tales of the Southwest.* Alfred A. Knopf, New York, 1930

MERWIN, HENRY CHILDS. *The Life of Bret Harte.* Houghton Mifflin Co., Boston, 1911

MEYER, HAROLD. "Mark Twain on the Comstock," *Southwest Review,* XII (1927), 197–207

MIGHELS, HENRY R. *Sage Brush Leaves.* Edward Bosqui & Co., San Francisco, 1879

MILLARD, BAILEY. "Mark Twain in San Francisco," *Bookman,* XXXI (June, 1910), 369–73

PAINE, ALBERT BIGELOW. *Mark Twain: A Biography.* 4 vols. Harper & Brothers, New York, 1912

————. *Mark Twain's Letters.* 2 vols. Harper & Brothers, New York, 1917

PAINE, ALBERT BIGELOW. *Mark Twain's Notebook.* Harper & Brothers, New York, 1935

————. *A Short Life of Mark Twain.* Harper & Brothers, New York, 1920

PATTEE, FRED LEWIS. *A History of American Literature since 1870.* The Century Co., New York, 1915

————. *Mark Twain.* American Book Co., New York, 1935

PEMBERTON, T. EDGAR. *Life of Bret Harte.* C. Arthur Pearson, London, 1903

POTTER, JOHN KELLY. *Samuel L. Clemens, First Editions and Values.* The Black Archer Press, Chicago, 1932

RABB, KATE MILNER (Ed.). *Wit and Humor of America.* 6 vols. Bobbs-Merrill Co., Indianapolis, 1907

ROURKE, CONSTANCE. *American Humor.* Harcourt, Brace & Co., New York, 1931

SCHONEMANN, FRIEDERICH. *Mark Twain als Literarische Personlichkeit.* Verlag der Frommanschen Buchhandlung, Walter Biedermann, Jena, 1925

SEITZ, DAN C. *Artemus Ward: A Biography and Bibliography.* Harper & Brothers, New York, 1919

SHERMAN, STUART. "Mark Twain," *Cambridge History of American Literature,* Vol. III. G. P. Putnam's Sons, New York, 1921

STELLMAN, L. J. *Mother Lode.* Harr Wagner Publishing Co., San Francisco, 1935

STEWART, GEORGE R., JR. *A Bibliography of the Writings of Bret Harte in the Magazines and Newspapers of California, 1857–1871.* University of California Press, Berkeley, California, 1933

————. *Bret Harte, Argonaut and Exile.* Houghton Mifflin Co., Boston, 1931

STEWART, WILLIAM M. *Reminiscences.* Edited by GEORGE ROTHWELL BROWN. The Neale Publishing Co., New York, 1908

WAGENKNECHT, EDWARD. *Mark Twain: The Man and His Work.* Yale University Press, New Haven, Connecticut, 1935

WALKER, FRANKLIN (Ed.). *The Washoe Giant in San Francisco.* Being sketches by Mark Twain published in the *Golden Era* in the Sixties . . . . George Fields, San Francisco, 1938

WHITE, EDGAR. "Mark Twain's Printer Days," *Overland Monthly,* LXX (1917), 573–76

WHITE, FRANK M. "Mark Twain as a Newspaper Reporter," *Outlook,* XCVI (1910), 961–67

WRIGHT, WILLIAM (DAN DE QUILLE). *History of the Big Bonanza.* American Publishing Co., Hartford, Connecticut; A. L. Bancroft & Co., San Francisco, California, 1876

YOUNG, JOHN P. *Journalism in California.* Chronicle Publishing Co., San Francisco, 1915

PERIODICAL BIBLIOGRAPHY

BIBLIOGRAPHY OF THE WRITINGS OF MARK TWAIN IN THE NEWSPAPERS AND MAGAZINES OF NEVADA AND CALIFORNIA, 1861–1866

Alta California, San Francisco
1866 Dec. 14 "So-Long"
     15 Address, "Mark Twain's Farewell," delivered at Congress Hall, San Francisco, December 10, 1866

The fifty "Holy Land Excursion Letters" to the *Alta California,* published from August 25, 1867, to May 17, 1868, were rewritten for *Innocents Abroad* (1869).

Bulletin, San Francisco
1866 Nov. 30 "Mark Twain's Interior Notes"
     Dec. 6 "Mark Twain's Interior Notes"
          7 "Mark Twain's Interior Notes"
          7 "Mark Twain Mystified"

Californian, San Francisco
1864 Oct. 1 "A Notable Conundrum" (*Sketches of the Sixties*)
          8 "Concerning the Answer to That Conundrum" (*Sketches of the Sixties*)
         15 "Still Further Concerning That Conundrum" (*Sketches of the Sixties*)
         22 "Whereas"—("Love's Bakery" and "Aurelia's Unfortunate Young Man") (part in *The Jumping Frog,* complete in *Sketches of the Sixties*)
         29 "A Touching Story of George Washington's Boyhood" (*The Jumping Frog*)

1864 Nov. 5 "Daniel in the Lion's Den—and Out Again All Right"
                 (*Sketches of the Sixties*)
       12 "The Killing of Julius Caesar Localized" (*The Jumping
                 Frog*)
       19 "A Full and Reliable Account of the Extra-ordinary
                 Meteoric Shower of Last Saturday Night" (*Sketches of
                 the Sixties*)
      Dec. 3 "Lucretia Smith's Soldier" (*The Jumping Frog*)
1865 Mar. 18 "An Unbiased Criticism" (*Sketches of the Sixties*)
      May 6 "Important Correspondence. Between Mr. Mark Twain
                 of San Francisco, and Rev. Bishop Hawks, D.D., of
                 New York, Rev. Phillips Brooks of Philadelphia, and
                 Rev. Dr. Cummings of Chicago, concerning the Occu-
                 pancy of Grace Cathedral" (*Sketches of the Sixties*)
       13 "Further of Mr. Mark Twain's Important Correspondence"
                 (*Sketches of the Sixties*)
       27 "How I Went to the Great Race between Lodi and Nor-
                 folk"
      June 3 "Answers to Correspondents" (some in *The Jumping Frog*)
                 "Discarded Lover"
                 "Arabella"
                 "Persecuted Unfortunate"
                 "Arthur Augustus"
       10 "Answers to Correspondents" (some in *The Jumping Frog*)
                 "Amateur Serenader"
                 "St. Clair Higgins, Los Angeles"
                 "Arithmeticus, Virginia, Nevada"
                 "Ambitious Learner, Oakland"
                 "Julia Maria"
                 "Nom de Plume"
                 "Melton Mowbray, Dutch Flat"
                 "Laura Matilda"
                 "Professional Beggar"
       17 "Answers to Correspondents" (some in *The Jumping Frog*)
                 "Moral Statistician"
                 "Simon Wheeler, Sonora"
                 "Inquirer"
                 "Anna Maria"
                 "Charming Simplicity"
                 "Literary Connoisseur"
                 "Etiquetticus, Monitor Silver Mines"
       24 "Answers to Correspondents" (some in *The Jumping Frog*)
                 "True Son of the Union"
                 "Socrates Murphy"

1865 June 24 "Arithmeticus, Virginia, Nevada"
                "Young Mother"
                "Blue-Stocking, San Francisco"
                "Agnes St. Clair Smith"

      July 1 "Answers to Correspondents" (some in *The Jumping Frog*)
                "Young Actor"
                "Mary, Rincon School"
                "Anxiety, S. F."
                "Mark Twain"
                "Gold Hill News"

          8 "Answers to Correspondents" (some in *The Jumping Frog*)
                "Inquirer, Sacramento"
                "Student of Etiquette"
                "Mary, Rincon School"

      Aug. 26 "The Facts. Concerning the recent trouble between Mr. Mark Twain and Mr. John William Skae of Virginia City—Wherein it is attempted to be proved that the former was not to blame in the matter" (part in *The Jumping Frog*, complete in *Sketches of the Sixties*)

      Oct. 28 "Real Estate Versus Imaginary Possessions, Poetically Considered" (*Sketches of the Sixties*)

      Nov. 18 "On the Launch of the Steamer Capital" (includes "The Entertaining History of the Scriptural Panoramist," which was published in *Beadle's Dime Fun Book, No. 3*, 1866; and later in *The Jumping Frog*)

      Dec. 2 "Mark Twain Overpowered" (*Sketches of the Sixties*)
          23 "The Christmas Fireside. For good little girls and boys by Grandfather Twain" (*The Jumping Frog*)
          23 "Enigma" (*Sketches of the Sixties*)

1866 Apr. 7 "On Linden, etc." (*Sketches of the Sixties*)
      Aug. 25 "The Moral Phenomenon" (*Sketches of the Sixties*)
      Sept. 29 "Origin of Illustrious Men" (*The Jumping Frog*)

Call, San Francisco

1863 July 9 "Mark Twain's Letter, Virginia City, N.T., July 5, 1863"
         15 "Mark Twain's Letter, Virginia City, N.T., July 12, 1863"
         18 "Mark Twain's Letter, Virginia City, N.T., July 16, 12 M"
         23 "Mark Twain's Letter, Virginia City, N.T., July 19"
         30 "Mark Twain's Letter, Virginia City, N.T., July 26"
      Aug. 6 "Mark Twain's Letter, Virginia City, Aug. 2, 1863"
         13 "Mark Twain's Letter, Virginia City, Aug. 8, 1863"
         30 "Mark Twain's Letter, Steamboat Springs, Aug. 20, 1863"
      Sept. 3 "Mark Twain's Letter, Carson City, Nov. 14, 1863"

1863 Nov. 19 "Mark Twain's Letter"
        (22) "Mark Twain on Murders" (reprinted in *Golden Era*)
      Dec. 2 "Death—Robbery, Carson, Dec. 1"
           11 "Assassination in Carson, Carson, Dec. 10"
1864 Sept. 6 "A Small Piece of Spite"

Dramatic Chronicle, San Francisco
1865   "Earthquake Almanac" (reprinted in *Golden Era,* Oct. 22,
                  1865; *The Jumping Frog*)

Golden Era, San Francisco
1863 Sept. 20 "How to Cure a Cold" (*The Jumping Frog*)
      Oct. 11 "The Great Prize Fight" (*Wit and Humor of America*)
1864 June 26 "Evidence in the Case of Smith vs. Jones" (*Wit and Humor
                  of America*)
      July 3 "Early Rising as Regards Excursions to the Cliff House"
1865 July 2 "Smith Brown Jones"
           9 "S. Browne Jones"
          16 "S. Browne Jones"
1866 Feb. 25 "Mark Twain on Fashions"
          25 "Mark Twain on California Critics"
      Mar. 4 "Mark Twain on the New Wild Cat Religion"
          11 "Mark Twain on Boot-Blacks"
          11 "More Spiritual Investigations by Mark Twain"
          18 "Reflections on the Sabbath, by Mark Twain"

Hawaiian Herald, Honolulu
1866 Oct. 17 "An Epistle from Mark Twain"

Napa County Reporter, Napa
1865 Nov. 11 Letter—San Francisco, Nov. 8, 1865
                  "Similar Accident"
                  "A Daniel Come to Judgment"
                  "The Addisonians"
                  "Amusements"
                  "Jump's Last"
          25 Letter—San Francisco, Nov. 23, 1865
                  "On Guard of a Bender"
                  "Benkert Cometh"
                  "Kip, Kip, Hurrah!"
                  "Death of Gen. De Russy"

1865   Dec.   2   Letter—San Francisco, Nov. 30, 1865
                    "Webb's Benefit"
                    "Banished"
                    "Wretched Summerville"
                    "Too Bad"

Parts of these letters are reprinted in *Cornelius Cole* (California pioneer and United States Senator), by Catherine Coffin Philips (John Henry Nash, San Francisco, 1929).

Sacramento Union, Sacramento

1864   May 26   Duel correspondence with Laird (reprinted from *Territorial Enterprise*)
            26   Duel correspondence with Laird (reprinted from *Territorial Enterprise*)
            26   Duel correspondence with Laird (reprinted from *Territorial Enterprise*)
1866   Apr. 16   (Honolulu, March 18) "Climatic"
            17   (Honolulu, March 19) "The Ajax Voyage Continued"
            18   (Honolulu, March —) "Still at Sea"
            19   (Honolulu, March —) "Our Arrival Elaborated a Little More"
            20   (Honolulu, March —) "Board and Lodging Secured"
            21   (Honolulu, March —) "Coming Home from Prison"
            24   (Honolulu, March —) "The Equestrian Excursion Concluded"
       May 21   (Honolulu, April —) "Off"
            22   (Honolulu, April —) "Sad Accident"
            23   (Honolulu, April —) "The Whaling Trade"
            24   (Honolulu, April —) "Paradise and the Pari (Joke)"
       June 20   (Honolulu, May 23) "Hawaiian Legislature"
            21   (Honolulu, May 23) "Legislature Continued"
       July 16   (Honolulu, June 22) "Home Again"
            19   (Honolulu, June 25) "Burning of the Clipper Ship Hornet at Sea"
            30   (Honolulu, June 30) "A Month of Mourning"
       Aug. 1   (Honolulu, July 1) "Funeral of the Princess"
            18   (Honolulu, July —) "At Sea Again"
            24   (Kona, July —) "Still in Kona"
            30   (Kealakekua Bay, 1866) "Great Britain's Queer Monument to Captain Cook"
       Sept. 6   (Kealakekua Bay, July) "A Funny Scrap of History"
            22   (Kealakekua Bay, July) "The Romantic God Lono"
            26   (Honolulu, Sept. 10) "The High Chief of Sugardom"
       Oct. 25   (Kilauea, June —) "A Notable Discovery"
       Nov. 16   (Volcano House, June 3) "The Great Volcano of Kileaua"

Part of the letter published by the *Union* on April 20 is reprinted in *The Jumping Frog* under the title, "Honored as a Curiosity in Honolulu." Part of the letter published on April 21 is reprinted in *The Jumping Frog* under the title, "The Steed 'Oahu'." The letter published on July 16 was rewritten for *Harper's Magazine,* December 1866, appearing later in *Library of Universal Adventure,* 1888. The letters for April 16, 17, 18, 19, and 20 were reprinted in the *Union,* March 21, 1921, and the entire series was issued (550 copies) by The Grabhorn Press as *Letters from the Sandwich Islands,* with introduction and conclusion by G. Ezra Dane, San Francisco, 1937 (trade edition, Stanford University Press, 1938).

Territorial Enterprise, Virginia City

Letters from Mark Twain to the *Territorial Enterprise,* from "Mark Twain's Scrap Book," which is in Willard S. Morse's collection. (The dates given are the dates shown on letters, not the dates of publication):

1863 Dec. 13 Carson
"Third House—Reported by Mark Twain in 'Phonographic Short Hand'." (Thompson & West's *History of Nevada*)
"Our Carson Dispatch—Second Session" (by Telegraph)

1865 "Mark Twain on the Ballad Infliction" (reprinted in *Californian,* Nov. 4, 1865. This item is included in the list of *Californian* reprints)

Dec. 11 San Francisco
"Personal"
"Christian Spectator"
"The Police Judge Trouble"
"More Romance"
"Telegraphic"

13 San Francisco
"Managerial"
"Not a Suicide"
"Reopening of the Plaza"
"More Fashions—Exit 'Waterfall' "

19 San Francisco
"Caustic"
"Thief Catching"
"I Knew It!"
"MacDougal vs. Maguire"
"Louis Aldrich"
"Gould and Curry"

20 San Francisco
"The New Swimming Bath"
"Buckingham"
"Mining Corporations"

1865 Dec. 20 "Major Farren"
"Sam Brannan"
"The Excentrics"
"MacDougal vs. Maguire"
"Nursery Rhyme"
"Uncle Joe Trench"

22 San Francisco
"How Long, O Lord, How Long?"
"Editorial Poem"
"Facetious"
"Mayo and Aldrich"
"Financial"
"Personal"
"Mock Duel—Almost"
"More Wisdom"

23 San Francisco
"Extraordinary Delicacy"
"Shooting"
"Another Enterprise"
"Spirit of the Local Press"
"Gardiner Indicted"

29 San Francisco
"The Black Hole of San Francisco"
"Busted"
"Inspiration of Louderback"
"Personal"

1866 Jan. 8 San Francisco
"Whiteman Mighty Unsartain"
"The Opening Nights"
"The Portraits"
"The Mint Defalcation"

11 San Francisco
"Gorgeous New Romance by Fitz Smythe"
"Another Romance"
"Precious Stones"
"Premature"
"A Handsome Testimonial"
"The Californian Art Union"
"Theatrical"

24 San Francisco
"More Outcroppings"
"Among the Spiritualists"
"Personal"
"How They Take It"

1866 Jan. 28 San Francisco
          "Bearding the Fenian in His Lair" (*The Jumping Frog*,
             under title, "Among the Fenians")
          "Sabbath Recollections"
          "Neddamode"
    Feb. 3 San Francisco
          "Personal"
          "More Cemeterial Ghastliness"
          "Rev. Charles Ellis"
          "More Outcroppings"
          "I Feel I'm Growing Mirk—Poem"
          "Take the Stand, Fitz Smythe"
       6 San Francisco
          "Remarkable Dream"
          "Personal"
          "Dogberry's Lecture"
     12 San Francisco
          "Michael"
          "Liberality of Michael"
          "Liberality of His Heir"
          "The Fashions"
          "The New Play"
          "Personal"
    Feb. 15 San Francisco
          "Funny"
          "Montana"
          "Literary"
          "Personal"
          "Specie and Currency"
     23 San Francisco
          "A Voyage of the Ajax"
          "Pleasing Incident"
          "Off for the Snow Belt"
          "After Them"
          "Theatrical"
     25 Sacramento
          "Sacramento"
          "Boot-Blacking"
          "Brief Climate Paragraph"
          "The Lullaby of the Rain"
          "Try to Out 'Sass' the Landlord and Fail"
          "Mr. John Paul's Baggage"
    Aug. — San Francisco
          "An Inquiry about Insurance" (*The Jumping Frog*)

Items written by Mark Twain for the *Territorial Enterprise,* not included in "Mark Twain's Scrap Book." (The dates given are the dates of publication):

1866 Nov. 4 "Card from Mark Twain"
           11 "Card to the Highwaymen"

Miscellaneous

1863 Nov. — " 'Ingomar' over the Mountains. The Argument" (reprinted by *Yankee Notions,* New York, April, 1863. Also reprinted by *Golden Era,* Nov. 29, 1863)

1865 Nov. — "Grand Theatrical Banquet" (Theatrical barbecue at Occidental Hotel, San Francisco, Nov. 1865)
          "Steamer Departures"

Territorial Enterprise

Enterprise articles by Mark Twain reprinted in *Californian,* with date of that publication:

1865 Nov. 4 "Mark Twain on the Ballad Infliction"
           25 "The Pioneer Ball." "After Jenkins" (*The Jumping Frog*)
           25 "The Old Thing." "What Cheer Robbery" (in *Territorial Enterprise,* Nov. 18)
1866 Mar. 3 "A New Biography of George Washington" (*The Jumping Frog*)
            3 "Presence of Mind" (*The Jumping Frog*)

Enterprise articles by Mark Twain reprinted in *Golden Era,* with date of that publication:

1863 Sept. 27 "All About the Fashions" (San Francisco letter dated June 19)
      Nov. 29 "Announcing Artemus Ward's Coming"
           29 "Play Acting over the Mountains. The play of 'Barbarian,' by Maguire's Dramatic Troupe at Virginia City." (Also reprinted in *Yankee Notions,* April 1864. This item is listed under *Territorial Enterprise,* Miscellaneous)
      Dec. 6 "A Tide of Eloquence"
1864 Feb. 28 "Washoe Wit." "Mark Twain on the Rampage." "Concerning Notaries"
      May 1 " 'Mark Twain' and 'Dan De Quille,' Hors De Combat"
           22 "Information Wanted" ("Information for the Million," *The Jumping Frog*)
      June 26 " 'Mark Twain' in the Metropolis"

1866 Jan. 14 "Mark Twain's New Year's Day"
          21 "What Have the Police Been Doing?"
          21 "Fitz Smythe's Horse" (*Beadle's Dime Fun Book*, 1866)
          28 "Mark Twain's Kearny Street Ghost Story"
          28 "Captain Montgomery." "The Chapman Family." "Miseries of Washoe Men." "Busted, and Gone Abroad"
     Feb.   4 "Mark Twain Among the Spirits" (published in *Territorial Enterprise*, Nov. 4; rewritten for *The Jumping Frog*)
          11 "Mark Twain a Committee Man." "Ghostly Gatherings Down Among the Dead Men" (rewritten for "Among the Spirits" in *The Jumping Frog*). "A Phantom Fandango"
          18 "Mark Twain on the Signal Corps"
          18 "Mark Twain on Spiritual Insanity"
          18 "The Russian American Telegraph Company"

Enterprise articles by Mark Twain reprinted in *San Francisco Bulletin*, with date of that publication:

1862 Oct. 15 "The Petrified Man" (published in *Territorial Enterprise*, Oct. 5)
1863 Oct. 31 "The Latest Sensation" (Empire City Massacre story, which was published in *Territorial Enterprise;* edited for Paine's biography of Mark Twain, Appendix C)

SELECTED MARK TWAIN
WESTERN ITEMS

A WASHOE JOKE.

[From *San Francisco Bulletin,* October 15, 1862.]

The *Territorial Enterprise* has a joke of a "petrified man" having been found on the plains, which the interior journals seem to be copying in good faith. Our authority gravely says:

A petrified man was found some time ago in the mountains south of Gravelly Ford. Every limb and feature of the stony mummy was perfect, not even excepting the left leg, which has evidently been a wooden one during the lifetime of the owner—which lifetime, by the way, came to a close about a century ago, in the opinion of a *savan* who has examined the defunct. The body was in a sitting posture and leaning against a huge mass of croppings; the attitude was pensive, the right thumb resting against the side of the nose; the left thumb partially supported the chin, the forefinger pressing the inner corner of the left eye and drawing it partly open; the right eye was closed, and the fingers of the right hand spread apart. [!] This strange freak of nature created a profound sensation in the vicinity, and our informant states that, by request, Justice Sewell or Sowell of Humboldt City at once proceeded to the spot and held an inquest on the body. The verdict of the jury was that "deceased came to his death from protracted exposure," etc. The people of the neighborhood volunteered to bury the poor unfortunate, and were even anxious to do so; but it was discovered, when they attempted to remove him, that the water which had dripped upon him for ages from the crag above, had coursed down his back and deposited a limestone sediment under him which had glued him to the bed rock upon which he sat, as with a cement of adamant, and Judge S. refused to allow the charitable citizens to blast him from his position. The opinion expressed by his Honor that such a course would be little less than sacrilege, was eminently just and proper. Everybody goes to see the stone man, as many as 300 persons having visited the hardened creature during the past five or six weeks.

THE LATEST SENSATION.

[From *San Francisco Bulletin*, October 31, 1863.]

A Victim to Jeremy Diddling Trustees—He Cuts His Throat from Ear to Ear, Scalps His Wife, and Dashes out the Brains of Six Helpless Children!

[From the "Territorial Enterprise" of 28th October.]

From Abram Curry, who arrived here yesterday afternoon from Carson, we have learned the following particulars concerning a bloody massacre which was committed in Ormsby county night before last. It seems that during the past six months a man named P. Hopkins, or Philip Hopkins, has been residing with his family in the old log house just at the edge of the great pine forest which lies between Empire City and Dutch Nick's. The family consisted of 9 children—5 girls and 4 boys—the oldest of the group, Mary, being 19 years old, and the youngest, Tommy, about a year and a half. Twice in the past two months Mrs. Hopkins, while visiting in Carson, expressed fears concerning the sanity of her husband, remarking that of late he had been subject to fits of violence, and that during the prevalence of one of these he had threatened to take her life. It was Mrs. Hopkins's misfortune to be given to exaggeration, however, and but little attention was paid to what she said.

About 10 o'clock on Monday evening Hopkins dashed into Carson on horseback, with his throat cut from ear to ear, and bearing in his hand a reeking scalp from which the warm, smoking blood was still dripping, and fell in a dying condition in front of the Magnolia saloon. Hopkins expired in the course of five minutes, without speaking. The long red hair of the scalp he bore marked it as that of Mrs. Hopkins. A number of citizens, headed by Sheriff Gasherie, mounted at once and rode down to Hopkins' house, where a ghastly scene met their gaze. The scalpless corpse of Mrs. Hopkins lay across the threshhold, with her head split open and her right hand almost severed from the wrist. Near her lay the ax with which the murderous deed had been committed. In one of the bedrooms six of the children were found, one in bed and the others scattered about the floor. They were all dead. Their brains had evidently been dashed out with a club, and every mark about them seemed to have been made with a blunt instrument. The children must have struggled hard for their lives, as articles of clothing and broken furniture were strewn about the room in the utmost confusion. Julia and Emma, aged respectively 14 and 17, were found in the kitchen, bruised and insensible, but it is thought their recovery is possible. The eldest girl, Mary, must have sought refuge in her terror in the garret, as her body was found there frightfully mutilated, and the knife with which her wounds had been inflicted still sticking in her side. The two girls Julia and Emma, who had recovered sufficiently to be able to talk yesterday morning, state that their father knocked them down with a billet of wood and stamped on them. They think they were the first attacked. They further state that Hopkins had shown evidence of derangement all day, but had exhibited no violence. He flew into a passion and attempted to murder them because they advised him to go to bed and compose his mind.

Curry says Hopkins was about 42 years of age, and a native of Western Pennsylvania; he was always affable and polite, and until very recently we had never heard of his ill treating his family. He had been a heavy owner in the best mines of Virginia and Gold Hill, but when the San Francisco papers exposed the game of cooking dividends in order to bolster up our stocks he grew afraid and sold out, and invested to an immense amount in the Spring Valley Water Company of San Francisco. He was advised to do this by a relative of his, one of the editors of the San Francisco *Bulletin,* who had suffered pecuniarily by the dividend-cooking system as applied to the Daney Mining Company recently. Hopkins had not long ceased to own in the various claims on the Com-

stock lead, however, when several dividends were cooked on his newly acquired property, their water totally dried up, and Spring Valley stock went down to nothing. It is presumed that this misfortune drove him mad and resulted in his killing himself and the greater portion of his family. The newspapers of San Francisco permitted this water company to go on borrowing money and cooking dividends, under cover of which cunning financiers crept out of the tottering concern, leaving the crash to come upon poor and unsuspecting stockholders, without offering to expose the villainy at work. We hope the fearful massacre detailed above may prove the saddest result of their silence.

———

[From the "Territorial Enterprise" of 29th October.]

I take it all back. * * * * *

MARK TWAIN.

[ARTEMUS WARD.]

[From *Golden Era,* November 29, 1863.]

Artemus Ward announces his coming to Washoe, and "Mark Twain" of the *Territorial Enterprise* sends him greeting:

We understand that Artemus Ward contemplates visiting this region to deliver his lectures, and perhaps make some additions to his big "sho." In his last letter to us he appeared particularly anxious to "sekure a kupple ov horned todes; alsowe, a lizard which it may be persessed of 2 tales, or any komical snaix, an enny sich little unconsidered trifles, as the poets say, which they do not interest the kommun mind. Further, be it nown, that I

would like a opportunity for to maik a moddel in wax of a average size wash-owe man, with feet attached, as an kompanion pictur to a waxen figger of a nigger I have sekured, at an large outlaye, whitch it has a unnatural big hed onto it. Could you alsowe manage to gobbel up the skulp of the layte Missus Hoppins? I adore sich foot-prints of atrocity as it were, muchly. I was roominatin on gittin a bust of mark Twain, but I've kwit kontemplatin the work. They tell me down heer too the Ba that the busts air so kommon it wood only bee an waist of wax too git un kounterfit presentiment." We shall assist Mr. Ward in every possible way about making his Washoe collection and have no doubt but he will pick up many curious things during his sojourn.

[From *Daily Morning Call*, San Francisco, December 2, 1863.]

DISPATCHES BY THE STATE LINE.

(Exclusively to the *Morning Call*.)

DEATH—ROBBERY.

CARSON, December 1. — Hon. Charles S. Potter, member of the Constitutional Convention, from Washoe county, died at his residence at three o'clock P.M., to-day. The Convention adjourned over to-night, in consequence.

A teamster was murdered and robbed on the public highway, between Carson and Virginia, to-day. Our sprightly and efficient officers are on the alert. They calculate to inquire into this thing next week. They are tired of these daily outrages in sight of town, you know.

TWAIN.

[From *Daily Morning Call*, San Francisco, December 11, 1863.]

ASSASSINATION IN CARSON.

CARSON, December 10.—Joe Magee was assassinated in the St. Nicholas Saloon, at four o'clock this morning. The gun was fired through the window, from the street.

The murderer is not known. It is thought Magee assassinated Jack Williams in Virginia last Winter.

MARK TWAIN.

[From *Golden Era,* February 28, 1864]

WASHOE WIT.

MARK TWAIN ON THE RAMPAGE.

CONCERNING NOTARIES.

Mark Twain, the wild humorist of the Sage Brush Hills, writes from Carson City to the *Territorial Enterprise,* telling all about the Legislature, Governor Nye, and the rest of mankind at Nevada's Capital. He says:

A strange, strange thing occurred here yesterday, to wit:

A MAN APPLIED FOR A NOTARY'S COMMISSION.

Think of it. Ponder over it. He wanted a notarial commission—he said so himself. He was from Storey county. He brought his little petition along with him. He brought it on two stages. It is voluminous. The County Surveyor is chaining it off. Three shifts of clerks will be employed night and day on it, decyphering the signatures and testing their genuineness. They began unrolling the petition at noon, and people of strong mining proclivities at once commenced locating claims on it. We are too late, you know. But then they say the extensions are just as good as the original. I believe you.

Since writing the above, I have discovered that the foregoing does not amount to much as a sensation item, after all. The reason is, because there are seventeen hundred and forty-two applications for notaryships already on file in the Governor's office. I was not aware of it, you know. There are also as much as eleven cords of petitions stacked up in his back yard. A watchman stands guard over this combustible material—the back yard is not insured.

Since writing the above, strange events have happened. I started down town, and had not gone far, when I met a seedy, ornery, ratty, hang-dog-looking stranger, who approached me in the most insinuating manner, and said he was glad to see me. He said he had often sighed for an opportunity of becoming acquainted with me—that he had read my effusions (he called them "effusions,") with solemn delight, and had yearned to meet the author face to face. He said he was Billson—Billson of Lander—I might have heard of him. I told him I had—many a time—which was an infamous falsehood. He said "D—n it, old Quill-driver, you must come and take a drink with me;" and says I, "D—n it, old Vermin-ranch, I'll do it." [I had him there.] We took a drink, and he told the bar-keeper to charge it. After which, he opened a well-filled carpet-sack and took out a shirt-collar and a petition. He then threw the empty carpet sack aside and unrolled several yards of the petition—"just for a starter," he said. "Now," says he, "Mark, have you got a good deal of influence with Governor Nye?" "Unbounded," says I, with honest pride; "when I go and use my influence

with Governor Nye, and tell him it will be a great personal favor to me if he will do so and so, he always says it will be a real pleasure to him—that if it were any other man—any other man in the world—but seeing it's me, he won't." Mr. Billson then remarked that I was the very man; he wanted a little notarial appointment, and he would like me to mention it to the Governor. I said I would, and turned away, resolved to damn young Billson's official aspirations with a mild dose of my influence.

I walked about ten steps, and met a cordial man, with the dust of travel upon his garments. He mashed my hands in his, and as I stood straightening the joints back into their places again, says he, "Why, darn it, Mark, how well you're looking! Thunder! It's been an age since I saw you. Turn around and let's look at you good. 'Gad, it's the same old Mark! Well, how've you been—and what have you been doing with yourself lately? Why don't you never come down and see a fellow? Every time I come to town, the old woman's sure to get after me for not bringing you out, as soon as I get back. Why she takes them articles of yourn, and slathers 'em into her old scrap-book, along with deaths, and marriages, and receipts for the itch, and the small-pox, and hell knows what all, and if it warn't that you talk too slow to ever make love, dang my cats if I wouldn't be jealous of you. I would, by the eternal. But what's the use fooling away time here?—let's go and gobble a cock-tail." This was old Boreas, from Washoe. I went and gobbled a cock-tail with him. He mentioned incidentally, that he wanted a notaryship, and showed me a good deal of his petition. I said I would use my influence in his behalf, and requested him to call at the Governor's office in the morning, and get his commission. He thanked me most heartily, and said he would. [I think I see him doing of it.]

I met another stranger before I got to the corner—a pompous little man with a crooked-handled cane and sorrel moustache. Says he, "How do you do, Mr. Twain—how do you do, sir? I am happy to see you, sir—very happy indeed, sir. My name is——. Pardon me, sir, but I perceive you do not entirely recollect me—I am J. Bidlecome Dusenberry, of Esmeralda, formerly of the city of New York, sir." "Well," says I "I'm glad to meet you, Dysintery, and—" "No, no—Dusenberry, sir, Dusenberry!—you—" "Oh, I beg your pardon," says I; "Dusenberry —yes, I understand, now; but it's all the same, you know—Dusenberry, by any other name would—however, I see you have a bale of dry goods—for me, perhaps." He said it was only a little petition, and proceeded to show me a few acres of it, observing casually that he was a candidate in the notarial line—that he had read my lucumbrations (he called it all that) with absorbing interest, and he would like me to use my influence with the Governor in his behalf. I assured him his commission would be ready for him as soon as it was signed. He appeared overcome with gratitude, and insisted, and insisted, and insisted, until at last I went and took a drink with him.

On the next corner I met Chief Justice Turner, on his way to the Governor's office with a petition. He said, "God bless you, my *dear* fellow—I'm delighted to see you—" and hurried on, after receiving my solemn promise that he should be a Notary Public if I could secure his appointment. Next I met William Stewart, grinning in his engaging way, and stroking his prodigious whiskers from his nose to his stomach. Sandy Baldwin was with him, and they both had measureless petitions on a dray, with the names all signed in their own hand writing. I knew those fellows pretty well, and I didn't promise them my influence. I knew if the Governor refused to appoint them, they would have an injunction on him in less than twenty-four hours, and stop the issuance of any more Notary commissions. I met John B. Winters, next, and Judge North, and Mayor Arick, and Washoe Jim, and John O. Earl, and Ah Foo, and John H. Atchinson, and Hong Wo, and Wells Fargo, and Charley Strong, and Bob Morrow, and Gen. Williams, and seventy-two other prominent citizens of Storey county, with a long pack-train laden with their several petitions. I examined their documents, and promised to use my influence toward procuring notaryships for the whole tribe. I also drank with them.

I wandered down the street, conversing with every man I met, examining his petition. It became a sort of monomania with me, and I kept it up for two hours with unflagging interest. Finally, I stumbled upon a pensive, travel-worn stranger, leaning against an awning-post. I went up and looked at him. He looked at me. I looked at him again, and again he looked at me. I bent my gaze upon him once more, and says I, "Well?" He looked at me very hard, and says he "Well—well what?" Says I, "Well—I would like to examine your petition, if you please." He looked very much astonished—I may say amazed. When he had recovered his presence of mind, he says "what the devil do you mean?" I explained to him that I only wanted to glance over his petition for a notaryship. He said he believed I was a lunatic—he didn't like the unhealthy light in my eye, and he didn't want me to come any closer to him. I asked him if he had escaped the epidemic, and he shuddered and said he didn't know of any epidemic. I pointed to the large placard on the wall: "Coaches will leave the Ormsby House punctually every fifteen minutes, for the Governor's mansion, for the accommodation of Notarial aspirants, etc., etc.—Schemerhorn, Agent"— and I asked him if he didn't know enough to understand what that meant? I also pointed to the long procession of petition-laden citizens filing up the street toward the Governor's house, and asked him if he was not aware that all those fellows were going after notarial commissions— that the balance of the people had already gone, and that he and I had the whole town to ourselves? He was astonished again. Then he placed his hand upon his heart, and swore a frightful oath that he had just arrived from over the mountains, and had no petition, and didn't want a notaryship. I gazed upon him a moment in silent rapture, and then clasped him to my breast. Af-

ter which, I told him it was my turn to treat, by thunder. Whereupon, we entered a deserted saloon, and drank up its contents. We lay upon a billiard table in a torpid condition for many minutes, but at last my exile rose up and muttered in a sepulchral voice, "I feel it—O Heavens, I feel it in me veins!" "Feel what?" says I, alarmed. Says he, "I feel—O me sainted mother!— I feel —feel—a hankering to be a Notary Public!" And he tore down several yards of wall-paper, and fell to writing a petition on it. Poor devil—he had got it at last, and got it bad. I was seized with the fatal distemper a moment afterward. I wrote a petition with frantic haste, appended a copy of the Directory of Nevada Territory to it, and we fled down the deserted streets to the Governor's office.

But I must draw the curtain upon these harrowing scenes—the very memory of them scorches my brain. Ah, this Legislature has much to answer for in cutting down the number of Notaries Public in this Territory, with their infernal new law.

MARK TWAIN

[From *Yankee Notions,* New York, April, 1864.]

DRAMATIC AND MUSICAL.
"INGOMAR" OVER THE MOUNTAINS. THE "ARGUMENT."

During the Fall Season of Mr. Maguire's Dramatic troupe at his new Opera House in Virginia City, the *Territorial Enterprise* has indulged its readers with an extraordinary succession of humorous, pungent and peculiar *critiques.* The player-folk presented "Ingomar, the Barbarian," and "Mark Twain" did the piece after this funny fashion:

Act I—Mrs. Claughley appears in the costume of a healthy Greek ma-

tron (from Limerick). She urges Parthenia, her daughter, to marry Polydor, and save her father from being sold out by the sheriff—the old man being in debt for assessments.

Scene 2 — Polydor — who is a wealthy, spindle-shanked, stingy old stockbroker—prefers his suit and is refused by the Greek maiden—by the accomplished Greek maiden, we may say, since she speaks English without any perceptible foreign accent.

Scene 3—The Comanches capture Parthenia's father, Old Myron (who is the chief and only blacksmith in his native village), they tear him from his humble cot, and carry him away, to Reese River. They hold him as a slave. It will cost thirty ounces of silver to get him out of soak.

Scene 4—Dusty times in the Myron family. Their house is mortgaged—they are without dividends —they cannot "stand the raise."

Parthenia, in this extremity, applies to Polydor. He sneeringly advises her to shove out after her exiled parent herself.

She shoves!

Act II—Camp of the Comanches. In the foreground, several of the tribe throwing dice for tickets in Wright's Gift Entertainment. In the background, old Myron packing faggots on a jack. The weary slave weeps—he sighs—he slobbers. Grief lays her heavy hand upon him.

Scene 2—Comanches on the warpath, headed by the Chief, Ingomar. Parthenia arrives and offers to remain as a hostage while old Myron returns home and borrows thirty dollars to pay his ransom with. It was pleasant to note the varieties of dress displayed in the costumes of Ingomar and his comrades. It was also pleasant to observe that in those ancient times the better class of citizens were able to dress in ornamental carriage robes, and even the rank and file indulged in Benkert boots, albeit some of the latter appeared not to have been blacked for several days.

Scene 3—Parthenia and Ingomar alone in the woods. "Two souls with but a single thought, etc." She tells him that is love. He "can't see it."

Scene 4 — The thing works around about as we expected it would in the first place. Ingomar gets stuck after Parthenia.

Scene 5 — Ingomar declares his love—he attempts to embrace her— she waves him off, gently, but firmly —she remarks, "Not too brash, Ing., not too brash, now!" Ingomar subsides. They finally flee away, and hie them to Parthenia's home.

Acts III and IV—Joy! joy! From the summit of a hill, Parthenia beholds once more the spires and domes of Silver City.

Scene 2—Silver City. Enter Myron. Tableau. Myron begs for an extension on his note—he has not yet raised the whole ransom, but he is ready to pay two dollars and a half on account.

Scene 3—Myron tells Ingomar he must shuck himself and dress like a Christian; he must shave; he must work; he must give up his sword! His rebellious spirit rises. Behold Parthenia tames it with the mightier spirit of Love. Ingomar weakens— he lets down—he is utterly demoralized.

Scene 4 — Enter old Timarch, Chief of Police. He offers Ingomar —but this scene is too noble to be trifled with in burlesque.

Scene 5—Polydor presents his bill —213 drachmas. Busted again—the old man cannot pay. Ingomar compromises by becoming the slave of Polydor.

Scene 6—The Comanches again, with Thorne at their head! He asks who enslaved the Chief? Ingomar points to Polydor. Lo! Thorne seizes the trembling broker, and snatches him bald-headed!

Scene 7—Enter the Chief of Police again. He makes a treaty with the Comanches. He gives them a ranch apiece. He decrees that they shall build a town on the American Flat, and appoints great Ingomar to be its Mayor! (Applause by the supes.)

Scene 8—Grand tableau—Comanches, police, Pi-Utes, and citizens generally—Ingomar and Parthenia hanging together in the centre. The old thing. The old poetical quota-tion, we mean. They double on it— Ingomar observing "Two souls with but a single Thought," and she slinging in the other line, "Two Hearts that Beat as one." Thus united at last in a fond embrace, they sweetly smiled up at the orchestra and the curtain fell.

[From *Sacramento Union*, May 26, 1864.]

PERSONAL CORRESPONDENCE.

Several quite sharp notes appear in a late number of the Virginia *Enterprise,* between Samuel Clemens, of that paper, and J. W. Wilmington and James Laird, of the *Union* office, on account of the appearance in the latter journal of two articles which reflected somewhat severely on Clemens. Clemens demanded of Laird, one of the publishers of the *Union,* a retraction of, or satisfaction for, the alleged insults. The following correspondence ensued:

OFFICE OF THE
VIRGINIA DAILY UNION,
VIRGINIA, May 21, 1864.

Samuel Clemens: James Laird has just handed me your note of this date. Permit me to say that I am the author of the article appearing in this morning's *Union.* I am responsible for it. I have nothing to retract.

Respectfully,

J. W. WILMINGTON.

—

ENTERPRISE OFFICE,
Saturday evening, May 21, 1864.

James Laird—Sir: I wrote you a note this afternoon, demanding a published retraction of insults that appeared in two articles in the *Union* of this morning, or satisfaction. I have since received what purports to be a reply, written by a person who signs himself "J. W. Wilmington," in which he assumes the authorship and responsibility of one of said infamous articles. Wilmington is a person entirely unknown to me in the matter, and has nothing to do with it. In the columns of your paper you have declared your own responsibility for all articles appearing in it, and any farther attempt to make a catspaw of any other individual, and thus shirk a responsibility that you had previously assumed, will show that you are a cowardly sneak. I now peremptorily demand of you the satisfaction due to a gentleman, without alternative.

SAM. L. CLEMENS.

—

OFFICE OF THE
VIRGINIA DAILY UNION,
VIRGINIA, Saturday Evening,
May 21, 1864.

Samuel Clemens, Esq.: Your note of this evening is received. To the first portion of it I will briefly reply, that Mr. J. W. Wilmington, the avowed author of the article to which you object, is a gentleman now in the employ of the *Union* office. He formerly was one of the proprietors of the Cincinnati *En-*

quirer. He was Captain of a company in the Sixth Ohio Regiment, and fought at Shiloh. His responsibility and character can be vouched for to your abundant satisfaction.

For all editorials appearing in the *Union,* the proprietors are personally responsible; for communications, they hold themselves ready, when properly called upon, either to give the name and address of the author; or, failing that, to be themselves responsible.

The editorial in the *Enterprise* headed "How is it?" out of which this controversy grew, was an attack made upon the printers of the *Union.* It was replied to by a *Union* printer, and a representative of the printers, who in a communication denounced the writer of that article as a liar, a poltroon and a puppy. You announce yourself as the writer of that article which provoked this communication, and demand "satisfaction" —which satisfaction the writer informs you, over his own signature, he is quite ready to afford. I have no right, under the rulings of the code you have invoked, to step in and assume Wilmington's position, nor would he allow me to do so. You demand of me, in your last letter, the satisfaction due to a gentleman, and couple the demand with offensive remarks. When you have earned the right to the title by complying with the usual custom, I shall be most happy to afford you any satisfaction you desire at any time and in any place. In short, Wilmington has a prior claim upon your attention. When he is through with you, I shall be at your service. If you decline to meet him after challenging him, you will prove yourself to be what he has charged you with being, "a liar, a poltroon and a puppy," and as such, cannot of

course, be entitled to the consideration of a gentleman.

Respectfully,
JAMES L. LAIRD.

—

ENTERPRISE OFFICE, }
VIRGINIA CITY, }
May 21, 1864—9 o'clock P.M.}

James L. Laird—Sir: Your reply to my note—in which I peremptorily demanded satisfaction of you, without alternative—is just received, and to my utter astonishment you still endeavor to shield your craven carcass behind the person of an individual who in spite of your introduction is entirely unknown to me, and upon whose shoulders you cannot throw the whole responsibility. You acknowledge and reaffirm in this note that "For all editorials appearing in the *Union* the proprietors are personally responsible." Now, sir, had there appeared no editorial on the subject indorsing and reiterating the slanderous and disgraceful insults heaped upon me in the "communication," I would have simply called upon you and demanded the name of its author, and upon your answer would have depended my further action. But the "editorial" alluded to was equally vile and slanderous as the "communication," and being an "editorial" would naturally have more weight in the minds of readers. It was the following undignified and abominably insulting slander appearing in your "editorial" headed "The 'How is it' Issue," that occasioned my sending you first an alternative and then a peremptory challenge:

"Never before in a long period of newspaper intercourse—never before in any contact with a cotemporary, however unprincipled he might have been—have we found an opponent, in statement or in discussion, who had no gentlemanly sense of professional propriety, who conveyed in every word, and in every purpose of all his words, such a groveling disregard for truth, decency and courtesy as to seem to court the distinction only of being understood as a vulgar liar. Meeting one who prefers falsehood; whose instincts are all toward falsehood; whose thought is falsification; whose aim is villification through insincere professions of honesty; one whose only merit is thus described, and who evidently desires to be thus known, the obstacles presented are entirely insurmountable, and whoever would touch them fully should expect to be abominably defiled."—*Union, May 21st.*

You assume in your last note, that I "have challenged Wilmington," and that he has informed me, "over his own signature," that he is quite ready to afford me "satisfaction." Both assumptions are utterly false. I have twice challenged you, and you have twice attempted to shirk the responsibility. Wilmington's note could not possibly be an answer to my demand for satisfaction from you; and besides, his note simply avowed authorship of a certain "communication" that appeared simultaneously with your libelous "editorial," and stated that its author had "nothing to retract." For your gratification, however, I will remark that Wilmington's case will be attended to in due time by a distant acquaintance of his who is not willing to see him suffer in obscurity. In the meantime, if you do not wish yourself posted as a coward, you will at once accept my peremptory challenge, which I now reiterate.

SAM. L. CLEMENS.

OFFICE OF THE
VIRGINIA DAILY UNION
MONDAY MORNING, May 23, 1864.

Samuel Clemens: In reply to your lengthy communication, I have only to say that in your note opening this correspondence, you demanded satisfaction for a communication in the *Union* which branded the writer of an article in the *Enterprise* as a liar, a poltroon and a puppy. You declare yourself to be the writer of the *Enterprise* article, and the avowed author of the *Union* communication stands ready to afford satisfaction. Any attempt to evade a meeting with him and force one upon me will utterly fail, as I have no right under the rulings of the code to meet or hold any communication with you in this connection. The threat of being posted as a coward cannot have the slightest effect upon the position I have assumed in the matter. If you think this correspondence reflects credit upon you I advise you by all means to publish it. In the meantime you must excuse me from receiving any more long epistles from you.

JAMES L. LAIRD.

—

I denounce Laird as an unmitigated liar, because he says I published an editorial in which I attacked the printers employed on the *Union,* whereas there is nothing in that editorial which can be so construed. Moreover, he is a liar on general principles, and from natural instinct. I denounce him as an abject coward, because it has been stated in his paper that its proprietors are responsible for all articles appearing in its columns, yet he backs down from that position; because he acknowledges the "code," but will not live up to it; because he says himself that he is responsible for all "editorials," and then backs down from that also; and because he insults me in his note marked "IV," and yet refuses to fight me. Finally, he is a fool, because he cannot understand that a publisher is bound to stand responsible for any and all articles printed by him, whether he wants to do it or not.

SAM. L. CLEMENS.

There was no fighting at last accounts.

[From *Golden Era,* July 3, 1864.]

EARLY RISING,

AS REGARDS

EXCURSIONS TO THE CLIFF HOUSE.

BY MARK TWAIN

Early to bed, and early to rise,
Makes a man healthy, wealthy and wise.
—*Benjamin Franklin*

I don't see it—*George Washington*

Now both of these are high authorities—very high and respectable authorities—but I am with General Washington first, last, and all the time on this proposition.

Because I don't see it, either.

I have tried getting up early, and I have tried getting up late—and the latter agrees with me best. As for a man's growing any wiser, or any richer, or any healthier, by getting up early, I know it is not so; because I have got up early in the station-house many and many a time, and got poorer and poorer for the next half a day, in consequence, instead of richer and richer. And sometimes, on the same terms, I have seen the sun rise four times a week up there at Virginia, and so far from my growing healthier on account of it, I got to looking blue, and pulpy, and swelled, like a drowned man, and my relations grew alarmed and thought they were going to lose me. They entirely despaired of my recovery, at one time, and began to grieve for me as one whose days were numbered—whose fate was sealed—who was soon to pass away from them forever, and from the glad sunshine, and the birds, and the odorous flowers, and murmuring brooks, and whispering winds, and all the cheerful scenes of life, and go down into the dark and silent tomb —and they went forth sorrowing, and jumped a lot in the graveyard, and made up their minds to grin and bear it with that fortitude which is the true Christian's brightest ornament.

You observe that I have put a stronger test on the matter than even Benjamin Franklin contemplated, and yet it would not work. Therefore, how is a man to grow healthier, and wealthier, and wiser by going to bed early and getting up early, when he fails to accomplish these things even when he does not go to bed at all? And as far as becoming wiser is concerned, you might put all the wisdom I acquired in these experiments in your eye, without obstructing your vision any to speak of.

As I said before, my voice is with George Washington's on this question.

Another philosopher encourages the world to get up at sunrise because "it is the early bird that catches the worm."

It is a seductive proposition, and well calculated to trap the unsuspecting. But its attractions are all wasted on me, because I have no use for the worm. If I had, I would adopt the Unreliable's plan. He was much interested in this quaint proverb, and directed the powers of his great mind to its consideration for three or four consecutive hours. He was supposing a case. He was supposing for instance, that he really wanted the worm—that the possession of the worm was actually necessary to his happiness—that he yearned for it and hankered after it, therefore, as much as a man *could* yearn for and hanker after a worm under such circumstances—and he was supposing, further, that he was opposed to getting up early in order to catch it (which was much the more plausible of the two suppositions). Well, at the end of three or four hours' profound meditation upon the subject, the Unreliable rose up and said: "If he were so anxious about the worm, and he couldn't get along without him, and he didn't want to get up early in the morning to catch him—why then, by George, he would just lay for him the night before?" I never would have thought of that. I looked at the youth, and said to myself, he is malicious, and dishonest, and undhandsome, and does not smell good—yet how quickly do these trivial demerits disappear in the shadow when the glare from his great intellect shines out above them!

I have always heard that the only time in the day that a trip to the Cliff House could be thoroughly enjoyed, was early in the morning; (and I suppose it might be as well to withhold an adverse impression while the flow-tide of public opinion continues to set in that direction.)

I tried it the other morning with Harry, the stock-broker, rising at 4 A.M., to delight in the following described things, to wit:

A road unencumbered by carriages, and free from wind and dust; a bracing atmosphere; the gorgeous spectacle of the sun in the dawn of his glory; the fresh perfume of flowers still damp with dew; a solitary drive on the beach while its smoothness was yet unmarred by wheel or hoof, and a vision of white sails glinting in the morning light far out at sea.

These were the considerations, and they seemed worthy a sacrifice of seven or eight hours' sleep.

We sat in the stable, and yawned, and gaped, and stretched, until the horse was hitched up, and then drove out into the bracing atmosphere. (When another early voyage is proposed to me, I want it understood that there is to be no bracing atmosphere in the programme. I can worry along without it.) In half an hour we were so thoroughly braced up with it that it was just a scratch that we were not frozen to death. Then the harness came unshipped, or got broken, or something, and I waxed colder and drowsier while Harry fixed it. I am not fastidious about clothes, but I am not used to wearing fragrant, sweaty horse-blankets, and not partial to them, either; I am not proud, though, when I am freezing, and I added the horse-blanket to my overcoats, and tried to wake up and feel warm and cheerful. It was useless, however—all my senses slumbered, and continued to slumber, save the sense of smell.

When my friend drove past suburban gardens and said the flowers never exhaled so sweet an odor before, in his experience, I dreamily but honestly endeavored to think so too, but in my secret soul I was conscious that they only smelled like horse-blankets. (When another early voyage is proposed to me, I want it understood that there is to be no "fresh perfume of flowers" in the programme," either. I do not enjoy it. My senses are not attuned to the flavor—there is too much horse about it and not enough eau de cologne.)

The wind was cold and benumbing, and blew with such force that we could hardly make headway against it. It came straight from the ocean, and I think there are icebergs out there somewhere. True, there was not much dust, because the gale blew it all to Oregon in two minutes; and by good fortune, it blew no gravel-stones, to speak of—only one, of any consequence, I believe—a three-cornered one—it struck me in the eye. I have it there yet. However, it does not matter—for the future I suppose I can manage to see tolerably well out of the other. (Still, when another early voyage is proposed to me, I want it understood that the dust is to be put in, and the gravel left out of the programme. I might want my other eye if I continue to hang on until my time comes; and besides, I shall not mind the dust much hereafter, because I have only got to shut one eye, now, when it is around.)

No, the road was not encumbered by carriages—we had it all to ourselves. I suppose the reason was, that most people do not like to enjoy themselves too much, and therefore they do not go out to the Cliff House in the cold and the fog, and the dread silence and solitude of four o'clock in the morning. They are right. The impressive solemnity of such a pleasure trip is only equalled by an excursion to Lone Mountain in a hearse. Whatever of advantage there may be in having that Cliff House road all to yourself, we had—but to my mind a greater advantage would lie in dividing it up in small sections among the entire community; because, in consequence of the repairs in progress on it just now, it is as rough as a corduroy bridge—(in a good many places,) and consequently the less you have of it, the happier you are likely to be, and the less shaken up and disarranged on the inside. (Wherefore, when another early voyage is proposed to me, I want it understood that the road is not to be unencumbered with carriages, but just the reverse—so that the balance of the people shall be made to stand their share of the jolting and the desperate lonesomeness of the thing.)

From the moment we left the stable, almost, the fog was so thick that we could scarcely see fifty yards behind or before, or overhead; and for a while, as we approached the Cliff House, we could not see the horse at all, and were obliged to steer by his ears, which stood up dimly out of the dense white mist that enveloped him. But for those friendly beacons, we must have been cast away and lost.

I have no opinion of a six-mile ride in the clouds; but if I ever have to take another, I want to leave the horse in the stable and go in a balloon. I shall prefer to go in the afternoon, also, when it is warm, so that I may gape, and yawn, and stretch, if I am drowsy, without disarranging my horse-blanket and letting in a blast of cold wind.

We could scarcely see the sportive seals out on the rocks, writhing and squirming like exaggerated maggots, and there was nothing soothing in their discordant barking, to a spirit so depressed as mine was.

Harry took a cocktail at the Cliff House, but I scorned such ineffectual stimulus; I yearned for fire, and there was none there; they were about to make one, but the barkeeper looked altogether too cheerful for me—I could not bear his unnatural happiness in the midst of such a ghastly picture of fog, and damp, and frosty surf, and dreary solitude. I could not bear the sacrilegious presence of a pleasant face at such a time; it was too much like sprightliness at a funeral, and we fled from it down the smooth and vacant beach.

We had that all to ourselves, too, like the road—and I want it divided up, also, hereafter. We could not drive in the roaring surf and seem to float abroad on the foamy sea, as one is wont to do in the sunny afternoon, because the very thought of any of that icy-looking water splashing on you was enough to congeal your blood, almost. We saw no white-winged ships sailing away on the billowy ocean, with the pearly light of morning descending upon them like a benediction—"because the fog had the bulge on the pearly light," as the Unreliable observed when I mentioned it to him afterwards; and we saw not the sun in the dawn of his glory, for the same reason. Hill and beach, and sea and sun were all wrapped in a ghostly mantle of mist, and hidden from our mortal vision. [When another early voyage is proposed to me, I want it understood that the sun in his glory, and the morning light, and the ships at sea, and all that sort of thing are to be left out of the programme, so that when we fail to see them, we shall not be so infernally disappointed.]

We were human icicles when we got to the Ocean House, and there was no fire there, either. I banished all hope, then, and succumbed to despair; I went back on my religion, and sought surcease of sorrow in soothing blasphemy. I am sorry I did it, now, but it was a great comfort to me, then. We could have had breakfast at the Ocean House, but we did not want it; can statues of ice feel hunger? But we adjourned to a private room and ordered red-hot coffee, and it was a sort of balm to my troubled mind to observe that the man who brought it was as cold, and as silent, and as solemn as the grave itself. His gravity was so impressive, and so appropriate and becoming to the melancholy surroundings, that it won upon me and thawed out some of the better instincts of my nature, and I told him he might ask a blessing if he thought it would lighten him up any—because he looked as if he wanted to, very bad—but he only shook his head resignedly and sighed.

That coffee did the business for us. It was made by a master-artist, and it had not a fault; and the cream that came with it was so rich and thick that you could hardly have strained it through a wire fence. As the generous beverage flowed down our frigid throats, our blood grew warm again, our muscles relaxed, our torpid bodies awoke to life and feeling, anger and uncharitableness departed from us and we were cheerful once more. We got good cigars, also, at the Ocean House, and drove into town over a smooth road, lighted by the sun and unclouded by fog.

Near the Jewish cemeteries we turned a corner too suddenly, and got upset, but sustained no damage, although the horse did what he honestly could to kick the buggy out of the State while we were grovelling in the sand. We went on down to the steamer, and while we were on board, the buggy was upset again by some outlaw, and an axle broken.

However, these little accidents, and all the deviltry and misfortune that preceded them, were only just and natural consequences of the absurd experiment of getting up at an hour in the morning when all God-fearing Christians ought to be in bed. I consider that the man who leaves his pillow, deliberately, at sun-rise, is taking his life in his own hands, and he ought to feel proud if he don't have to put it down again at the coroner's office before dark.

Now, for that early trip, I am not any healthier or any wealthier than I was before, and only wiser in that I know a good deal better than to go and do it again. And as for all those notable advantages, such as the sun in the dawn of his glory, and the ships, and the perfume of the flowers, etc., etc., etc., I don't see them, any more than myself and Washington see the soundness of Benjamin Franklin's attractive little poem.

If you go to the Cliff House at any time after seven in the morning, you cannot fail to enjoy it—but never start out there before daylight, under the impression that you are going to have a pleasant time and come back insufferably healthier and wealthier and wiser than your betters on account of it. Because if you do you will miss your calculation, and it will keep you swearing about it right straight along for a week to get even again.

Put no trust in the benefits to accrue from early rising, as set forth by the infatuated Franklin—but stake the last cent of your substance on the judgment of old George Washington, the Father of his Country, who said "he couldn't see it."

And you hear me endorsing that sentiment.   MARK TWAIN

[From *San Francisco Call,* September 6, 1864.]

A SMALL PIECE OF SPITE.

Some witless practical joker made a false entry, a few days ago, on a slate kept at the dead-house for the information of the public, concerning dead bodies found, deaths by accident, etc. The Alta, Bulletin, and Flag, administered a deserved rebuke to the Coroner's understrappers, for permitting the entry to remain there, and pass into the newspapers and mislead the public, and for this reason the slate has been removed from the office. Now it is too late in the day for such men as these to presume to deny to the public, information which belongs to them, and which they have a right to demand, merely to gratify a ridiculous spite against two or three reporters. It is a matter of no consequence to reporters whether the slate is kept there or not; but it *is* a matter of consequence to the public at large, who are the real injured parties when the newspapers are denied the opportunity of conveying it to them. If the Coroner permits his servants to close the door against reporters, many a man may lose a friend in the Bay, or by assassination, or suicide, and never hear of it, or know nothing about it; in that case, the public and their servant, the Coroner, are the victims, not the reporter. Coroner Sheldon needs not to be told that he is a public officer; that his doings, and those of his underlings at the coffin-shop, belong to the people; that the public do not recognize his right or theirs to suppress the transactions of his department of the public service; and, finally, that the people will not see the propriety of the affairs of his office being hidden from them, in order that the small-potato malice of his employés against two or three newspaper reporters may be gratified. Those employés have *always* shown a strong disinclination to tell a reporter anything about their ghastly share in the Coroner's business, and it was easy to see that they longed for some excuse to abolish that slate. Their motive for such conduct did not concern reporters, but it might interest the public and the Coroner if they would explain it. Those official corpse-planters always put on as many airs as if the public and their master, the Coroner, belonged to them, and they had a right to do as they pleased with both. They told us yesterday that their Coronial affairs should henceforth be a sealed book, and they would give us *no* information. As if *they*— a lot of forty-dollar understrappers —had authority to proclaim that the affairs of a public office like the Coroner's should be kept secret from the people, whose minions they are! If the credit of that office suffers from their impertinence, who is the victim, Mr. Sheldon or the reporters? We cannot suffer greatly, for we never succeeded in getting any information out of one of those fellows yet. You see the dead-cart leaving the place, and ask one of them where it is bound, and without looking up from his newspaper, he grunts, lazily, and says, *"Stiff,"* meaning that it is going in quest of the corpse of some poor creature whose earthly troubles are over. You ask one of them a dozen questions calculated to throw more light upon a meagre entry in the slate, and he invariably answers, *"Don't know"*—as if the grand end and aim of his poor existence was not to know anything, and to come as near accomplishing his mission as his opportunities would permit. They would vote for General Jackson at the "Body-snatchers' Retreat," but for the misfortune that they "don't know" such a person ever existed. What do you suppose the people would ever know about how their interests were being attended to if the employés in all public offices were such unmitigated ignoramuses as these? One of these fellows said to us yesterday, "We have taken away the slate; we are not going to give you any more information; the reporters have got too sharp—by George, they know more'n *we* do!" God help the reporter that don't! It is as fervent a prayer as ever welled up from the bottom of our heart. Now, a reporter can start any day and travel through the whole of the long list of employés in the public offices in this city, and in not a solitary instance will he find any difficulty in getting any information which the public have a right to know, until he arrives at the inquest office of the Coroner. There all knowledge concerning the dead who die in mysterious ways and mysterious places, and who may have friends and relatives near at hand who would give the world and all its wealth for even the poor consolation of knowing their fate, is denied us. Who are the sufferers by this contemptible contumacy—we or the hundred thousand citizens of San Francisco? The responsibility of this state of things rests with the Coroner, and it is only right and just that he should amend it.

[From *San Francisco Californian,* May 27, 1865.]

(For the Californian.)

HOW I WENT TO THE GREAT RACE BETWEEN LODI AND NORFOLK.

There can be no use in my writing any account whatever of the great race, because that matter has already been attended to in the daily papers. Therefore, I will simply describe to you *how* I went to the race. But before I begin, I would like to tell you about Homestead—Benj. W. Homestead, of the Incidental Hotel. [I do not wish to be too severe, though, and so I use fictitious names, to prevent your finding out who it is I refer to, and where his place of business is.]

It will ease my mind to tell you about him. You know Homestead, clerk at the Incidental Hotel, and you know he has the reputation of being chatty, and sociable, and accommodating—a man, in fact, eminently fitted to make a guest feel more at home in the hotel than in his own house with his own wife, and his own mother, and his wife's mother, and her various friends and relatives, and all the other little comforts that go to make married life a blessing, and create what is known as "Sweet Home," and which is so deservedly popular—I mean among people who have not tried it. You know Homestead as that kind of a man. Therefore, you would not suppose that attractive exterior of his, and that smiling visage, and that seductive tongue capable of dark and mysterious crimes.

Very well, I will ask you to listen to a plain, unprejudiced statement of facts:

On or about the 21st of the present month, it became apparent to me that the forthcoming race between *Norfolk* and *Lodi* was awakening extraordinary attention all over the Pacific coast, and even far away in the Atlantic States. I saw that if I failed to see this race I might live a century, perhaps, without ever having an opportunity to see its equal. I went at once to a livery stable—the man said his teams had all been engaged a week before I called. I got the same answer at all the other livery stables, except one. They told me there that they had a nice dray, almost new, and a part of a horse—they said part of a horse because a good deal of him was gone, in the way of a tail, and one ear and a portion of the other, and his upper lip, and one eye; and, inasmuch as his teeth were exposed, and he had a villainous cast in his remaining eye, these defects, added to his damaged ears and departed tail, gave him an extremely "gallus" and unprepossessing aspect — but they only asked two hundred and forty dollars for the turn-out for the day.

I resisted the yearning I felt to hire this unique establishment.

Then they said they had a capacious riding-horse left, but all the seats on him except one had been engaged; they said he was an unusually long horse, and he could seat seven very comfortably; and that he was very gentle, and would not kick up behind; and that one of the choicest places on him for observation was still vacant, and I could have it for nineteen dollars—and so on and so on; and while the passenger agent was talking, he was busy measuring off a space of nine inches for me pretty high up on the commodious animal's neck.

It seemed to me that the prospect of going to the races was beginning to assume a very "neck-or-nothing" condition, but nevertheless I steadfastly refused the supercargo's offer, and he sold the vacancy to a politician who was used to being on the fence and would naturally consider a seat astride a horse's neck in the light of a pleasant variety.

I then walked thoughtfully down to the Incidental, turning over in my mind various impossible expedients for getting out to the Ocean Race - Course. I thought of the horse-cars and the steam-cars, but without relief, for neither of these conveyances could carry me within four miles of the place. At the hotel I met the abandoned Homestead, and as nearly as I can recollect, the following conversation ensued:

"Ah, Mark, you're the very man I was looking for. Take a drink?"

I cannot be positive, but it is my impression that I either stated that I would, or else signified assent by a scarcely perceptible eagerness of manner common to me under circumstances of this nature.

While we were drinking, Homestead remarked, with considerable vivacity:

"Yes, I was just looking for you. I am going out to the great race on Tuesday, and I've a vacancy and want company. I'd like to have you go along with me if you will."

I set my glass down with a suddenness and decision unusual with me on such occasions, and seizing his hand, I wrung it with heartfelt warmth and cordiality. It is humiliating to me to reflect, now, that at that moment I even shed some tears of gratitude, and felt them coursing down the backbone of my nose and dripping from the end of it.

Never mind the remainder of the conversation—suffice it that I was charged to be at the Incidental punctually at ten o'clock on Tuesday morning, and that I promised to do so.

Well, at the appointed time, I *was* there. That is, I was as near as I could get—I was on the outskirts of a crowd that occupied all the pavement outside and filled the office inside. Young Smith, of Buncombe and Brimstone, approached me with an air of superiority, and remarked languidly that he guessed he would go to the races. He dropped his airs, though, very suddenly, and came down to my level when I told him *I* was going to the races also. He said he thought all the conveyances in town had been secured a week ago. I assumed a crushing demeanor of wealthy indifference, and remarked, rather patronizingly, that I had seen greater races—in Europe and other places—and did not care about seeing this one, but then Homestead had insisted so on my going with him that—

"The very devil!" says young Smith, "give us your hand! we're *compangyongs dew vo-yaj!*" (he affects the French, does young Smith,) —"*I'm* going with Homestead, too, my boy!"

We grew cordial in a moment, and went around, arm-in-arm, patronizing the balance of the crowd. But somehow, every man we accosted silenced our batteries as I had silenced young Smith's in the first place — they were all going with Homestead. I tell you candidly, and in all seriousness, that when I came to find out that there were a hundred and fifty men there, all going to the races, and all going with Homestead, I began to think it was —was—singular, at the very least, not to say exceedingly strange.

But I am tired of this infamous subject—I am tired of this disgraceful narrative, and I shall not finish it.

However, as I have gone this far, I *will* quote from a conversation that occurred in front of the hotel at ten o'clock. The degraded Homestead stepped out at the door, and bowed, and smiled his hated smile, and said, blandly:

"Ah, you are all here, I see. I am glad you are so punctual, for there is nothing that worries me so much

when I am going on a little trip like this for recreation, as to be delayed. Well, boys, time presses— let's make a start."

"I guess we're all ready, Mr. Homestead," said one gentleman, "but—but how are you going?"

The depraved Homestead smiled, as if he were going to say something very smart, and then, "Oh," says he, "I'M GOING TO WALK!"

I have made a plain, simple statement of the facts connected with this outrage, and they can be substantiated by every man who was present upon that occasion. I will now drop this subject forever.

MARK TWAIN.

[From *San Francisco Californian,* November 4, 1865.]

"MARK TWAIN" ON THE BALLAD INFLICTION.

It is bound to come! There is no help for it. I smell it afar off—I see the signs in the air! Every day and every hour of every day I grow more and more nervous, for with every minute of waning time the dreadful infliction comes nearer and nearer in its inexorable march! In another week, maybe, all San Francisco will be singing "Wearing of the Green!" I know it. I have suffered before, and I know the symptoms. This holds off long, but it is partly that the calamity may gather irresistible worrying-power, and partly because it is harder to learn than Chinese. But that is all the worse; for when the people do learn it they will learn it bad—and terrible will be the distress it will bring upon the community. A year ago "Johnny came marching home!" That song was sung by everybody, in every key, in every locality, at all hours of the day and night, and always out of tune. It sent many unoffending persons

to the Stockton asylum. There was no stopping the epidemic, and so it had to be permitted to run its course and wear itself out. Short was our respite, and then a still more malignant distemper broke out in the midst of this harried and suffering community. It was "You'll not forget me, mother, mother, mother, mother!" with an ever-accumulating aggravation of expression upon each successive "mother." The fire-boys sat up all night to sing it; and bands of sentimental stevedores and militia soldiers patroled the streets and howled its lugubrious strains. A passion for serenading attacked the youth of the city, and they sang it under verandahs in the back streets until the dogs and cats destroyed their voices in unavailing efforts to lay the devilish spirit that was driving happiness from their hearts. Finally there came a season of repose, and the community slowly recovered from the effects of the musical calamity. The respite was not long. In an unexpected moment they were attacked, front and rear, by a new enemy—"When we were marching through Georgia!" Tongue cannot tell what we suffered while this frightful disaster was upon us. Young misses sang it to the guitar and the piano; young men sang it to the banjo and the fiddle; the un-blood-stained soldier yelled it with enthusiasm as he marched through the imaginary swamps and cotton plantations of the drill-room; the firemen sang it as they trundled their engines home from conflagrations; and the hated serenader tortured it with his damned accordeon. Some of us survived, and some have gone the old road to a haven of rest at Stockton, where the wicked cease from troubling and the popular songs are allowed. For the space of four weeks the survivors have been happy.

But as I have said before, it is bound to come! *Arrah-na-Pogue* is breeding a song that will bedeck some mountain with new - made graves! In another week we shall be "Wearing of the Green," and in a fortnight some will be wearing of the black in consequence. Three repetitions of this song will produce lunacy, and five will kill—it is that much more virulent than its predecessors. People are finding it hard to learn, but when they get it learned they will find it potent for harm. It is Wheatleigh's song. He sings it in *Arrah-na-Pogue,* with a sprig of shamrock in his hat. Wheatleigh sings it with such aggravated solemnity as to make an audience long for the grave. It is doled out slowly, and every note settles deliberately to its place on one's heart like a solid iceberg—and by the time it is finished the temperature of the theatre has fallen to twenty degrees. Think what a dead-cold winter we shall have here when this Arctic funeral melody becomes popular! Think of it being performed at midnight, in lonely places, upon the spirit-depressing accordeon! Think of being driven to blow your brains out under such circumstances, and then dying to the grave-yard cadences of "Wearing of the Green!" But it is bound to come, and we may as well bow our heads and submit with such degree of Christian resignation as we are able to command.— *Territorial Enterprise.*

[From *San Francisco Californian,* November 25, 1865.]

[WHAT CHEER ROBBERY]

"MARK TWAIN," in summing up the facts and theories of the What Cheer House robbery, says (correspondence Virginia *Enterprise,* Nov. 18th):

"The Old Thing.—As usual, the *Alta* reporter fastens the mysterious What Cheer robbery on the same horrible person who knocked young Myers in the head with a slung-shot a year ago and robbed his father's pawnbroker shop of some brass jewelry and crippled revolvers, in broad daylight; and he laid that exploit on the horrible wretch who robbed the Mayor's Clerk, who half-murdered detective officer Rose in a lonely spot below Santa Clara; and he proved that this same monster killed the lone woman in a secluded house up a dark alley with a carpenter's chisel, months before; and he demonstrated

by inspired argument that the same villain who chiselled the woman tomahawked a couple of defenseless women in the most mysterious manner up another dark alley a few months before that. Now, the perpetrator of these veiled crimes has never been discovered, yet this wicked reporter has taken the whole batch and piled them coolly and relentlessly upon the shoulders of one imaginary scoundrel, with a comfortable, 'Here, these are yours,' and with an air that says plainly that no denial, and no argument in the case, will be entertained. And every time anything happens that is unlawful and dreadful, and has a spice of mystery about it, this reporter, without waiting to see if maybe somebody else didn't do it, goes off at once and jams it on top of the old pile, as much as to say, 'Here—here's some more of your work.' Now this isn't right, you know. It is all well enough for Mr. Smythe to divert sus-

picion from himself—nobody objects to that—but it is not right for him to lay every solitary thing on this mysterious stranger, whoever he is—it is not right, you know. He ought to give the poor devil a show. The idea of accusing 'The Mysterious' of the What Cheer burglary, considering who was the last boarder to bed and the first one up!

"Smythe is endeavoring to get on the detective police force. I think it will be wronging the community to give this man such a position as that —now you know that yourself, don't you? He would settle down on some particular fellow, and every time there was a rape committed, or a steamship stolen, or an oyster cellar rifled, or a church burned down, or a family massacred, or a black-and-tan pup stolen, he would march off with portentous mien and snatch that fellow and say, 'Here, you are at it again, you know,' and snake him off to the Station House."

[From *Golden Era*, January 28, 1866; reprint from *Territorial Enterprise*.]

MARK TWAIN'S KEARNY STREET GHOST STORY

Disembodied spirits have been on the rampage now for more than a month past in the house of one Albert Krum, in Kearny street—so much so that the family find it impossible to keep a servant forty-eight hours. The moment a new and unsuspecting servant maid gets fairly to bed and her light blown out, one of those dead and damned scalliwags takes her by the hair and just "hazes" her; grabs her by the waterfall and snakes her out of bed and bounces her on the floor two or three times; other disorderly corpses shy old boots at her head, and bootjacks, and brittle chamber furniture—washbowls, pitchers, hair-oil,

teeth-brushes, hoop-skirts—anything that comes handy those phantoms seize and hurl at Bridget, and pay no more attention to her howling than if it were music. The spirits tramp, tramp, tramp, about the house at dead of night, and when a light is struck the footsteps cease and the promenader is not visible, and just as soon as the light is out that dead man goes to waltzing around again. They are a bloody lot. The young lady of the house was lying in bed one night with the gas turned down low, when a figure approached her through the gloom, whose ghastly aspect and solemn carriage chilled her to the heart. What do you suppose she did?—jumped up and seized the intruder?—threw a slipper at him?—"laid" him with a misquotation from Scripture? No—none of these. But with admirable presence of mind she covered up her head and yelled. That is what she did. Few young women would have thought of doing that. The ghost came and stood by the bed and groaned—a deep, agonizing, heartbroken groan—and laid a bloody kitten on the pillow by the girl's head. And then it groaned again, and sighed, "Oh, God, and must it be?" and bet another bloody kitten. It groaned a third time in sorrow and tribulation, and went one kitten better. And thus the sorrowing spirit stood there, moaning in its anguish and unloading its mewing cargo, until it had stacked up a whole litter of nine little bloody kittens on the girl's pillow, and then, still moaning, moved away and vanished. When lights were brought, there were the kittens, with the fingermarks of bloody hands upon their white fur—and the old mother cat, that had come after them, swelled her tail in mortal fear and refused to take hold of them. What do you think of that? What would you think of a ghost that came to your bedside at dead of night and had kittens?—*Territorial Enterprise.*

[From *Golden Era,* March 4, 1866.]

MARK TWAIN ON THE NEW WILD CAT RELIGION

Another spiritual investigator— G. C. De-Merrit—passed his examination to-day, after a faithful attendance on the *seances* of the Friends of Progress, and was shipped, a raving maniac, to the insane asylum at Stockton—an institution which is getting to be quite a College of Progress.

People grow exasperated over these frequently occurring announcements of madness occasioned by fighting the tiger of spiritualism, and I think it is not fair. They abuse the spiritualists unsparingly, but I can remember when Methodist camp meetings and Campbellite revivals used to stock the asylums with religious lunatics, and yet the public kept their temper and said never a word. We don't cut up when madmen are bred by the old legitimate regular stock religions, but we can't allow wildcat religions to indulge in such disastrous experiments. I do not really own in the old regular stock, but I lean strongly toward it, and I naturally feel some little prejudice against all wildcat religions— still, I protest that it is not fair to excuse the one and abuse the other for the self-same rascality. I do not love the wildcat, but at the same time I do not like to see the wildcat imposed on merely because it is friendless. I know a great many spiritualists—good and worthy persons who sincerely and devotedly love their wildcat religion, (but not regarding it as wildcat themselves, though, of course,)—and I know them to be persons in every way worthy of respect. They are men of business habits and good sense.

Now when I see such men as these, quietly but boldly come forward and consent to be pointed at as supporters of a wildcat religion, I almost feel as if it were presumptuous in some of us to assert without qualification that spiritualism *is* wildcat. And when I see these same persons cherishing, and taking to their honest bosoms and fondling this wildcat, with genuine affection and confidence, I feel like saying, "Well, if this is a wildcat religion, it pans out wonderfully like the old regular, after all." No—it goes against the grain; but still, loyalty to my Presbyterian bringing-up compels me to stick to the Presbyterian decision that spiritualism is neither more nor less than wildcat.

I do not take any credit to my better-balanced head because I never went crazy on Presbyterianism. We go too slow for that. You never see us ranting and shouting and tearing up the ground. You never heard of a Presbyterian going crazy on religion. Notice us, and you will see how we do. We get up of a Sunday morning and put on the best harness we have got and trip cheerfully down town; we subside into solemnity and enter the church; we stand up and duck our heads and bear down on a hymn book propped on the pew in front when the minister prays; we stand up again while our hired choir are singing, and look in the hymn book and check off the verses to see that they don't shirk any of the stanzas; we sit silent and grave while the minister is preaching, and count the waterfalls and bonnets furtively, and catch flies; we grab our hats and bonnets when the benediction is begun; when it is finished, we shove, so to speak. No frenzy—no fanaticism—no skirmishing; everything perfectly serene. You never see any of us Presbyterians getting in a sweat about religion and trying to massacre the neighbors. Let us all be content with the tried and safe old regular religions, and take no chances on wildcat.

[From *Daily Hawaiian Herald,* Honolulu, Wednesday Morning, October 17, 1866.]

AN EPISTLE FROM MARK TWAIN.

SAN FRANCISCO, Sept. 24th.

THE QUEEN'S ARRIVAL.

Queen Emma and suite arrived at noon to-day in the P. M. S. S. Sacramento, and was received by Mr. Hitchcock, the Hawaiian Consul, and escorted to the Occidental Hotel, where a suite of neatly decorated apartments had been got ready for her. The U. S. revenue cutter Shubrick went to sea and received the guest with a royal salute of 21 guns, and then escorted her ship to the city; Fort Point saluted again, and the colors of the other fortifications and on board the U. S. war steamer Vanderbilt were dipped as the Sacramento passed. The commander of the fleet in these waters has been instructed to tender the Vanderbilt to Queen Emma to convey her to the Islands when she shall have concluded her visit. The City government worried for days together over a public reception programme, and then, when the time arrived to carry it into execution, failed. But a crowd of gaping American kings besieged the Occidental Hotel and peered anxiously into every carriage that arrived and criticized every woman who emerged from it. Not a lady arrived from the steamer but was taken for Queen Emma, and her personal appearance subjected to remarks—some of them flattering and some otherwise. C. W. Brooks and Jerome Leland, and other gentlemen, are out of pocket and a day's time, in making preparations all day yesterday for a state reception—but at midnight no steamer had been telegraphed, and so they sent their sumptuous carriages and spirited four-horse teams back to the stables and went to bed in sorrow and disappointment.

The Queen was expected at the public tables at dinner to-night, (in the simplicity of the American heart,) and every lady was covertly scrutinized as she entered the dining room—but to no purpose—Her Majesty dined in her rooms, with her suite and the Consul.

She will be serenaded to-night, however, and to-morrow a numerous cortege will march in procession before the hotel and give her three cheers and a tiger, and then, no doubt, the public will be on hand to see her if she shows herself.

ALPHABET WARREN.

I believe I do not know of anything further to write about that will interest you, except that in Sacramento, a few days ago, when I went to report the horse-fair of the State Agricultural Society, I found Mr. John Quincy Adams Warren, late of the Islands, and he was well dressed and looked happy. He had on exhibition a hundred thousand varieties of lava and worms, and vegetables, and other valuables which he had collected in Hawaii-nei. I smiled on him, but he wouldn't smile back again. I did not mind it a great deal, though I could not help thinking it was ungrateful in him. I made him famous in California with a paragraph which I need not have written unless I wanted to—and this is the thanks I get for it. He would never have been heard of if I had let him alone—and now he declines to smile. I will never do a man a kindness again.

MISCELLANEOUS.

Charles L. Richards, of Honolulu, sails to-morrow for the Islands with a fast team he purchased here.

The great steamer Colorado is undergoing the alterations necessary to fit her for the China Mail Company's service, and will sail about the first of January with about all the cabin passengers she can carry. She will touch at Honolulu, as I now understand. I expect to go out in her, in order to see that everything is done right. Commodore Watson is to command her I believe. I am going chiefly, however, to eat the editor of the *Commercial Advertiser* for saying I do not write the truth about the Hawaiian Islands, and for exposing my highway robbery in carrying off Father Damon's book—History of the Islands. I shall go there mighty hungry. Mr. Whitney is jealous of me because I speak the truth so naturally, and he can't do it without taking the lock-jaw. But he ought not to be jealous; he ought not to try to ruin me because I am more virtuous than he is; *I* cannot help it—it is my nature to be reliable, just as it is his to be shaky on matters of fact—we cannot alter these natures—us leopards cannot change our spots. Therefore, why growl? —why go and try to make trouble? If he cannot tell when I am writing seriously and when I am burlesquing—if he sits down solemnly and takes one of my palpable burlesques and reads it with a funereal aspect, and swallows it as petrified truth,— how am I going to help it? I cannot give him the keen perception that nature denied him—now, can I? Whitney knows that. Whitney knows he has done me many a kindness, and that I do not forget it, and am still grateful—and he knows that if I could scour him up so that he could tell a broad burlesque from a plain statement of fact, I would get up in the night and walk any distance to do it. You know that, Whitney. But I am coming down there mighty hungry—most uncommonly hungry, Whitney.

MARK TWAIN.

[From *Territorial Enterprise,* Sunday, November 4, 1866.]

CARD FROM MARK TWAIN.

The following characteristic card from Mark Twain is in reply to a general invitation of the residents of Carson extended to him to visit the State Capital and deliver his lecture on the Sandwich Islands:

CARD.

VIRGINIA, November 1.

His Excellency H. G. Blasdel, Governor, and Messrs. A. Helm, O. A. F. Gilbert, H. F. Rice and others:

Gentlemen: Your kind and cordial invitation to lecture before my old friends in Carson has reached me, and I hasten to thank you gratefully for this generous recognition — this generous toleration, I should say—of one who has shamefully deserted the high office of Governor of the Third House of Nevada and gone into the Missionary business, thus leaving you to the mercy of scheming politicians — an act which, but for your forgiving disposition, must have stamped my name with infamy.

I take a natural pride in being welcomed home by so long a list of old personal friends, and shall do my level best to please them, hoping at the same time that they will be more indulgent toward my shortcomings than they would feel called upon to be toward those of a stranger.

Kindly thanking you again, gentlemen, I gladly accept your invitation, and shall appear on the stage of the Carson Theatre on Saturday evening, November 3d, and disgorge a few lines and as much truth as I can pump out without damaging my constitution.

Yours sincerely,

MARK TWAIN.

Ex-Gov. Third House, and late Independent Missionary to the Sandwich Islands.

P.S.—I would have answered yesterday, but I was on the sick list, and I thought I had better wait a day and see whether I was going to get well or not.

M. T.

[From *Territorial Enterprise,* Sunday, November 11, 1866.]

CARD TO THE HIGHWAYMEN.

Last night I lectured in Gold Hill, on the Sandwich Islands. At ten o'clock I started on foot to Virginia, to meet a lot of personal friends who were going to set up all night with me and start me off in good shape for San Francisco in the morning. This social programme proved my downfall. But for it, I would have remained in Gold Hill. As we "raised the hill" and straightened up on the "Divide," a man just ahead of us (Mac, my agent, and myself), blew an ordinary policemen's whistle, and Mac said, "Thunder! this is an improvement—they didn't use to keep policemen on the Divide." I coincided. The infernal whistle was only a signal to you road agents. About half a minute afterwards, a small man emerged from some ambuscade or other and crowded close up to me. I was smoking and supposed he wanted a light. But this humorist instead of asking for a light, thrust a horrible six-shooter in my face and simply said, "Stand and deliver!" I said, "My son, your arguments are powerful—take what I have, but uncock that infamous pistol." The young man uncocked the pistol (but he requested three other gentlemen to present theirs at my head) and then he took all the money I had ($20 or $25), and my watch. Then he said to one of his party, "Beauregard, go

through that man!"—meaning Mac —and the distinguished rebel did go through Mac. Then the little Captain said, "Stonewall Jackson, seat these men by the roadside, and hide yourself; if they move within five minutes, blow their brains out!" Stonewall said, "All right, sire." Then the party (six in number) started toward Virginia and disappeared.

Now, I want to say to you road agents as follows: My watch was given to me by Judge Sandy Baldwin and Theodore Winters, and I value it above anything else I own. If you will send that to me (to the Enterprise office, or to any prominent man in San Francisco) you may keep the money and welcome. You know you got all the money Mac had—and Mac is an orphan—and besides, the money he had belonged to me.

Adieu, my romantic young friends.

MARK TWAIN.

[From *San Francisco Bulletin,* November 30, 1866.]

MARK TWAIN'S INTERIOR NOTES.

[CORRESPONDENCE OF THE "BULLETIN."]

Sacramento.

I have recently returned from a missionary trip to the interior. I have nothing new to report concerning Sacramento; it was rather warm there. They haven't got the grade finished yet. The grade has proven of high sanitary importance to Sacramento; nothing else could have so happily affected the health of the city as the new grade. Constant exercise on a dead level is too monotonous — the human system eventually ceases to receive any benefit from it. What the people there

needed was a chance for up-hill and down-hill exercise, and now they have got it. You see, they have raised some of the houses up about eight or ten feet, to correspond with the new grade, and raised the sidewalks up accordingly; the other houses remain as they were before, and so do the sidewalks in front of them; the high walks are reached from the low ones by inclined staging similar to the horse stairways in livery stables. This arrangement gives infinite variety to a promenade there, now. The more the grade progresses the more the people are exercised and the healthier they become. The patience, money and energy required to prosecute the work to a successful completion are fearful to contemplate, but I think the citizens are equal to the emergency. Sacramento, with its broad, straight avenues, shaded by stately trees and bordered with flower-gardens, is already handsome, and some day it will be beautiful.

The new Capitol is a slow coach. I would like to be Superintendent of it for life, with the privilege of transmitting the office to my heirs and assigns forever.

Marysville.

This is the most generally well built town in California—nothing in it, hardly, but fine, substantial brick houses. I found there many a man who had made his fortune in Washoe, and didn't have the shrewdness to hold on to it, and so had wandered back to his old Marysville home. It is a pity to see such a town as this go down, but the citizens say the railroads are sapping its trade and killing it. They are a sociable, cheerful-spirited community, and if the town should die, they would hardly die with it.

Grass Valley.

Reminded me somewhat of Virginia in her palmy days. There are a great many old time Washoe miners there, and some are doing remarkably well. There are ten dividend-paying mines in the camp, (some of them very heavy concerns in this respect,) and a dozen more that are in a fair way to come under the same head. The bullion shipments are large and gradually increasing. Grass Valley is an old quartz mining camp—one of the oldest in the State—and it has al-

ways been the wise policy of her thoughtful business men to preserve the prosperity of the place from the injurious effects of exaggerated newspaper reports and mining excitements, and the plan has worked well as a general thing. Still, business promises to be overdone there, notwithstanding. The place can very comfortably support its present population, but additions are being made to it every day, and there is a disposition to open two stores and two shops where one would suffice for the present. Miners, also, go there from various parts of this State and Nevada, to apply for work, and they are not likely to get it, because none but men like those Cornishmen, who are used to working in extremely hard rock, are of much account there.

The Eureka.

In so short a letter as this will be, I can say but little upon any one subject, but I will give a specimen of what a good mine can be made to do when economically worked. The Eureka is doubtless the best mine in Grass Valley, and is also the most prosperous. It was purchased, (together with its 20-stamp mill,) something over a year ago, for the sum of $400,000, and it paid for itself in 13 months. I got permission to take some figures from the official books of the Eureka. The gross product of the mine for the year ending September 30, 1866, was $536,431.41. After deducting stores, repairs, labor and all other expenses, a net profit remained of $368,042.18. The average yield of the rock, per ton, was $47.15. The total cost of mining and working it, per ton, was $13.75. The mill was not running full time during the greater part of the year. The rock grew much richer during the last four months; the mill ran full time and this is the result: Gross yield for last four months, $255,072.35; nett, $187,-751.72. Latterly, the rock paid $65.33 per ton, including the sulphurets. There are about $5 worth of sulphurets in a ton. These are separated, stored away and sold to the agents of a Swansea establishment for shipment to England. A ton of clean sulphurets is worth from $300 to $400. When I was at the mine a contract was about being entered into for the sale of a large quantity at $320 a ton. The mine and mill together employ 175 men, and the expenses of the establishment are about $17,000 a month. The shaft was down about 400 feet; the lowest working level was 320 feet. The Eureka stock comprises 20 shares; one-fourth is owned in Grass Valley, and, (if I recollect rightly,) a fourth in San Francisco, and the remaining half in the East. Prof. Silliman is the possessor of half a share. The mine is now paying princely dividends, and is ably and economically managed.

The Ophir Hill mill is the Gould and Curry of California. It is a superb affair, is as neat as a parlor and cost $125,000—but it has been a month since I was there, and if I can remember how many stamps it has got I wish I may be shot—thirty, I think. They had just struck a rich place in the mine, and I saw chunks of quartz as large as a child's head, which were plastered nearly all over with gleaming leaves and plates of the purest gold; jewelers had already bought a handful or so—$600 worth, to work up into watch-seals, cane-heads, etc.

I only visited one other mine—the Ione (the printer will please not put that Jones,)—owned by five or six Washoe men. It is said to be doing well. Its shaft was not well arranged for visitors, and I did not go down.

The thing that touches a traveler's heart nearest, is to come drearily into a strange place and find himself at home in a good hotel. I found such in Grass Valley, and also in

Nevada.

There are plenty of good mines around this camp, but I know very little about them. I took more interest in the people and the town than in anything else. I enjoyed myself rather too well to bother much about statistics. Nevada is the capital of the county, and within it is collected a notably refined and intelligent society. But just here I am reminded that between Grass Valley and Nevada (they are pretty close together) began the series of practical jokes with which I have been assailed lately. I have paid the jokers back faithfully every time, and never lost my temper but once, (and then only for a short time,) and I will pay this one off if I live long enough. I had a letter of introduction to Hon. A. A. S., of Nevada, and I went up there from the Valley, one day, purposely to present it, and then got to talking to a young man there by the name of Blaze, who keeps petrified wood, quartz specimens, and other attractions, in his establishment—and forgot it. As the coach left Grass Valley the next day, with the Orphan in it who traveled with me, I ran and handed him the letter, and told him to give it to Mr. S., and say I would call on him soon. An apparently feeble-minded, unprepossessing-looking man on the back seat said:

"Who did you say it was for?"

"Mr. S——."

"Very well—I'll take it!"

"Are you Mr. S——?"

"That is my name."

"*Honorable* A. A. S——?"

"The same."

I handed him the letter and said: "Well, by George, I'm glad to see you! You must excuse me for my seeming impertinence—but that's all right, you know—I'm exceedingly glad I met you!" (and I thought to myself, "What infernally cheap material they make honorables out of up here in this part of the country!")

The next afternoon I was in Nevada, and a gentleman approached the group I was conversing with, and was introduced to me as Hon. A. A. S——. I said to myself, "Well, this looks something like an honorable," and then I began to inquire into things. The truth soon leaked out. One of the party said, "Why that fellow in the stage was named Duell—he don't know enough to come in when it rains!" I said that that was what I thought in the first place, but after all, that was as much intelligence as a practical joker requires—any idiot can tell a lie, and no practical joke is anything more than a spoken or acted deception. You can carefully analyze the best one you ever heard of, and you will find that that is exactly all it consists of.

The letter had passed through some fifty hands, and when Mr. S—— received it it was about worn out. However, I accepted the harmless joke, and some time or other when an opportunity offers, I will try to "get even" on the festive ass they call Duell. I will not tell about his celebrated law case now.

MARK TWAIN.

[From *San Francisco Bulletin,* December 6, 1866.]

MARK TWAIN'S INTERIOR NOTES—No. 2.

[CORRESPONDENCE OF THE "BULLETIN."]

To Red Dog and Back.

We visited the mining camps of Red Dog and You Bet, and returned to Nevada in the night, through a forest country cut up into innumerable roads. In our simplicity we depended on the horses to choose the route for themselves, because by many romantic books we had been taught a wild and absurd admiration for the instinct of that species of brute. The only instinct ours had was one which moved them to hunt for places where there wasn't any road, and it was unerring—it never failed them. However, our horses did not go lame. It was very singular. My experience of horses is that they never throw away a chance to go lame, and that in all respects they are well meaning and unreliable animals. I have also observed that if you refuse a high price for a favorite horse, he will go and lay down somewhere and die.

A Memento of Speculation.

We traveled by stage to Meadow Lake, over a villainous road, which usually led through beautiful and picturesque mountain scenery, variegated with taverns, where they charge reasonable rates for dinners and get them up satisfactorily.

We reached the town of Meadow Lake at 9 P. M. It is built on a level plat of ground shut in by rugged mountains well clad with heavy timber. The lake itself is a very handsome sheet of water a mile long and perhaps a quarter of a mile wide. Meadow Lake is the prettiest site for a town I know of; and the town already built there is the wildest exemplar of the spirit of speculation I have ever stumbled upon. Here you find Washoe recklessness and improvidence repeated: A lot of highly promising but unprospected ledges, and behold! on such guarantees as these they have built a handsome town and painted it neatly, and planned wide, long streets, and got ready for a rush of business, and then—jumped aboard the stage coaches and deserted it! And they have done all this on what? Why, if I am correctly informed, only three or four mines are barely opened, and all the bullion ever shipped from this place would not foot up $30,000. Yet all this bad business was the work of men who had done such things before, and been scorched at Kern River, Gold Lake, Washoe and other theatres of fierce mining excitement. Here is a really handsome town, built of two-story frame houses—a town capable of housing 3,000 persons with ease, and how many inhabitants has it got? A hundred! You can have a house all to yourself merely by promising to take care of it. The place is perfectly citified with signs. There are the inevitable "Bank Exchanges" and Metropolitan Hotels, and wholesale hardware stores, printing, and lawyers' and doctors' offices, and restaurants and billiard saloons of a pretentious city. One man has even had the temerity to build a large, handsome dressed stone house, at great expense. A bright, new, pretty town, all melancholy and deserted, and yet showing not one sign of decay or dilapidation! I never saw the like before.

The people who are there have strong faith in the ultimate prosperity of the place, though, and from all I hear I am a good deal of their opinion myself. Their rock pays all the way from $15 to $50 in free gold, and the sulphurets (they seem to be of an unusually rebellious character,) are uncommonly rich. Machinery has lately been erected there for working them, and my opinion that experimenting on those things outside of Swansea is a frittering away of valuable time, is not entitled to consideration, and is nothing against the enterprise.

There are five quartz mills in Meadow Lake, and they are jogging along comfortably and doing very well with the free gold. They shipped $4,000 one month, $6,000 another, and expected in October to yield $10,000. There is no question but that the leads are good, and there is also no question but that Meadow Lake can easily support its present population; but that they should go and provide house-room for 3,000 people so very early in the day was rather foolish. Wood is as cheap as dirt there, and water is plenty. Snow falls to the depth of six feet in winter, but the mill men do not seriously object to that, because it is easier to haul wood and quartz in sleds than in wagons. The winter cannot be excessively cold, else the snow would not fall so freely. It is expected that the camp will be as lively and populous as ever in the spring.

An Aristocratic Turn-out.

The next morning we started to Virginia. The stage was small (and had a wheel of questionable stability,) and the four horses were rather small for their age, especially the wheel horse on the port side, which had been staging some 38 years, it was said. We had 14 passengers, (there was comfortable room for 9,) and baggage for 150. That is a little extravagant—but we did have the hind boot full of trunks, (and a cooking-stove,) and the forward boot full of carpet sacks and rolls of blankets, and on the roof was a stack of valises, several chairs and a few joints of stove-pipe—and I think if a menagerie had offered, we would have tried to take it along. Take notice, I am not doing our stage man any injury with these remarks, because he has hauled his line off for the winter—otherwise, I would keep silence, for I would not wantonly injure so good-natured and accommodating a fellow as he was. We crossed little depressions very gently, on account of our shaky wheel, and got out and walked, when we were not going down hill, so as to give the horses a chance. We generally walked, anyway. Occasionally we would come back and encourage the driver a little, and then go off and leave him again. I thought the team we started with was rather a hard lot, but those were circus horses compared to what we had afterwards. Every change we made was for the worse. Or rather, the worse culminated in the next to the last change. They brought out a weird-looking, bowlegged crowbait, and the boys laughed; next a thoughtful, Senator-looking skeleton, that looked as grave as a hearse and had an expression of more than earthly wisdom in his lean face; next came a prodigiously long animal, whose ridgy backbone stood out prominently all the way from his shoulders to his tail, like the croppings of a quartz ledge; and the bridge of his nose was broken and he breathed

with a blubbering snort that was exquisitely annoying; and last and most notable, came a horse with only one ear that stood boldly up, and the other had been chopped off close to his head—and if ever I saw a comical looking beast, it was he. Altogether, it was the most forlorn team I have come across yet. We only had one set of harness, and it had to be let out for the long horses and taken up for the short ones. The driver cracked his whip, and we started— one horse galloping, another trotting, another pacing, and the long horse with the curb-stone backbone walking with a martial stride that defied all imitation except with stilts. The boys made so much fun of the earless horse that in self-defense the driver said he bought him especially to afford passengers an entertaining topic of conversation. They thought he might well have bought the others for the same purpose, and they conferred the title on the whole team. Wherefore, whenever anything went wrong, they observed, for instance, that "The topic of conversation with the broken nose has unshipped his check-rein." However, we had a right jolly trip of it and got into Virginia at about 10 o'clock at night.

Silver Land.

I did not observe any very great changes in Nevada. There were many teams on the roads, and the towns looked about as they formerly did. Virginia bore quite a business-like aspect, and it was said that she was enjoying a very fair degree of prosperity. Business there now is on a good, firm, healthy basis, and she is steadily recovering from the collapse brought upon her by reckless speculation.

Gold Hill is doing far better than she was when I was there last. She is shipping an average of $800,000 a month in bullion—an increase of half a million since my time. The principal mine is the Yellow Jacket. It was a shaky affair for a long time, but good management has brought it out all right at last. On the first of July, 1865, its liabilities were $404,875.65, and its assets $256,-120.02. A year later, on the first of July, 1866, the Company were out of debt and had a cash balance on hand amounting to $142,915.38. The mine has been paying dividends regularly for several months, now, and a recent rich strike has sent the stock up to a high figure. During the year, $1,895,228.70 in bullion has been produced from the mine and shipped.

The Silver City mills are doing profitable work. Dayton, like Virginia, has suffered from a disastrous fire, but the native energy of her people has not been crushed by the misfortune. I could not discover any change in Carson, scarcely. It was never much of a speculative town, and its business affairs seem to go along about as smoothly as ever. The new Mint building is being rapidly erected—Abraham Curry is the Superintendent, and his energy is not of a flagging nature. The Mint will be an exceedingly ornamental edifice when completed, and will add considerably to the appearance of Carson. It is being constructed partly of brick and partly of a fine species of granite found near the city. The Mint is to cost $150,000 in greenbacks.

The mills around Washoe City are driving ahead and doing a lively business, especially those of the New York and Nevada and the Savage. The Savage is an excellent mine now, even in its deepest levels, and has the pay streak (at a depth of some 700 feet,) which has made the Hale and Norcross such a valuable property since I got out of it. If I were mean enough to bear malice, I would buy in again and kill that mine.

I cannot see but that all these towns are getting along well enough, and I cordially wish their prosperity may increase. They have always treated me well. I had heard that Nevada was as good as dead, and I am glad to know it was false.

Some of my friends in Virginia met me on the Divide one night and robbed me—for fun, they said—and I forgive them, because they returned the stolen property, whereas, when they blew up Wells, Fargo's stage and robbed it they kept the proceeds. I have been told that these were two different parties, but I think not. I never saw such hang-dog countenances in my life as the gang wore that captured me. And besides, they transacted the business with a degree of artistic excellence that could only have been attained by long experience. I know them, and they are none too good to dig up a grave and carry it off, if they had any use for such an article.

MARK TWAIN.

[From *San Francisco Bulletin,* December 7, 1866.]

MARK TWAIN'S INTERIOR NOTES—No. 3.

[CORRESPONDENCE OF THE "BULLETIN."]

San Jose.

As some persons already know, this is a handsome city of 6,000 inhabitants, and has wide, level streets. Some uncommonly fine buildings for such a town, a couple of ample public squares in addition to the usual plaza, a pretty park adorned with shrubbery, half a dozen newspapers, and several first class schools. But there are almost incredible items of interest connected with the place which are not so well known. For instance: The county is said to be out of debt; the $150,000 of scrip appropriated for the stately Courthouse now in course of erection has sold at figures ranging all the way from one up to five per cent. premium; the city is also out of debt and has $150,000 in its treasury. I give these marvels as they were told to me—I dare not vouch for them. Cities and counties that are out of debt are very rare; the official virtue that permits them to remain so is still rarer—wherefore we must receive such statements as the above with caution.

The Academy of Notre Dame is a fine structure, and its elegant grounds are kept in perfect order. The establishment cost $130,000. The people of San Jose propose to build a preparatory school for the reception of pupils destined for college, which shall rank with the finest in the Union. I paid full price at the principal hotel—without abatement on the score of being a newspaper man—and this ought to entitle me to say it is much the best hotel on the coast outside of San Francisco, without being accused of compounding for my board with puffs.

Silk.

I spent two hours in questioning Mr. Prevost about the silk culture—and crowding him down to categorical answers without permitting him to wander off into other departments of the subject—and what I don't know about this business now is hardly worth knowing.

The dry, sunny, mild and balmy atmosphere of California, and especially of San Jose Valley, is unsurpassed in all the world in its peculiar adaptation to the production of raw silk. The mulberry tree springs up in a shorter time, flourishes more luxuriantly, and is blessed with a greater freedom from disease or blemish of any kind, in this State than in almost any other country. Its trunk attains a circumference of two or three feet in six or seven years, and slips will grow to the height of 10 or 12 feet in a single year. In writing about these things to that officer of the French Government whose duty it is to keep the nation posted on the agriculture of the world, Mr. Prevost subtracted several inches from the first statement and knocked off several feet from the second, so as to bring them within the limits of that officer's credulity! It was a piece of noteworthy sagacity.

Mr. P. raises his cocoons in a garret about 40 by 12, which has no ventilation, and where the thermometer gets up to 107 sometimes—a state of things which no silk worm would put up with in any other country—yet the beasts eat ravenously, live happily, and curl up in July or August and die with unalloyed satisfaction. They weave a silken winding-sheet for themselves, and always take a pride in getting it up the best they know how. If these shrouds are to be sent to the factory, the life of the imprisoned worm must be destroyed. If not, that worm turns into a very imbecile looking and inferior quality of butterfly and bites a hole in the end of the cocoon and climbs out. And as long as it lives, it never takes any interest in anything but laying eggs. It lays them by the thousand, and they turn to worms and fall to eating mulberry leaves with an avidity that shows they mean business. A hundred thousand silk worms at dinner at once make a noise with their teeth something like the racket of a steam printing press.

There were about 200,000 cocoons produced in California this year, half of them by Prevost. He reserved half for the market and saved the rest to breed eggs from. Mr. Prevost is the old original pioneer of the silk culture in this State, and furnished eggs and information to one farmer after another, until, after six years of persevering labor, he has now the satisfaction of seeing the silk business surely and steadily gathering strength and establishing itself as one of the permanent sources of the State's wealth and importance. But for the fact that some chattering, pretentious impostor too frequently steps in at the eleventh hour and robs the pioneer of his laurels, I would expect Prevost to be honored with the title of Father of California Silk Culture, some day. But let him look out that he don't confer affluence and distinction upon the State,

and then die in poverty and neglect at last.

A silk manufacturing company has been formed, machinery has been purchased, and the buildings are now in process of erection. The grounds — 26 acres — were donated by citizens of San Jose.

Mulberry trees should be planted 10 feet apart, so that the sunshine can have free access to all the foliage. Thus planted, an acre will contain 435 trees. Any farmer can have four or five acres of trees, and his young children, useless for all other purposes, can feed silk worms, and produce cocoons for the factory. There is no trouble and no expense connected with the operation. Mr. Prevost has about 30 acres of trees, and the 100,000 cocoons he reared the present season would produce 2,000 yards of silk fabric, a yard wide—worth $4,000 or $5,000, I suppose. Being a bachelor, I never have occasion to buy silk goods, and am not well acquainted with prices. A cocoon averages 800 yards of fibre, or 200 to 250 yards of thread—about one spool, I should say. Woven into cloth, it will make a strip of silk goods a yard long and an inch wide.

Silk can be manufactured in San Jose, with Chinese labor, cheaper than it can be imported. One great advantage the culture of silk has over many other products is that it is not in any wise cramped—it has the whole world for its market. There are hundreds of thousands of acres in California, well situated to do the silk culture.

The State Legislature has instituted very fair premiums for the encouragement of the silk interest, and latterly, the agricultural and industrial societies have given assistance in the same direction, though at first they gave lop-eared rabbits and incomprehensible pictures done with a needle on the general plan of a darned stocking, the preference over the silk culture.

Mr. Prevost has been obliged to give lengthy instructions to farmers so often by word of mouth, that he has finally concluded to write a complete manual of the silk culture and publish it for the benefit of all who are interested, and he is hard at work at it now.

When a climate can be found which insures the mulberry tree against disease, no occupation is so free from risk and so surely profitable as the silk culture; and California furnishes that climate. Therefore, there is little question that she will one day become a great silk-growing State.

MARK TWAIN.

———

Mark Twain Mystified.

EDITOR BULLETIN.—I cannot understand the telegraphic despatches now-a-days, with their odd punctuation—I mean with so many question marks thrust in where no questions are asked. The despatches appear to be in the last degree mysterious. I fear we are on the eve of fearful things. Now, read this ominous telegram. I cut it out of this morning's papers, and have been studying over it most of the day, but still I don't consider that I understand it now any better than I did at first:

NEW YORK, December 6.—The World's Brownsville special says: The city of Matamoras was surrounded[?] to General Sedgwick, commanding the United States horses[?] on the Rio Grande, on the evening of the 24th ult. Col. T. G. Perkins, of the Nineteenth U.S. Infantry, being the only artil-

lery[?] regiment now on duty there, was stationed in command of eleven[?] men of the French[?] cavalry, who crossed over and stultified [occupied?] the city that day, but did not return until the previous[?] day, on account of having to remove [remodel?] the pontoon bridge, to let his baggage train cross over, whereby he did not get back again [where?] in time to prevent it, or at least not as much as he might if he had, and certainly not otherwise if he did not or was unable, or even could not and went back on him. So Gen. Wxgrclvtkrvw [?] thinks.

Come, now, this is not right, you know. I have got to lecture Monday night, and my mind ought to be in repose. It is ruinous to me to have my mind torn up in this way on the eve of a lecture. Now, just at the very time that I ought to be serene and undisturbed, comes this dreadful news about Col. T. G. Perkins and his incomprehensible (but I think, wicked) conduct, and Gen. Wxrg(insert remainder of alphabet)'s bloodcurdling though unintelligible opinion of it. I wish to Heaven I knew what Perkins was trying to do, and what he wanted to do it for, and what he expected to gain by it, and whether he ever accomplished it or not.

I have studied it over patiently and carefully, and it appears that he, with his regiment of American infantry, being the only artillery there, crossed over with his French cavalry and occupied some city or other; and then returned the day before he went over and sent his baggage train across to the other side (of course returning again at some other time not mentioned,) but too late, unfortunately, to prevent it, which this Gen. Wxgr, etc., thinks he might if he had, or otherwise if he did not or was unable; he therefore— However, it ain't any use. This

telegram is too many for *me*. Despondently,

MARK TWAIN.

[From *Alta California,* December 14, 1866.]

SO-LONG.

EDITORS ALTA: I leave for the States in the Opposition steamer to-morrow, and I ask, as a special favor, that you will allow me to say good-bye to my highway-robber friends of the Gold Hill and Virginia Divide, and convince them that I have got ahead of them. They had their joke in robbing me and returning the money, and I had mine in the satisfaction of knowing that they came near freezing to death while they were waiting two hours for me to come along the night of the robbery. And at this day, so far from bearing them any ill will, I want to thank them kindly for their rascality. I am pecuniarily ahead on the transaction. I got a telegram from New York, last night, which reads as follows:

"NEW YORK, December 12th.

"MARK TWAIN: Go to Nudd, Lord & Co., Front street, collect amount of money equal to what highwaymen took from you.

"(Signed.) A.D.N."

I took that telegram and went to that store and called for a thousand dollars, with my customary modesty; but when I found they were going to pay it, my conscience smote me and I reduced the demand to a hundred. It was promptly paid, in coin, and now if the robbers think *they* have got the best end of the joke, they are welcome—they have my free consent to go on thinking so. (It is barely possible that the heft of the joke is on A.D.N., now.)

Good-bye, felons — good-bye. I bear you no malice. And I sincerely pray that when your cheerful career is closing, and you appear finally before a delighted and appreciative audience to be hanged, that you will be prepared to go, and that it will be as a ray of sunshine amid the gathering blackness of your damning recollections, to call to mind that you never got a cent out of *me*. So-long, brigands.

MARK TWAIN.

[From *Alta California,* December 15, 1866.]

"MARK TWAIN'S" FAREWELL.

Samuel Clemens, ("Mark Twain,") the talented humorist and brilliant writer, leaves San Francisco on the steamer *America,* to-day, and we take occasion to print the farewell address delivered on Monday night, at Congress Hall. After having kept the audience listening in rapt atten-

tion to his gorgeous imagery, in describing the scenes at the Sandwich Islands, or convulsed with laughter at the humorous sallies interspersed through the lecture, he seemed to come reluctantly to the promised "good-bye," and then his whole manner changed—the words were evidently the language of the heart, and the convictions of his judgment. He said:

"My Friends and Fellow-Citizens: I have been treated with extreme kindness and cordiality by San Francisco, and I wish to return my sincerest thanks and acknowledgments. I have also been treated with marked and unusual generosity, forbearance and good-fellowship, by my ancient comrades, my brethren of the Press —a thing which has peculiarly touched me, because long experience in the service has taught me that we of the Press are slow to praise but quick to censure each other, as a general thing—wherefore, in thanking them I am anxious to convince them, at the same time, that they have not lavished their kind offices upon one who cannot appreciate or is insensible to them.

"I am now about to bid farewell to San Francisco for a season, and to go back to that common home we all tenderly remember in our waking hours and fondly revisit in dreams of the night—a home which is familiar to my recollection, but will be an unknown land to my unaccustomed eyes. I shall share the fate of many another longing exile who wanders back to his early home to find gray hairs where he expected youth, graves where he looked for firesides, grief where he had pictured joy—everywhere change! remorseless change where he had heedlessly dreamed that desolating Time had stood still!—to find his cherished anticipations a mockery, and to drink the lees of disappointment instead of the beaded wine of a hope that is crowned with its fruition!

"And while I linger here upon the threshold of this, my new home, to say to you, my kindest and my truest friends, a warm good-bye and an honest peace and prosperity attend you, I accept the warning that mighty changes will have come over this home also when my returning feet shall walk these streets again.

"I read the signs of the times, and I, that am no prophet, behold the things that are in store for you. Over slumbering California is stealing the dawn of a radiant future! The great China Mail Line is established, the Pacific Railroad is creeping across the continent, the commerce of the world is about to be revolutionized. California is Crown Princess of the new dispensation! She stands in the centre of the grand highway of the nations; she stands midway between the Old World and the New, and both shall pay her tribute. From the far East and from Europe, multitudes of stout hearts and willing hands are preparing to flock hither; to throng her hamlets and villages; to till her fruitful soil; to unveil the riches of her countless mines; to build up an empire on these distant shores that shall shame the bravest dreams of her visionaries. From the opulent lands of the Orient, from India, from China, Japan, the Amoor; from tributary regions that stretch from the Arctic circle to the equator, is about to pour in upon her the princely commerce of a teeming population of four hundred and fifty million souls. Half the world stands ready to lay its contributions at her feet! Has any other State so brilliant a future? Has any other city a future like San Francisco?

"This straggling town shall be a vast metropolis; this sparsely populated land shall become a crowded hive of busy men; your waste places shall blossom like the rose, and your deserted hills and valleys shall yield bread and wine for unnumbered thousands; railroads shall be spread hither and thither and carry the invigorating blood of commerce to regions that are languishing now; mills and workshops, yea, and *factories* shall spring up everywhere, and mines that have neither name nor place to-day shall dazzle the world with their affluence. The time is drawing on apace when the clouds shall pass away from your firmament, and a splendid prosperity shall descend like a glory upon the whole land!

"I am bidding the old city and my old friends a kind, but not a sad farewell, for I know that when I see this home again, the changes that will have been wrought upon it will suggest no sentiment of sadness; its estate will be brighter, happier and prouder a hundred fold than it is this day. This is its destiny, and in all sincerity I can say, So mote it be!"

"Mark Twain" goes off on his journey over the world as the Travelling Correspondent of the ALTA CALIFORNIA, not stinted as to time, place or direction — writing his weekly letters on such subjects and from such places as will best suit him; but we may say that he will first visit the home of his youth— St. Louis—thence through the principal cities to the Atlantic seaboard again, crossing the ocean to visit the "Universal Exposition" at Paris, through Italy, the Mediterranean, India, China, Japan, and back to San Francisco by the China Mail Steamship line. That his letters will be read with interest needs no assurance from us—his reputation has been made here in California, and his great ability is well known; but he has been known principally as a humorist, while he really has no superior as a descriptive writer—a keen observer of men and their surroundings—and we feel confident his letters to the ALTA, from his new field of observation, will give him a world-wide reputation.

INDEX